A Reader's Guide to the *Roman de la Rose*

A Reader's Guide
to the
Roman de la Rose

Maxwell Luria

1982

ARCHON BOOKS

Library of Congress Cataloging in Publication Data
Luria, Maxwell, 1932-
    A reader's guide to the Roman de la Rose.

    Bibliography: p.
    Includes index.
    1. Roman de la Rose.   I. Title.
PQ1528.L8   841.'1   81-22767
ISBN 0-208-01838-7   AACR2

Pages 160–163 reprinted from Alan of Lille, *Anticlaudianus*, translated by James J. Sheridan, by permission of
the publishers; © 1973 by the Pontifical Institute of Mediaeval Studies.

for Clarence Eugene Turner

Ce tres noble livre de la Rose.

Car son propos fu de poursuir la matiere commensee et touchee par Guillaume de Lorris, et en ce faisant parler de toutes choses selonc leur estat au proufit de creature humainne, tant a l'ame come au corps.

Pierre Col

Contents

Preface

The *Roman de la Rose* is the preeminent achievement of French poetry in the Middle Ages. It was a work of enormous consequence in its day and for long after, and it continues to engage new generations of readers with its own special range of aesthetic and intellectual satisfactions. The *Divine Comedy* apart, no other medieval poem in any vernacular survives in so many manuscript copies, and none was more influential, or more controversial. Chaucer was profoundly influenced by it, and, consequently, Chaucerians are fascinated by it. In fact, the current tide of interest in things medieval has brought it renewed attention in the Anglo-Saxon world, as the fine English translation of Charles Dahlberg and the important scholarship of Robertson, Tuve, Fleming, and others have recently testified.

But there are inevitable difficulties attendant upon the reading or study of a seven-hundred-year-old poem: a distant cultural milieu to be evoked, subtle philosophical and religious issues to be clarified, forgotten mythological or historical allusions to be explained, old language to be defined, literary modes to be illuminated, forms to be appreciated. The *Roman* is a vast, difficult, and complex poem, as well as a delightful and interesting one. It is a densely allusive allegory, and, like the *Divine Comedy* or the *Canterbury Tales*, it reserves most of its copious rewards of beauty and truth for those who are prepared to receive them.

However, readers of Dante and Chaucer have long enjoyed a choice of introductory surveys, reader's guides, collections of criticism, and the like. Readers of the *Roman de la Rose* have not. Except for a very few publications such as Jean Batany's *Approches du*

Roman de la Rose (Paris, 1974), which is directed toward French university students, there is no book on the *Roman* for the cultivated general reader or student as distinct from the scholarly specialist, least of all in English. I became aware of this lack several years ago when I happened to be working with a manuscript of the *Roman* and, myself a nonspecialist, wished for a book whose two covers might enclose the diverse but basic data I needed, along with directions for getting more—something comparable to R. D. French's well-known *Chaucer Handbook*. Finding myself obliged to assemble this material and suspecting that others had experienced the same need, I decided to prepare my own reader's guide to the *Roman* as soon as the work I had in hand was completed.

The present volume, however, has grown, as such things will, into something more than a fact book. In Part One, I have tried to provide a great deal of information about the *Roman* and *Roman* studies, along with a survey of some of the critical issues which it raises, together with excerpts from the critical and scholarly literature. (Some of these, such as the discussions by Langlois and Lecoy, have not been translated before.) Naturally, this survey is selective, and the selection is determined by my own point of view. Nor, in fact, have I always tried to submerge this point of view; but I think the reader will have no trouble finding when my remarks express my own view rather than another's. Part One is intended, then, to form a general introduction to the poem.

Parts Two and Three supply the reader with outlines and summaries to aide in analyzing the poem, and cross-referenced glossaries to help in understanding it. I do not believe that anything of the sort has hitherto appeared in English.

In Part Four, I have gathered a number of texts which may enlarge the reader's understanding of the origins of the *Roman* and of the kinds of responses which it elicited. (All these texts are discussed in Part One, and cross-references are provided.) The first six texts—by Macrobius, Alanus de Insulis, Andreas Capellanus, Pierre Col, and Christine de Pisan—are available in modern scholarly editions for specialists, but these are not always accessible, and I believe that many readers will welcome the excerpts collected here. The other four texts have not, so far as I know, been translated into English before; certainly none is available in a modern edition, even in the French. The selections from the Collins gloss are published here for the first time.

This book is intended for use by readers and students at all levels of sophistication, who are drawn for whatever fortuitous reason to the *Roman de la Rose*. Beginners, for instance, will find in certain sections of Part One, and in the summaries in Part Two and glossaries in Part Three, a functional introduction to the poem and an orientation to its study. Advanced readers will perhaps consider especially valuable the materials in Part Four, the research bibliographies in Part Five, as well as certain sections of Part One.

Moreover, I hope that students of Chaucer will find the book both useful and accessible: all important French and Latin materials have been translated (with bibliographical information to lead interested readers to texts in the original languages); the Chaucerian *Romaunt of the Rose*, and the important influence which the *Roman* exerted on Chaucer, are discussed in the last section of Part One; and both these subjects are fully covered in the bibliographies in Part Five.

I have used the Lecoy text and Dahlberg translation throughout. With two exceptions, I have generally adopted the conventional English versions of the names in the *Roman*. (These can easily be converted to the French originals by consulting the Glossary of Personifications in Part Three.) The exceptions are *Deduit* and *Dangier*: there is no consensus translation for these, and none of the English versions is altogether satisfactory. I thought it best, therefore, to leave them in the original. (Their meanings and roles are, of course, explained in the Glossary of Personifications.) All translations into English not otherwise attributed are by me.

It is an agreeable task to acknowledge, with gratitude, the cooperation and assistance I received while preparing this book. The Philadelphia Museum of Art kindly permitted me to reproduce parts of the gloss in Collins MS 45-65-3. Harvard University Library, the Library of Congress, and the Rosenwald Collection in Alverthorpe Library generously put certain of their treasures at my disposal. Repeated visits to the New York Public Library confirmed my admiration for that great and indispensable institution. The staff of the Princeton University Library, where most of my research was accomplished, were unfailingly helpful in providing access to its splendid resources. The Bibliothèque Nationale, the British Library, and the Bodleian Library responded promptly to my requests for information about their manuscript holdings. *Mediaeval Studies* has allowed me to use here, in somewhat different form, materials which I originally prepared for publication in that journal.

Inevitably, many books have gone into the making of this one. I am grateful to their authors for writing them and to their publishers for permitting me to quote from them and otherwise to use them: above all, the standard editions of Langlois and Lecoy, and the English version of Dahlberg. Parts Two and Three are based on these works, and I have freely drawn on their notes, glossaries, and summaries. Similarly, in preparing Part Five, I made extensive use of all the printed bibliographies at my disposal, especially the ones listed on pp. 226–27.

When I turned to my colleagues and students for insight, information, books, or encouragement, I was never denied, and it is a particular satisfaction to thank Raymond Cormier, Charles Dahlberg, John V. Fleming, Morton Levitt, David Perry, and Marilyn Rosenthal. Jeanne Krochalis gave generously of her paleographical expertness, and much more. Richard Hoffman helped me in innumerable ways, and tolerated my almost weekly importunities; his recent death at forty-four has deprived us of a scholar-teacher of rare gifts, and me personally of a precious friend and collaborator. Richard Brewer and Jerome Steen provided good ideas; good fellowship, and sometimes good gin, as they have been doing for thirty years or so. Margaret McGuire contributed significantly to Part Five by surveying scholarly materials on the *Roman*. Stephen A. Barney provided several valuable suggestions for improving the book.

There remain two final acknowledgements. It was in D. W. Robertson's unforgettable seminars at Princeton twenty years ago that my interest in the *Roman de la Rose* was kindled. A few years earlier, I had had the good fortune to study French literature at Rutgers with C. E. Turner, a great teacher whose insight, gusto, and aversion to all pedantry and cant left an indelible impression on his students. He has allowed me to ensure my book a measure of distinction by dedicating it to him.

January 1982

Abbreviations

B.L.	British Library
B.N.	Bibliothèque Nationale
CL	*Comparative Literature*
DAI	*Dissertation Abstracts International*
EETS-ES	Early English Text Society, Extra Series
ELN	*English Language Notes*
fr.	français
JEGP	*Journal of English and Germanic Philology*
MLA	Modern Language Association
MLN	*Modern Language Notes*
MLQ	*Modern Language Quarterly*
MLR	*Modern Language Review*
MP	*Modern Philology*
MS, MSS	manuscript, manuscripts
n.a.	nouvelles acquisitions
PL	*Patrologia Latina*
PMLA	*Publications of the Modern Language Association*
SATF	Société des Anciens Textes Français
SP	*Studies in Philology*

ONE

In Search of the Rose

1

The Poem and Its Authors

The *Roman de la Rose* is the work of two poets, Guillaume de Lorris and Jean de Meun. The first of these composed lines 1–4,028, and left his poem unfinished; the second picked up the thread and wove a vast "conclusion," lines 4,029–21,750.[1] The *Roman* is therefore a very long poem, though in an age of monumental literary conceptions it is by no means the longest.[2] Neither is the fragmentary character of Guillaume's original *Roman*, nor the dual authorship of the poem as we have it today, without parallel in medieval French writing. What is, however, unique about this work, in all of European literature, is that a poem of the very first magnitude, qualitatively as well as historically, should have been the product of two authors, separated by a generation in time and by more than a little divergence of taste and style.

Early scribes, commentators, and editors seem indifferent to this aspect of the *Roman*, and treat the work unhesitatingly as a unitary piece.[3] In modern times, however, critics and readers have become more conscientious about classical standards of literary unity; and especially since 1936, when C. S. Lewis aroused much interest in the English-speaking world with his brilliant, characteristically eloquent chapter on the *Roman* in *The Allegory of Love*, substantial critical discussion has hinged on the question of the work's essential unity or doubleness; on whether, for all their undeniable differences of manner and matter, Guillaume's and Jean's moral and imaginative visions are or are not fundamentally congruent.[4]

As to the importance of the *Roman de la Rose*, there has rarely been any doubt, except for the two centuries (1538–1735) during

3

which the *Roman*, like most of medieval literature, was considered rude and old-fashioned, a relic from the barbarous "gothick" past.[5] Even then, the poem had its partisans. Thomas Sibilet wrote in 1573, in his *Art Poétique François*, that the *Roman* "is one of the greatest works which we read today in our French poetry."[6] In the seventeenth century, Agrippa d'Aubigny still considered it an admired work.[7] The very large number of surviving manuscripts and of early printed editions, as well as its enormous influence on French and European poetry, attest to the *Roman's* unsurpassed importance in its own day and long after. As Lewis remarked: "The poems that derive from it constitute the most important literary phenomenon of the later Middle Ages. As a germinal book during these centuries, it ranks second to none except the Bible and the *Consolation of Philosophy*."[8] Alan Gunn, whose critical study of 1952 remains the most comprehensive treatment of the poem in any language, described its current status:

> Concerning the primacy and influence of the *Roman de la Rose*, if not concerning its artistic merit, the critics and literary historians of the past hundred years have spoken with one voice. To Désiré Nisard, the allegory merited "l'honneur d'être le premier inscrit sur la liste des ouvrages en vers qui ont eu le privilège de durer." With it he opened his study of "la vraie poésie française." Gaston Paris preferred to say that the allegory of the Rose closed the literature of the Middle Ages and opened that of the modern world. Of the truth of these sweeping claims, the researches of Langlois and other medievalists into the immense influence of the poem upon French, English, and Italian literature provide ample demonstration.[9]

Inevitably there has been less unanimity with respect to the merits of the poem. About the year 1400, when the "Quarrel" was in full swing and sharp-tongued epistles were racing across Paris, opinion was in vigorous conflict. Pierre Col thought it "this most noble book of the *Rose*," but Christine de Pisan found little in it to please her:

> I say that it can be a source of wicked and perverse encour-

agement to disgusting conduct, although it does contain some good things (the more authentic the good, the greater the evil, as I have said before), because mankind is naturally inclined to evil. This book can be, for many people, a supporter of the dissolute life; a doctrine full of deceit; the road to damnation; a public defamer; a source of suspicion, mistrust, shame, and perhaps of heresy. And in several places a most loathsome book![10]

Toward the end of the sixteenth century, Etienne Pasquier, expressing what we should probably consider a more strictly literary judgment, was, in Gunn's words, "ready to oppose Guillaume de Lorris and Jean de Meun, not only to Dante, but 'à tous les Poëtes d'Italie,' even though he recognized that 'l'oeconomie générale' of their work 'ne se rapporte à ce que nous pratiquons aujourd'huy.' "[11]

Modern critics have sometimes been more eager to explain the *Roman* than to praise it, and although some have joined C. S. Lewis in preferring Guillaume to Jean, the entire work has attracted its passionate admirers, as Gunn shows:

> "To comprehend a Gothic cathedral," declared George Saintsbury, "the *Rose* should be as familiar to us as the *Dies Irae*." W. J. Courthope expressed the view that Jean de Meun's portion of the poem was "the work of a poet of extraordinary power," and one illustrating, "more vividly than any [other] poem of the Middle Ages, the inward nature of the political and literary forces which combined, on the one hand for the overthrow of French feudalism, and on the other for the development of the French Renaissance." . . . George Lyman Kittredge hailed Jean de Meun as a medieval Montaigne. . . . Professors W. A. Nitze and E. P. Dargan declared the *Roman de la Rose* to be, save "for the *Divine Comedy*, which it foreshadows, the greatest allegory of European literature."[12]

Guillaume de Lorris, the first of the two begetters of the *Roman*, was evidently from Lorris, a small town some fifty kilometers east of

Orleans. Everything else we know, or think we know, about him is inferential.[13] In deliciously ironic words which he gives to the God of Love, Jean de Meun pretends to identify Guillaume with his persona, the *fol amoureux* or Lover, and puts "more than forty years" between the two poets:

> Here is Guillaume de Lorris, whose opponent, Jealousy, brings him so much anguish and sorrow that he is in danger of dying if I do not think about saving him. He took counsel with me willingly, like one who is wholly mine; and he was right, for it is for him that we put ourselves to the trouble of assembling all our barons to carry off Fair Welcoming or steal him. . . . Here Guillaume shall rest. May his tomb be full of balm, of incense, myrrh, and aloes, so well has he served me, so well did he praise me! Then will come Jean Chopinel with gay heart and lively body. He will be born at Meung-sur-Loire; he will serve me his whole life, feasting and fasting, without avarice or envy, and he will be such a very wise man that he will have no concern for Reason, who hates and blames my unguents, which exhale a perfume sweeter than balm. . . . He will be so fond of the romance that he will want to finish it right to the end, if time and place can be found. For when Guillaume shall cease, more than forty years after his death—may I not lie—Jean will continue it. . . .[14] [10,496–10,558]

Ernest Langlois determined that Jean concluded his work on the poem between 1275 and 1280, and that Guillaume's death should be ascribed to the period 1225–40.[15] Félix Lecoy would modify these dates only slightly: Guillaume, he believes, worked between 1225 and 1230; Jean, according to "his own" assertion, was born about the time of Guillaume's death, c. 1235–40, and worked on the *Roman* between 1269 and 1278. Jean's death, however, is documented: it occurred in 1305, or slightly earlier, at Paris.[16] Beyond his dates, Langlois can suggest of Guillaume only that he knew Latin but was not much of a scholar, since he mistook Scipio for a king.

If we know little enough about Guillaume de Lorris, the immediate reception which greeted his poem is almost equally obscure. Langlois thought that it enjoyed "un grand succès" in the mid-thirteenth century, and cited a number of supposed imitations.[17] But Lecoy persuasively shows that his evidence for these texts being imitations of Guillaume's poem, or being composed before Jean's continuation, is flimsy.[18]

The enthusiasm and the imitations would come in due course, at any rate, for Guillaume's fragment was an extraordinarily original creation, although, in the usual medieval way, its materials were mainly traditional. Lecoy has described these complementary characteristics of the work:

> The poem is indeed constructed of elements which had long been commonplaces of rhetoric, and even of the most trite kind of academic rhetoric. The dream was a hackneyed device, and from his first verses Guillaume alludes to the most famous of all, the dream of Scipio, as Macrobius had presented it in his commentary. The theme of the garden of Love goes back to a double source, whose waters are, moreover, quite mixed: ancient, if one thinks of Tibullus and elegiac poetry, Christian if one turns to the frequent descriptions of the earthly paradise. The fusion of these two inspirations had been accomplished more than once, in the famous Latin poem of *Phillis et Flora*, for example, of which we have several French versions, a sign of its success. The motif of the arrows of the God of Love is to be found in Ovid—who did not himself invent it—and had been used to the point of tedium by his followers. Nor was the use of a rose to symbolize the beloved lady a new idea: it was known to the Latins, and we find it several times in Plautus. As for the personification of spiritual tendencies or psychological states, of vices and virtues, one could fill a large volume in tracing its history, starting with the great models of late antiquity, Prudentius or Martianus Capella, up to the medieval theologians and moralists whom Guillaume had read. Finally, Guillaume's intention, stated in his opening verses, to give his public a work containing the *art* of love was not in itself original,

7

nor did it surprise an audience which enjoyed being addressed learnedly even with respect to frivolous things, and whose taste, not wholly free of pedantry, welcomed anything which smelled of instruction—above all, when the author declared . . . that his learning had roots in far-off antiquity, whose treasures would thus be put at the disposal of a *beau monde* ignorant of Latin. . . .

Nevertheless, despite all these models and precedents, Guillaume's originality remains unqualified. He was, surely, very refined, and, evidently, educated. But he was probably not a clerk, in the narrow sense of the word; rather, he was a worldly man, elegant and fluent. Doubtless, the story which he tells us is "exemplary" in that it is in the nature of instruction; but the didactic intention remains discreetly veiled. Even the speeches of Love, Reason, or Friend are introduced naturally into the action. To be sure, this action itself is extremely tenuous, and progresses with the greatest leisureliness. . . . The development of the abstractions, which is so heavy and arduous in so many of Guillaume's models or rivals, has in Guillaume the mark of a virtuosity and an imaginative freshness which makes us forget what is artificial and forced, and we have no trouble remembering the living portraits of such rational beings as Beauty, Youth, *Deduit*, Leisure, Openness, and even Foul Mouth or *Dangier*. Even the choice of these personages, however little it conforms to modern taste, reveals a most sincere and commendable effort of analysis, a sense of psychological truth which is, if not very delicate or subtle, at least firm and solid. Guillaume, finally, as a writer, is the master of a style at once brilliant, deft, and functional. He lacks, it is true, the verbal virtuosity—sometimes indeed mannered—of a Chrétien de Troyes; but this restraint even in expression helps him avoid the rocks of affectation which might menace his barque. A prevailing verisimilitude mitigates the bookish and academic features of his conception. A most authentic and delicate sense of the beauty of forms, of the elegance of attitudes, encompasses and clothes Guil-

laume's poem with a thin veil of youthful ardor, of tender-
ness and joy.[19]

Merely to survey the apparent sources of Guillaume's poem, as
Lecoy does, is to remind oneself how startlingly new was his general
conception. Most great innovative poets are good readers, endlessly
casting about and gathering together all manner of materials from
diverse sources, and then, by virtue of their magisterial imaginations,
shaping from these materials something quite different. Dante and
Chaucer were poets of this kind; so was Shakespeare. To be sure,
Guillaume's *Roman* presupposes certain Roman elegies and medieval
Latin allegories, but, in truth, neither Tibullus nor Prudentius nor
Alanus de Insulis, nor even Ovid, all great authors in their own right,
can give us more than the faintest foreshadowing of the *Roman de la
Rose.* Practically speaking, as Chrétien de Troyes had in the twelfth
century invented the Arthurian romance, so Guillaume de Lorris in
the first half of the thirteenth century invented the medieval dream
vision of love, and both inventions were to have a copious and sometimes brilliant progeny.

* * * * * * * * * * * *

Jean Chopinel, or Clopinel as he is sometimes called in the manuscripts, was born at Meung-sur-Loire, a town which, like Lorris, is
in the neighborhood of Orleans. He is better known to us than Guillaume—as an author, at any rate—for we have at least three other
productions of his, all translations: the *De Re Militari* of Vegetius (a
Latin writer probably of the fifth century), translated as *L'Art de
Chevalerie* and dated 1284; the epistles of Abelard and Heloïse; and
the *Consolatio Philosophiae* of Boethius. In addition, there are two
other poems which are ascribed to Jean in many of the MSS, and are
probably his: the *Testament Maistre Jehan de Meun* and the *Codicile
Maistre Jehan de Meun.* (Another poem, found with equal frequency
in the MSS, the *Tresor de Jean de Meun*, is actually the work of Jean
Chapuis.)[20]

Of his life apart from his bibliography, however, we know virtually nothing: only the approximate location of his house in Paris,
and the approximate date of his death (1305). As Lecoy remarks:

> We must admit that we are ignorant about his personality
> as such: that is, his social level, the milieu in which he
> lived, the vocation which he followed, and even his back-
> ground and education. Scholars have looked in vain for
> his name among the archives of that period. We must
> resign ourselves to knowing of him only what we can learn
> from his works.[21]

Jean completed Guillaume's unfinished *Roman* by writing a conclusion more than four times as long as the original poem, and—
whatever may be said of the two poets' ideas—in a drastically different style.[22] Critics have described the difference in many ways: if
Guillaume is courtly and elegant, Jean is bourgeois and realistic; if the
one is lyrical, pictorial, incisive, idealistic, the other is philosophical,
encyclopedic, digressive, satirical. The four thousand verses of Guillaume's *Roman* constitute a poem of almost classical compactness and
decorum, entirely centering about a libidinous youth, who is endowed with more sensibility than sense, at large in a garden of fleshly
delights. The allegorical scenes, personifications, and actions form a
kind of psychodrama of male sexuality pursuing female resistance and
scrupulosity, and issuing, as Guillaume's fragment ends, in the
Lover's frustration. Critics think it unlikely that Guillaume would
have left the matter there, and it is widely assumed that in his original scheme the Lover would sooner or later have got his "rose." So,
of course, he does when Jean is finally through with him, some
eighteen thousand lines later; but only after the mimetic unity and
psychological allegory of Guillaume have been largely supplanted by
a massive dialectical structure based upon a sequence of enormous
"discourses" advocating or expressing one or another of a series of
related attitudes, philosophies, or ways of life, and embodying exemplary matter, fables, myths, anecdotes, dramatic skits, historical
allusions, and all sorts of received knowledge. These discourses are
spoken by personifications called Reason, Friend, False Seeming, Old
Woman, Genius, and Nature. Ostensibly, they are part of the allegorical "action" of the poem, the conflict between the Lover's aggressive
libido and the lady's other-directed reluctance; but they soon come to
overshadow this action, and even to eclipse the reader's interest in
Guillaume's protagonist. Jean's part of the poem thus becomes an

"encyclopedic satire," in Northrop Frye's convenient phrase, a vast festival of ideas, abrasive wit, and consistently corrosive and unblinking reportage about women and men, sex, love, reproduction, marriage, religion, and human behavior generally.[23] It is the poem that Jonathan Swift and H. L. Mencken would have written. This, then, and not Guillaume's tapestried romance, in which satire is politely masked by myth and allusion, is what so annoyed the God of Love in Chaucer's *Legend of Good Women*, and, later, drove Christine de Pisan and Jean Gerson to extravagances of outrage and vituperation.[24] Nevertheless, as the profusion of MSS and early evidences of its influence make clear, the two-part *Roman de la Rose* found its audience, and very soon became a great literary success.[25]

Jean's contribution is just as traditional and just as original as Guillaume's, though the task of defining its form has often baffled and irritated critics. C. S. Lewis was not the only one to see in it a "huge, dishevelled, violent poem," nor to conclude that Jean

> utterly lacks, perhaps despises, Guillaume's architectonics and sense of proportion. We never know, at one page, what we shall be reading about on the next. . . . He chose to continue a work in which the unity of subject was conspicuous: but he himself had no interest in that subject. He escaped from it at every turn and always seems to come back to it with reluctance. And in those passages where he keeps himself to the matter in hand, his treatment is perfunctory and confused. . . . His digressions constitute a different but equally serious fault. . . . The meandering . . . is . . . fatal to his poem.[26]

Lewis, evidently, is deeply disturbed by the fact that Jean's style is not Guillaume's. Another modern critic, Charles Muscatine, is more inclined to accept Jean for himself, and is more just in his remarks:

> The form of Jean's realism is intimately bound up with its context, as the variety of the style in his poem is roughly coextensive with its variety of thought. Jean is capable of the whole range of vernacular style: ornate rhetorical word play, lyric and formal description, scholastic

argument, popular scientific exposition, and dramatic realism. His heavenly park is handled with as much elevation
as Guillaume's earthly one was. His satirical passages have
as much bite as those of the most vigorous fabliaux. What
attracts our attention most is his modeling of the latter to,
or at least toward, the invention of the dramatic
monologue.[27]

Lewis's charge of undisciplined digressiveness, however, is one
that is often levelled at Jean, and, as we have already observed, his
work is indeed loose and baggy by contrast with that of Guillaume.
He is a Dickens, not a Flaubert. But the point which ought chiefly to
be made is that within the limits of his style, he observes an artful
economy, and the more often one reads his verse the more evident
this becomes. Every episode and subepisode within those eighteen
thousand lines, narrative and exemplum, image and emblem, plays
its role in articulating a dialectical analysis not only of the Foolish
Lover and his problems, but of the tremendous subject of which the
Lover is after all only one expression: Love itself, man's multifarious
and conflicting and sometimes treacherous attraction toward the
whole spectrum of created goods and their uncreated Maker, which,
as medieval poets and philosophers generally believed, constitutes the
chief subject matter of our lives as well as our literature. Here, if
anywhere, is the Babylonian confusion—in the circumstances of
fallen humanity, not in the poem which imposes a most un-
Babylonian order upon this confusion. As befits the philosopher
which his admirers declared him to be, Jean de Meun explored the
implications of Guillaume's unfinished fable, and extended its
significance. He did not betray it; he fulfilled it. It may well be that
the Middle Ages were better able, or at any rate more disposed, than
we to perceive that all expressions of love are parts of the same
human impulse, and thus that the temptations, satisfactions, and
frustrations which come to young men in the garden of *Deduit* form
only a single facet of a many-sided, infinitely puzzling, and infinitely
interesting matter. The manuscript evidence, as we have noted, does
not reveal any reluctance among early scribes and readers to regard
Guillaume's and Jean's work as parts of a single poem.

One can say, finally, of Jean's originality what was said above of
Guillaume's: nobody had ever made such a poem before. And until

the reader knows it well enough to perceive the form beneath the apparent disorder, the reason behind the seeming chaos, he can at least be stimulated immediately by some excellent talk. As Lecoy points out, "The characters of Jean de Meun do indeed speak a lot—but then, they have a lot to say."[28]

2

Manuscripts, Editions, and Translations

The immense number of surviving MSS of the *Roman de la Rose* testifies to its great and enduring popularity. Ernest Langlois, surveying them at the turn of the century, knew of more than 215.[29] A more recent editor, Félix Lecoy, speaks of some 247, and assumes that still others will come to light in the future.[30] By contrast, we have 84 MSS of the *Canterbury Tales*, 54 of *Piers Plowman*, and unique MSS of *Beowulf* and of *Sir Gawain and the Green Knight*—but the unequalled aggregate of nearly 600 MSS of the *Divine Comedy*. The most abundantly preserved Middle English poem, the *Prick of Conscience*, exists in 117 manuscript copies.[31]

By far the most important holdings of *Roman* MSS are those of the Bibliothèque Nationale, with 73, including the base MS of both the principal twentieth-century editions (B.N. fr. 1573). The other preeminent European collections are those of the Bibliothèque de l'Arsenal in Paris (8 MSS), the British Library (16 MSS), and the Bodleian Library at Oxford (9 MSS).[32] In North America, there are 21 MSS in public and private collections, nine of these in the Pierpont Morgan Library in New York.[33] The others belong to Princeton University, Harvard University, Yale University, University of Pennsylvania, University of Illinois, Huntington Library (San Marino, California), Walters Art Gallery (Baltimore), Philadelphia Museum of Art, Library of William S. Glazier (New York), Library of Harry A. Walton (Covington, Virginia), Massachusetts Historical Society (Boston), and Library of George A. Plimpton (New York). The last two are fragments of two and six leaves, respectively.[34]

The only extensive survey of the *Roman* MSS is that of Langlois:

14

Les Manuscrits du Roman de la Rose: Description et Classement (Lille, 1910). The section of his book devoted to descriptions is, of course, limited by the incompleteness of the inventory of MSS known to him. In other ways as well, however, these chapters, useful and engaging as they are, are imperfect. His descriptions are sometimes more anecdotal than systematic, and they are not always accurate. Nor was Langlois able personally to inspect all the MSS whose existence he records. Many scholars will smile with sympathy when reading Langlois's explanation of one such frustration, at the Municipal Library in Chalon-sur-Saone:

> I was unable to see this manuscript. When I went to Chalon to collate it, I found the library closed for two months. During the next vacation, I wrote to the librarian to request a meeting; he wrote me back that he was ill. The town refused to let me see the volume outside the library.[35]

One consequence of the lacunae in Langlois's descriptive pages is that we cannot infer from them precisely which MSS are glossed, or how valuable these glosses may be, for his references to marginalia are casual and inconsistent. For example, the MS in the Philadelphia Museum of Art now identified as Collins 45-65-3 may have been known to Langlois, though he appears not to have seen it, and he does not mention its extensive and important gloss, which has recently been shown to provide a fascinating index of how the *Roman* could be read c. 1500.[36] No doubt other such commentaries will be uncovered and published. A major desideratum in any future examination of the MSS is, therefore, a full and systematic description of glosses.

Another must be a thorough description and classification of the iconography, for many of these MSS are extensively and richly illustrated; and here, too, Langlois is virtually silent. Though he will signal the existence of miniatures in a MS, he rarely tells us even their number, and virtually never provides any description or analysis of their iconography. The *Roman*'s descriptive and allegorical character made it particularly suitable for illustration, and this fact no doubt contributed to the proliferation and preservation of the MSS, as later of the printed editions. One scholar has suggested: "We see from the manuscripts that the work was regarded as preeminently a field for illustration, almost as if it had been a religious book; and the printed editions carried on the tradition."[37] Indeed, since Langlois, it is art historians who have shown most interest in the *Roman* MSS. Recently, such literary scholars as Robertson, Tuve, Fleming, and Dahlberg have used the manuscript illustrations to explicate the poem; but little attempt has been made to use the textual traditions themselves for interpretation and appreciation, and still less the manuscript glosses.[38]

The reader of the *Roman* who is lucky enough to have access to one of the illustrated MSS will have an experience as pleasurable as it will be rewarding. Unfortunately, no *Roman* MS has yet been published in facsimile, and there are no satisfactory color reproductions of the miniatures in book form. The largest gatherings of black-and-white reproductions are in John V. Fleming's *The Roman de la Rose: A Study in Allegory and Iconography* (Princeton, 1969) and in Charles Dahlberg's prose translation (Princeton, 1971). Fleming reproduces forty-two miniatures from diverse MSS; Dahlberg's sixty-four reproductions include the complete cycle of illustrations in MS B.N. fr. 378, and thirty miniatures from MS Douce 195 in the Bodleian. Study of these miniatures, in conjunction with a reading of the poem, can provide at least a skeletal sense of how the illustrated MSS of the fourteenth and fifteenth centuries used the painter's art to amplify and gloss the poets' narrative.[39]

Further examination of the MSS and their glosses should also throw more light on the relation between Guillaume's opening fragment and Jean's conclusion. Contrary to those modern scholars who believe that the unquestionable difference between the two poets' styles betokens a comparable difference between their ideas, values, and general literary aims, the design of the Collins MS, for example, implies no such distinction, and its gloss also treats the poem as a unitary work.[40] The matter has obvious relevance to such a rudimentary though unresolved critical issue as whether Guillaume advocates, approves, or at least tolerates the Lover's quest, whereas Jean satirizes it. A more searching inspection of the MSS than Langlois was able to perform may help us better to gauge the early views with respect to this problem, and to others which also arise from the *Roman*'s unusual origin.

* * * * * * * * * * * *

The *Roman de la Rose* was first printed by Ortuin and Schenck at Lyon, c. 1481; and the twenty editions which followed between that year and 1538 reveal how sustained was the work's vogue until well into the sixteenth century. The standard account of these early editions is still F. W. Bourdillon, *The Early Editions of the Roman de la Rose* (London, 1906), and it is from this indispensable volume that the following summary descriptions of them are taken.[41]

1. Folio, without title, printer's name, place, or date. [Lyon: Ortuin and Schenck, c. 1481.] The editio princeps.

2. Folio, without title, printer's name, place, or date. [Lyon: Jean Syber, c. 1485.]

3. Folio, without printer's name, place, or date. Title: "Le Rommant De La Rose." [Lyon: Guillaume Le Roy, c. 1487.]

4. Folio, without date. Title: "Le rommant de la rose / imprime a Paris." Device of Jehan Du Pré [c. 1494]. This edition was reproduced in facsimile by Delavue in Paris, 1878.

5. Folio, without date. Title: "Le rommant de la rose / imprime a Paris." Device of Antoine Vérard [1494–95].

6. Folio, without date. Title: "Le rommant de la rose / imprime a Paris." Device of Jean Petit, or of Vérard, or blank [c. 1497].

7. Folio, without date. Title: "Le rommant de la rose nou / uellement Imprime a Paris." Diverse imprints [1498–1505].

8. Quarto, without date. Title: "Le romant de la rose. / Codicille & testament de / maistre Jehã de meun: / Nouuellement Imprme a Paris." Device of Vérard [c. 1500].

9. Folio. Title: "Cest le romant de la rose / Moralisie cler et net / Translate de rime en prose / Par vostre humble molinet." Jean Molinet's prose version. Paris, device of Vérard; 1500.

10. Folio. Title: "Cest le romant de la rose / Moralise cler

et net / Trãslate de rime en prose / Par vostre hũble molinet." Jean Molinet's prose version. Lyon, device (on the last leaf) of Guillaume Balsarin; 1503.

11. Quarto. Title: "Le rommant de la / rose nouuellement im / prime a paris." Device (on the last leaf) of Michel Le Noir; 1509.

12. Quarto. Title: "Le rommant de la / rose. Nouuellement / imprime a paris." Device (on the last leaf) of Michel Le Noir; 1515.

13. Quarto. Title: "Le rommant de la rose / Nouuellement imprime / a paris." Device (on the last leaf) of Michel Le Noir; 1519.

14. Quarto, without date. Title: "Sensuyt le rõ- / mãt de la rose / aultremẽt dit / le sõge vergier / Nouuellement Imprime a Paris xxix." Device (on the last leaf) of Jehan Janot [1520–21].

15. Folio. Title: "Le romant de la Rose / Moralisie cler et net / Translate de rime en prose / Par vostre humble molinet." Jean Molinet's prose version. Paris, device (on the last leaf) of Michel Le Noir; 1521.

16. Quarto, without printer's name. Title: "Sensuyt le rõmant / de la Rose aultre- / ment dit le songe vergier Nou- / uellement Imprime a paris. xxix." [Philippe Le Noir] 1526.

17. Folio, without date. Title: "Cy est le Romãt de la roze / Ou tout lart damour est enclose / Histoires et auctoritez / Et maintz beaulx propos usitez / Qui a este nouuellement / Corrige suffisantement / Et cotte bien a lauantaige / Com on voit en chascune page." Paris, device of Galliot Du Pré, or of Jehan Petit [1526]. Clément Marot's modernization.

18. Quarto, without date. Title: "Sensuyt le Rom- / mant de la Rose: / Aultremẽt dit le / songe vergier. Nouuellement Imprime A. / Paris. xxx." Alain Lotrian [c. 1528].

19. Small octavo. Title: "Le Rommant de la Rose nou- / uellement Reueu et corrige / oultre les precedentes / Im-

pressions." Paris: Galliot Du Pré, 1529. Clément Marot's modernization.

20. Folio. Title: "Cy est le Rommant / de la Roze. / Ou tout lart damour est enclose / Hystoires et auctoritez / Et maintz beaulx propos usitez / Qui a este nouuellement / Corrige suffisantement / Et cotte bien a lauantaige / Com on voit en chascune page." Paris: Galliot Du Pré, 1531. Clément Marot's modernization.

21. Small octavo. Title: "Le rommant / de la Rose nouuellement reueu / et corrige oultre les pre / cedentes Im- / pressions." Paris: diverse imprints, 1537 and 1538. Clément Marot's modernization.

Nearly all these early editions are elaborately illustrated with cycles of woodcuts, which further attest to the poem's popularity, and doubtlessly contributed to it. There are five separate series of cuts which were largely imitated from one another, though designed for particular editions of the *Roman*. In addition, there were partial recuttings based on three of these series. The number of cuts in the several series ranged from thirty-three to eighty-six. Bourdillon accounts for their rather uninspired character:

A striking feature in the different series of illustrations to the *Roman de la Rose* is the lack of inventiveness displayed in the successive sets of designs. In fact, with few exceptions, they simply repeat each other more or less closely, and are all founded eventually upon the earliest series of all, the rude and archaic cuts of the first Lyon folio. But this sheep-like want of originality, whether due to mere parsimony and indolence, or to some instinctive love of convention, is very typical of all French illustrations of the time, and is quite as evident in the highest class of illustrated books, such as the *Livres d'Heures*; being seen also in the slavish copies of archaic German cuts which are handed down through various French editions of such works as the *Speculum Humanae Salvationis*. It may be supposed that the wider, less educated reading public, brought into existence by the development of the printed book, had actually a sort of childish fondness for conventional representations of scenes to which its eyes had first been opened by certain designs, and would have felt a shock of strangeness at seeing them presented in an unfamiliar way.[42]

The popular and imitative character of these editions is further emphasized by the cycle of some 103 chapter headings or rubrics, which were composed for the editio princeps and used in all twenty subsequent editions. Most of the MSS contain sectional rubrics of some kind, but they are brief, and they are in prose. The printed cycle, however, is in verse, and most of the rubrics are related to the woodcuts.[43] At least four of them are worthy of special note here because of the interpretation of the poem which they seem to presuppose. These are numbers 18, 24, 36, and 40. They all come from the early parts of the poem, in which the Lover commits himself to the God of Love, and Reason tries without success to persuade him to abrogate this commitment:

> Comment apres ce bel langage
> Lamant humblement fist homage
> Par jennesse qui le decoit
> Au dieu damours qui le recoit.

> Comment rayson de dieu aymee
> Est jus de sa tour devalee
> Qui lamant chastie et reprent
> De ce que folle amour emprent.

> Cy est la tres belle rayson
> Qui est preste en toute saison
> De donner bon conseil a ceulx
> Qui deulx sauver sont paresseux.

> Comment rayson monstre a lamant
> Fortune sa roe tournant
> Et luy dit que tout son pouoir
> Sil veult ne le fera douloir.[44]

Although the other rubrics are "objective" summaries or descriptions of the poem's content, these four appear to accept the accuracy of Reason's critique of the Lover and the God of Love. It may be that we have here an indication that these early printed editions, in their casual and rather businesslike way, took for granted the satirical view of our poem's protagonist, and consequently of the poem itself. But it would perhaps be a mistake to read very much into these rubrics, one way or another. The early printed editions—with the exceptions of the versions of Molinet and Marot, which we shall consider presently—were designed principally to satisfy a popular demand for the *Roman*, not to explicate its meaning.

By 1538, however, enthusiasm for the *Roman* had spent itself, and the poem would wait two centuries for another edition.[45] In 1724 a certain Coustelier announced that he was preparing one, but the project seems never to have attained fruition.[46] In 1735 the abbé Lenglet du Fresnoy brought out, in Paris and Amsterdam, his three-volume edition—a very poor one, based on Vérard's quarto of c. 1500, though prefaced by a perceptive essay that shows some real sympathy for the *Roman* at the same time that it reveals the cultural attitudes which had driven medieval literature from favor generations earlier.[47] In 1737, there appeared a volume of notes by J.B. Lantin de Damerey. Text and notes reached a second edition in 1798; but this latter printing, observed Méon drily, "n'est pas plus correcte." Langlois wrote of it: "Il est à peine besoin de noter que le prétendu correcteur de cette édition n'a utilisé aucun manuscrit."[48]

Méon's own edition, which was published at Paris in four volumes in 1814, is far better than any of its predecessors. It is, in fact, the first good edition of the *Roman*, and signals the beginning of modern scholarly interest in the poem. Méon was the first of the *Roman*'s editors to base his text on a comparison of MSS. He writes in his *avertissement*:

> I have, during a period of fifteen years, given all my leisure
> to collating this work from more than forty manuscripts,
> the oldest that I was able to obtain . . . . This procedure
> has given me the advantage of finding in one MS the word
> or verse which may be missing or incorrect in another MS.
> I have taken for my base MS one bearing the date 1330,
> whose language seems to me the purest for that time.[49]

This admirable first attempt at a critical text of the *Roman* was still,

21

by modern textual standards, rather naive. Langlois describes Méon's editorial method and its results:

> Méon only very rarely provides variants, and, with one exception, only when it is a question of a group of verses which he considers to have been interpolated, and which he prints in his notes. In any case, he does not reveal the MS whose reading he accepts or rejects. When Méon confronts divergent readings, he lacks any criterion for making a choice: he gives preference to the MSS which are most numerous; when there is no numerical preference, he accepts the reading of his base MS. His text is very superior to those of his predecessors, although he had the misfortune to allow himself often to be influenced by them. He retained the verse rubrics of the older editions, and added others, borrowed from MS B.N. fr. 1569. Nearly all his notes are by Lantin de Damerey.[50]

The most useful feature of Méon's edition is now the wealth of editorial matter which it contains. Volume one reprints the prefaces of Marot and of Lenglet, as well as Damerey's commentaries, and includes valuable and lengthy historical accounts. Volume four includes a glossary of archaic words. The text of the poem itself is furnished with explicatory footnotes. For anyone who is interested in how the *Roman* appeared at the start of the last century, Méon is of course essential.

This text was, practically speaking, the only one available to nineteenth-century readers. The 1864 edition of Francisque Michel (2 vols., Paris) and the five-volume edition of "Pierre Marteau" (pseudonym of Jules Croissandeau, a merchant and president of the Chamber of Commerce at Loiret), which appeared at Orleans and Paris, 1878–80, merely reprinted Méon. Langlois's acidulous comment on the first of these is worth including here:

> Francisque Michel consulted no manuscripts. His corrections, fortunately rare, generally replace correct readings with mistakes. He did not even try to correct some obvious errors of Méon: contradictions, lack of meaning, impossible rhymes, printer's errors. To the con-

trary, an unacceptable interpolation, which Méon gave only in a note, and which he ought simply to have rejected, was reintroduced into the text by Michel. The notes which he added are generally pointless. One must, however, acknowledge a happy innovation, which consists in providing modern translations opposite difficult words.[51]

The Marteau edition is, by contrast, an accurate reprinting of Méon, and in it the entire text is accompanied by a modern verse translation.

In 1914, exactly a century after Méon, Ernest Langlois published the first of the five volumes of his great critical edition, which had been long in preparation and was eagerly awaited (Paris, 1914–24). Langlois's object was to try to reconstitute the "original" text, using as his base MS B.N. fr. 1573, an excellent MS of the thirteenth century, which he normalized and "corrected" with reference to his survey of 215 extant MSS. Published by the Société des Anciens Textes Français, Langlois's edition became standard as soon as it appeared, and it remains today an invaluable work for the serious student of the *Roman*. It is furnished with an elaborate philological introduction (vol. one), abundant linguistic, explicatory, and source notes, a glossary (vol. five), and other useful tools.

Since the appearance of Langlois's volumes, the most important edition of the *Roman* to be published has been that of Félix Lecoy, issued in three volumes (Paris, 1965–70), and now widely considered to have supplanted Langlois's as the standard edition. Lecoy, like Langlois, based his text upon the superior B.N. fr. 1573, but he reproduced this MS with relative fidelity, avoiding normalization or the intention of constructing a critical text. He does, however, adopt readings from other MSS when he finds them necessary, especially in Guillaume's part of the poem, which is reproduced in the base MS less accurately than is Jean's. Lecoy's procedure of keeping as close as possible to a "best manuscript" is more in scholarly favor today than Langlois's attempt to approximate an "original" text, at least among romanists still under the influence of Joseph Bédier's theories of textual criticism. This is one reason for the approval which the newer edition has received. Lecoy's notes, which are chiefly devoted to sources, are excellent, but less comprehensive than Langlois's, with which they must be supplemented. His edition contains a glossary (vol. three), a brief *apparatus criticus*, and résumés of the text at the beginning of each volume.

* * * * * * * * * * * *

The Middle English version of sections of the *Roman de la Rose*, part of which is usually ascribed to Chaucer, is of course the earliest extant translation from the poem into English.[52] Usable texts of this *Romaunt of the Rose*, with good notes and glossary, may be found in the standard editions of Chaucer's works: those of W.W. Skeat (2d ed., Oxford, 1899) and F.N. Robinson (2d ed., Boston, 1957). The most recent edition of the *Romaunt* is edited by Ronald Sutherland, and is useful for its French text on facing pages as well as for its extensive discussion of textual problems in an introduction (Oxford, 1967).

The first essentially complete English translation was that of Frederick Startridge Ellis, in three volumes (London, 1900), based on Marteau's edition. Ellis (1830–1901) was a successful dealer in rare books and manuscripts, a buyer for the British Museum, and friend and collaborator of William Morris and other literary figures of the time. His rhymed octosyllabic couplets form a free rendering of the poem, fatally loose and inaccurate by modern standards. The edition has no notes or other critical aids except summaries. With Victorian reticence, and also in the spirit of Christine de Pisan (see p. 191–202 below), Ellis declined to translate the *Roman*'s conclusion, believing "that those who read [it] will allow that he is justified in leaving [it] in the obscurity of the original."[53] Ellis's version is now obsolete, although the preface will still interest those curious about the *Roman*'s reputation in the last century.

The blank-verse translation which Prof. Harry Robbins made from Langlois's text (New York, 1962) is more nearly literal than Ellis's; nor did Robbins share Ellis's scruples with regard to translating the conclusion. But this version, too, is freer than most scholarly readers would prefer, and is inadequate for those who wish to get as close to the original as possible. There are no notes or scholarly apparatus beyond the most rudimentary.

With the publication of Charles Dahlberg's prose translation (Princeton, 1971), we have at last an accurate, literal version of the poem. The absence of verse is more than compensated for by the literal precision and fluency of the translation. The long introduction, extensive notes, and copious reproduction of manuscript illustrations add to the utility of the volume. Dahlberg's is, therefore, now the English translation of preference for serious students and readers.[54]

3

"Li Romanz . . . ou l'Art d'Amors est Tote Enclose"

Guillaume starts his poem in the usual medieval fashion, by establishing the narrative situation and characterizing the work about to unfold:

> In the twentieth year of my life, at the time when Love exacts his tribute from young people, I lay down one night, as usual, and slept very soundly. During my sleep I saw a very beautiful and pleasing dream; but in this dream was nothing which did not happen almost as the dream told it. Now I wish to tell this dream in rhyme, the more to make your hearts rejoice, since Love both begs and commands me to do so. And if anyone asks what I wish the romance to be called, which I begin here, it is the Romance of the Rose, in which the whole art of love is contained. Its matter is good and new; and God grant that she for whom I have undertaken it may receive it with grace. It is she who is so precious and so worthy to be loved that she should be called Rose. [21—44]

Guillaume describes his poem as a "romance" which embraces an "art of love." In order to know how to read the *Roman de la Rose*, one must know something about the implications of both assertions.

* * * * * * * * * * *

Charles Dahlberg has pointed out, with reference to the frequent use of the word *art* (Latin *ars*) in medieval titles, that the expression "art of love" may mean either a how-to-do-it handbook or a comprehensive treatise: "'complete method of seduction' and 'organized inquiry into all kinds of love' are two of the possible, complementary meanings."[55] Ovid's *Ars Amatoria*, the fountainhead of this literary tradition and locus classicus of the expression, is, naturally, taken in the first of these senses, as is its most important twelfth-century imitation, the *De Arte Honeste Amandi* [*De Amore*] of Andreas Capellanus. However satirical or ironic one may conclude these works to have been, they certainly treat explicitly only one kind of love, not all kinds. The extended implication of the expression is, however, worth noticing in connection with the *Roman de la Rose*, precisely because Guillaume's poem is fragmentary and of disputed meaning, and also because Jean's continuation is manifestly concerned with love beyond the limits of sexual seduction. As Dahlberg says, the two notions are in any case complementary; especially is this so when a seduction manual is itself ironic. Even, therefore, if Guillaume understood "art of love" in the narrower sense, Jean, in drawing his part of the poem toward the more comprehensive, was not necessarily betraying either his predecessor or their common genre.

Lecoy surveys the twelfth-century Ovidian tradition on which Guillaume was drawing:

> With regard to didactic love books, there had already been in the preceding century Chrétien de Troyes's translation of Ovid's *Ars Amatoria*; Andreas Capellanus had written his *De Amore*, in Latin, to be sure, but the conception was modern and based entirely on the principles of medieval courtesy; in the schools, one read a poem—also in Latin—called *Pamphilus de Amore*, in the form of a comedy with four characters, which Guillaume unquestionably knew, and, though more coarse in its inspiration, perhaps provided our poet with the idea of presenting its notions in the form of an uninterrupted action.[56]

Chrétien's translation of Ovid is now lost, but, as Lecoy tells us, there were in the thirteenth century at least three other French versions of the *Ars Amatoria*, two French versions of Andreas, and "numerous treatises in which the same theme of the instruction of love is treated with more or less originality and felicity."[57] (These texts and their possible influence on Guillaume are discussed by Ernest Langlois in his *Origines et Sources du Roman de la Rose*, the classic treatment of the subject.)[58]

In contrast to Ovid's cynical and sensual *Ars* (which he supplemented with an equally cynical *Remedia Amoris*, explaining how to terminate an affair which has become more troublesome than pleasurable), Andreas is often elegant and "courtly," and treats his subject in a style assumed to have been acceptable to the Countess Marie of Champagne, the lady who is supposed to have directed him to write the book.[59] Marie was the daughter of Louis VII of France and Eleanor of Aquitaine, and the wife of Count Henry the Liberal, of Champagne. Their court at Troyes was an important center of the new literature and the home of Chrétien, the innovative master of courtly Arthurian romance.[60]

Much scholarly attention has been given in recent years to this court at Troyes and to its most influential literary figures, Chrétien and Andreas. Their importance to later European poetry is unquestioned, but their own intentions, and therefore the ways one ought to read their works, are matters of considerable controversy. Andreas's love treatise, the *De Amore*, is a prime case in point. Its English translator, J.J. Parry, who dates its composition c. 1186, believes that it "was almost certainly intended to portray conditions at Queen Eleanor's court at Poitiers between 1170 and 1174," and that its author

> seems to have felt little repugnance for the doctrines embodied in it. He takes care to remind gentlemen that they should be attentive to the services of the Church and generous in giving, but he is more concerned with establishing the fact that the clergy, by virtue of their cloth, rank above even the higher nobility. He does admit, grudgingly, that this kind of nobility, granted them by God and not to be taken away from them by men, cannot give them especial privilege in a love affair, so that in love a clerk can claim no more consideration than his original social status entitled him to; nevertheless a clerk makes the best lover because he has "an experienced knowledge of all things." Andreas boasts of his own skill in "the art of

soliciting nuns" and smacks his lips over an adventure he
once had with one of them; very regretfully he was forced
to decline her proffered advances because of the very
severe penalties which, in this world and the next, are in-
flicted upon a man who carries on a love affair with a nun.
The picture we get of Andreas from his book is that of a
man who is connected with the Church, but for whom
spiritual affairs are not the first consideration.[61]

Whether this is an accurate assessment—whether, that is, the *De
Amore* constitutes Andrew the Chaplain's "normative," uncritical account of Poitevin or Troyan amorous behavior, and expresses his
own values—is clearly of much interest to the reader of the *Roman*, for
on it may hinge Guillaume's notion of what an "art of love" was, or
might be. D.W. Robertson and other critics have warmly disputed
Parry's interpretation of Andreas, which is shared in essentials by
C.S. Lewis and others.[62] Each reader of the *Roman* must decide where
truth or probability lies.

One inconvenient matter which must be explained by those who
see Andreas as an advocate of unsanctioned sensual love is his Book
Three, which forms a rejection of the erotic values hitherto advanced
in the *De Amore*. But unlike Ovid's *Remedia Amoris*, which purports
merely to show how a stale or tiresome love affair can be terminated,
not to develop any principled position on the subject, Andreas's
palinode claims to represent the author's real opinion which he had
been rhetorically misrepresenting in the first parts of the *De Amore*:

> Now, friend Walter, if you will lend attentive ears to
> those things which after careful consideration we wrote
> down for you because you urged us so strongly, you can
> lack nothing in the art of love, since in this little book we
> gave you the theory of the subject, fully and completely,
> being willing to accede to your requests because of the
> great love we have for you. You should know that we did
> not do this because we consider it advisable for you or any
> other man to fall in love, but for fear lest you might think
> us stupid; we believe, though, that any man who devotes
> his efforts to love loses all his usefulness. Read this little
> book, then, not as one seeking to take up the life of a lover,

but that, invigorated by the theory and trained to excite the minds of women to love, you may, by refraining from so doing, win an eternal recompense and thereby deserve a greater reward from God. For God is more pleased with a man who is able to sin and does not, than with a man who has no opportunity to sin.[63]

Parry takes Andreas's rejection as mere Ovidian and patristic convention mongering, designed "to appease his ecclesiastical superiors, who may well have been offended by the tone of the first two books."[64] Lewis offers a curiously convoluted, though interesting, explanation: in the first two books, he says, Andreas was dealing with human, worldly values, in the third with divine and spiritual ones; and though he would, if pressed, have acknowledged final commitment to the latter, most of the time he was able to hold the two sets of values in a kind of suspension. The apparently conflicting parts of the *De Amore*, therefore, are both of them serious expressions of his beliefs.[65]

This problem is too important and complex to be further simplified here, and students of the *Roman* will, in any case, want to examine the primary and secondary literature for themselves. They will find Professor Robertson to be the most insistent, as he was the first, of those scholars who decline to accept that Andreas was an advocate of "courtly love" (even some of the time), and regard him rather as a highly entertaining moral satirist:

Andreas added the third book, not to contradict what he had already said before, but to make the implications of what he had already said explicit. There he explained that no man can devote himself to love and at the same time please God by doing anything else, since God detests the acts of Venus or fornication, and instituted marriage so that his people might multiply . . . . It is significant that what Andreas condemns in his last book is not some romantic conception of "courtly love" . . . . He condemns, instead, the foolishness and vice to which unbridled concupiscence leads. Concupiscence is something we all inherit, a thing which since the Fall we have had in common with the wild beasts, fish, cattle, and birds. When the bridle begins to slacken and we feel that the horse is running away with us, what will happen if we let it go? This is the problem with which Andreas concerned himself. Can we give the horse its rein and avoid offending and injuring our neighbors in society on the one hand and God on the other, keeping all the while our probity? The answer to this is "no". The "no" is implied from the start, in the definition of love which identifies it with cupidity and indicates that its development is simply the development of sin. It is implied again in the foolish and hypocritical behavior of the lovers in the dialogues and once more in the decisions of the ladies regarding problems of love. The last book simply states the same answer to the same question openly.[66]

* * * * * * * * * * * *

Guillaume calls his poem a "romance" as well as an "art of love." He composed it in the rhymed octosyllabic couplets which his greatest predecessor, Chrétien de Troyes, had used a few decades earlier, in turning the "matter of Britain" into shimmering enigmatic narratives of love and chivalric striving. Guillaume's *Roman* differs, of course, from Chrétien's romances in certain obvious ways. It is founded not on a received body of narrative material, some of it already old and probably somewhat obscure, but rather on an eclectic selection of literary materials, freely adapted, and shaped without any anterior fable or narrative structure in view. Whereas both Chrétien's matter and style favor the *gymnastique intellectuelle* of enigmatic action and dark symbolism, Guillaume's are relatively transparent, and the classical origin of much of his allusive and iconographic material enables his reader to use the conventional medieval interpretations and glosses of the classical texts as guides to his own poem. Most obvious, of course, is the difference of mimetic conceptions: Chrétien's figures, actions, and settings, however odd or emblematic they may actually be, are presented as imitations of real persons and of human experience; and, in fact, in his use of a sort of interior monologue for expressing erotic emotions—perhaps his chief technical innovation as a narrative poet—Chrétien may reasonably be credited with an early form of one of the leading devices of modern fictional realism. Guillaume, on the other hand, is thoroughly allegorical: that is *his* main technical characteristic. And although he too can cast a certain verisimilitude over his story, at least on occasions, and his own "characters" have "human" experiences and enjoy or endure "human" feelings, like those in other good medieval allegories, still his "characters" are personifications of abstractions, and his narrative engages the psychology of erotic experience primarily by means of this allegorical analysis.

With respect to other crucial features, however, Guillaume's romance is quite distinctly in line of descent from Chrétien. These features are perhaps best subsumed under the rubric "courtly," which—if we may leave aside for a moment the vexed matter of "courtly love"—refers to the thematic focus on amorous experience, the general air of elegance and luxury, the chivalry, the frequent moral idealism, above all the elevated, almost transcendent role of the Lady. All of these qualities are usually thought to define the values of certain twelfth-century courts where the new literature of romance was germinated. The way Guillaume fits into this context of courtly romance has been well stated by Charles Muscatine, whose *Chaucer and the French Tradition* (Berkeley, 1957) is a valuable study of Chaucer's relation to these French masters:

> At its beginnings, the courtly romance has a daring, experimental flavor. The earliest romances retain much of the epic and historiographic character of more popular contemporary literature, but they are attempts, at least, to imitate *classical* epic. Herein their matter is already more learned, more remote, and more wonderful than that of the *chanson de geste* and the chronicle. . . . Romance is soon at the point, though, where its style is overtaken by the full development of theme, and thus where style, rather than seeming merely *appliqué*, can have a functional relationship to meaning. Love and adventure are the two large topics of romance, and of those who manage to subsume both topics within a single theme, Chrétien de Troyes is pre-eminent. In his *Erec et Enide*, his *Yvain*, and his *Lancelot*, love is a cue for adventure, chivalry, and chivalry is a means of deserving love. . . . The Lady is traditionally desirable and difficult, and her favors are not lightly given. Love itself is a humbling and refining passion, open only

to the worthy. Chivalry, in the form of difficult adventure, is a means of achieving the respect of the Lady, or, in more complex movements, such as the plot of *Yvain*, to recapture it, often on a higher or deeper level than that on which it was previously held. . . . Love by itself, or with a minimum of adventure, is the topic of some of the best of the later romances, and finds its most elaborate treatment in the incomparable *Roman de la Rose* of Guillaume de Lorris. Here the field of external vision is acutely narrowed; for the movements of knights, giants, and damsels in distress are substituted the movements of the soul itself, and one's attention is focused, not on a set of defeats and victories in field and bower, but on the minutest events in the progress of a single love affair, rendered through allegory. . . . Partly indeed a handbook of love, the *Roman* brings the idealism and subjectivity of the courtly tradition to their most refined expression in French literature.[67]

* * * * * * * * * * * *

Whether the sexual adventures of courtly romance heroes form part of the "idealism" of which Professor Muscatine speaks, or whether they are as likely to be the objects of at least implied ridicule or disapproval, is hotly debated by scholars. This issue is closely related to the interpretation of Andreas Capellanus's *De Amore*, and, in fact, the two issues are really one, for the question which underlies them both is this: was there at certain courts of the twelfth and thirteenth centuries in France, and of the fourteenth in England, an ethos which may be called "courtly love," which, contrary to prevailing Christian orthodoxy, tolerated and even idealized certain kinds of sexual liaisons outside of marriage, and which we find embodied in the poetry of that period? No issue emerging from medieval literature has aroused more heated or persistent controversy in recent years than this, and any student of the *Roman de la Rose* will surely be familiar with some of its ramifications. The matter is one of particular urgency when we turn to Chrétien's *Lancelot* or Béroul's *Tristan*, in which the hero's love is adulterous, or to the *Roman de la Rose* (and a host of other medieval poems, including Chaucer's *Knight's Tale* and *Troilus and Criseyde*), in which it is obsessive and all-consuming as well as unsanctified.

C.S. Lewis was among those who believed in the historical existence of this ethos, or "sentiment," as he calls it, and in its straightforward expression in the poems under consideration:

> Everyone has heard of courtly love, and everyone knows that it appears quite suddenly at the end of the eleventh century in Languedoc. . . . The sentiment, of course, is love, but love of a highly specialized sort, whose characteristics may be enumerated as Humility, Courtesy, Adultery, and the Religion of Love. The lover is always abject. Obedience to his lady's lightest wish, however whimsical, and silent acquiescence in her rebukes, however unjust, are the only virtues he dares to claim. There is a service of love closely modelled on the service which a feudal vassal owes to his lord. The lover is the lady's "man". . . . It is possible only to those who are, in the old sense of the word, polite. It thus becomes, from one point of view the flower, from another the seed, of all those noble usages which distinguish the gentle from the vilein; only the courteous can love, but it is love that makes them courteous. Yet this love, though neither playful nor licentious in its expression, is always what the nineteenth century called "dishonourable" love.[68]

We find a quite different perspective in the writings of D.W. Robertson, the acknowledged leader of the anti-"courtly love" host:

> I have never been convinced that there was any such thing as what is usually called courtly love during the Middle Ages. However, it is obvious that courtly love does exist in modern scholarship and criticism, and that the idea appeals to a great many people today. . . . At various times in the past I have sought to show that works presumably illustrative of "courtly love" like the *De Amore* of Andreas Capellanus, or the *Lancelot* of Chrétien de Troyes, or the *Roman de la Rose*, are, in fact, ironic and humorous. . . . What is being satirized in the works in question is not "courtly love" at all, but idolatrous passion.[69]

To Robertson, as we see, a romance can also be a satire. No one
doubts that Jean's part of the *Roman de la Rose* is exactly that (though
there is less unanimity with regard to what Jean is satirizing)—but
Lewis, and like-minded critics, are also apt to assert that Jean's work
constitutes a "new poem," a work foreign to the spirit and intentions
of Guillaume, and, indeed, not really a romance at all. The originality of Robertson's position, which he now shares with others, is
that Guillaume, too, is a satirist—and that Jean's continuation, far
from being a new poem, is rather "an elaboration of the themes
established in the first part, ornamented with a wealth of
'humanistic' and philosophical material, and with satiric glances at
the institutions of the society in which he lived."[70]

If, then, the relation of Guillaume's *Roman* to its backgrounds in
Ovidian love manuals and twelfth-century romances must claim a
central place in any attempt to appreciate it, this relation—like the
meaning of these anterior texts themselves—remains a subject of lively controversy.

4

Allegory

The originality of Guillaume's genius is most brilliantly shown in his use of personification allegory. Jean later followed in his steps, modifying and amplifying his procedures. If Guillaume was not the first to join personification allegory to romance, he was the first to do it memorably; and after the *Roman de la Rose* this allegorical style of romance was to constitute virtually a new genre.[71] Chrétien's romances, with their luxuriance of narrative episode and their calculated obscurity, had suggested the dimness of some immense Gothic interior—say, the cathedral of Amiens—from whose recesses the dazzling windows and luminous niches leap to the eye at every turn. The *Roman*, however, is more like the great sun-drenched western facade of that same marvellous temple, where innumerable voices issue from the stone imagery in an eternal dialectic, and the whole vast wall somehow rises out of the monstrous into an overwhelming and transcendent symmetry.

* * * * * * * * * * *

Personification allegory is, to be sure, only one of several kinds of *allegoria* (using that word in its comprehensive sense) which flourished in medieval discourse, and hardly an author of consequence was exempt from one or more of them. The Middle Ages inherited allegory as part of the fabric of those antecedent civilizations which it cherished. Classical literary culture had, practically speaking, given birth to allegorical exegesis in the sixth century B.C., in an attempt to bypass perceived immoralities in Homeric theology. By late antiquity, the *Iliad* and *Odyssey* were nearly always read as allegories of natural forces, of metaphysical principles, or of human faculties; and although the details of the subject are often disputed, it is certain that Augustan authors such as Virgil and Ovid, as well as such later ones as Apuleius, were influenced by this tradition of allegorism.[72]

Jewish biblical culture, too, generated allegory. The exegetical *Midrashim* are traditionally attributed to the age of the scribes, the fifth and fourth centuries B.C. But the major development occurred in the Alexandrian community starting in the second century B.C. Alexandrian Jewish allegory is full of the awareness of Greek culture, and in fact constitutes one of the precious attempts in Western civilization, constantly recurring, to reconcile Hellenism with Hebraism. Thus, a certain Aristobulus tried to show that Homer and the Greek poets derived their substance largely from Moses; and his second-century B.C. contemporary, Artapanos, identified Moses with Musaeus, as well as with certain Greek and Egyptian deities. Still another contemporary, Eupolemos (their names speak as clearly as their books), identified the builders of the Tower of Babel with the giants in Hesiod. This tradition of Jewish allegorism reached its apogee in the voluminous works of Philo the Alexandrian (c. 20 B.C.–A.D. 40), whose attempts to explain the Bible in terms of Greek philosophy owe much to the moral allegorism of the Homeric exegetes, and were in turn to influence the scriptural interpretations of some of the early Christian church fathers.[73]

Christian culture inherited and transmuted both these traditions, making allegorism an integral part of its own apologetics, as well as its literary and figurative expression. By medieval times, then, not only scriptural exegesis and the interpretation of classical literature, but intellectual and literary expression themselves, often employed some mode of allegory, and it was assumed that in serious poetry, as in Scripture (though not, of course, in the same ways), the kernel of *sententia* could be got out of the husk of *littera* by allegorical analysis.[74] Certain poems embodied allegory in relatively consistent and highly visible ways: the *Roman*, followed at the end of the century by the *Divine Comedy*, are obvious cases in point. A rather larger body of literature—Chaucer's works can serve as an example—used allegory less obviously and systematically, but used it nevertheless. The impulse to mean more than one says was as natural an impulse among sophisticated medieval poets as the urge to describe things "as they are" was to writers of fiction in the nineteenth and twentieth centuries.

The earliest construction of an entire narrative from personified agents is to be found in the famous *Psychomachia* of the fourth-century Spanish Christian, Prudentius. A comparatively short poem (915 lines), the *Psychomachia* ("War within the Soul") is today more often cited than read, and with reason: though brief, it is tedious. But its influence on medieval iconography and literary expression was immense. With all the trappings of Virgilian epic, a group of Virtues, personified as female warriors, contest the soul with their opposites among the Vices: Faith wars against Worship of the Old Gods (*Veterum Cultura Deorum*), Chastity against Lust, Long-Suffering against Wrath, Lowliness against Pride, Sobriety against Indulgence (*Luxuria*), Good Works against Avarice, Concord against Discord. The following passage, which is somewhat condensed, will serve as a sample:

Avarice, her robe arranged to make a capacious fold in front, crooked her hand and seized on everything of price that gluttonous Indulgence left behind, gaping with mouth open wide, delighting to stuff her base gain in money bags and cram swollen purses to bursting with her pelf, keeping them in hiding behind her left hand under cover of her robe on the left side, for her quick right hand is busy scraping up all the plunder and plies nails hard as brass in gathering the booty. All the while, Crimes, the brood of their mother Avarice's black milk, like ravening wolves go prowling and leaping over the field. But now of a sudden Good Works dashes in anger on to the battlefield. Posted last on the field is she, but destined singly so as to put her hand to the war that nought shall remain to be feared. Every load she had cast off from her shoulders, and she moved along stripped of all coverings; of many a burden had she lightened herself, for once she had been borne down by riches and the weight of money. Like a thunderbolt to Avarice was the sight of the invincible conqueror. Cold with terror, she could not move. The brave Virtue sets upon her with the iron grip of her arms and strangles her, crushing the blood out of her throat till it is dry. Her arms, pressed tight like bands beneath the chin, squeeze the gorge and wrest the life away; no wound ravished it in the agony of death; the breath passage stopped, it suffers its end shut up in the prison of the body. As she struggles, the victor presses hard on her with knee and foot, stabs her through the ribs and pierces the heaving flanks.[75]

Prudentius's grandiloquent style enters the *Roman* most directly in the battle scenes of Jean's section. But in such a passage as the following, in which we may well detect a Prudentian echo, earnestness and propriety give way to parody and outrageous farce:

> Straightway Foul Mouth got down, knelt, and confessed, for he was already truly repentant; False Seeming seized him by the throat, squeezed with his two hands, strangled him, and then took away his chatter by removing his tongue with his razor. Thus they finished with their host; they did nothing else to kill him, but tumbled him into a moat. They broke down the undefended gate, passed through it, and found all the Norman soldiers within, so much had they vied with each other in drinking wine that I had not poured. They themselves had poured out so much that they all lay sleeping on their backs. False Seeming and Constrained Abstinence strangled them, drunk and sleeping as they were. They will never again be capable of chattering. [12,331–12,350]

This is indeed Prudentius turned inside out: both Foul Mouth and False Seeming are morally ambiguous figures, effectively "good" or "bad" depending on whether one supports the Lover's cause or not; but neither of them is a particularly savory character in his own right, and the introduction into this allegorical context of crapulous Norman soldiers verges on the surreal. But, of course, this is not really Prudentius at all, and the *Roman* is not a psychomachy. It is immeasurably more complex at every level than Prudentius's noisy but tidy confrontation between virtue and vice. From the opening pages of Guillaume, the allegorical personifications represent diverse ontological orders; and although their multiple conflicts do in fact often suggest contention within the human soul, as well as other kinds of actions, they do this on multiple levels. Guillaume's figures, though more mimetic and consistent than Jean's, are nevertheless altogether liberated from their ultimate origins in Prudentius and intervening authors; and Jean, ringing ever more daring changes on these allegorical techniques, avails himself of possibilities which he found in his inheritance from Guillaume.

* * * * * * * * * * * *

The first allegorical personification we meet is the narrator/ dreamer, and he is one of the most complex and elusive. As Charles Dahlberg has reminded us, the *Roman* "is probably the first major French narrative poem that uses a first-person narrator to control the point of view from beginning to end."[76] The kind and degree of control vary widely during the course of the poem, and to say that the narrator ever represents Guillaume himself (not to say Jean), as the older critics assumed, is no more satisfactory than to identify Geoffrey Chaucer with the narrators of *his* poems. The narrator/dreamer is a persona, a representative of the type of the libidinous young man of quality. He is nameless in the poem (except for Jean's mock identification of him with his inventor), though he is sometimes referred to by others as "lamant," and so the critics usually call him "the Lover." (The authors of the Quarrel, and later such commentaries as the Collins gloss, regularly call him "Fol Amoureux"—Foolish Lover—which serves at least equally well.)

The relation to the dreamer of the narrative voice which introduces the dream is much less than transparent. Did the dream in fact occur "five years or more ago," or was that impression merely part of the dream? What order of "she" is it to whom the poem is dedicated? What kind of dream (in Macrobian categories) is this one, and does the narrator understand the consequent implications?[77] What precisely was it that happened "almost as the dream told it"? Above all, is there any evidence that the narrator, now that he has experienced the dream and certain real-life consequences, is aware of the ironies which attend the Lover's quest and ultimate "success"? The more one ponders such matters, the more problematic they are apt to seem.

Once the account of the dream starts, however, and till the end of Guillaume's fragment, the dreamer/narrator is consistently the personification of Lover or *Fol Amoureux*, whose devotion to the God of Love is never seriously threatened, and who thus serves as an iconic representation of a certain human type and disposition. Jean, however, immediately introduces complications by allowing this figure for the first time (though only fleetingly) to contemplate the possibility that Reason's doctrine may be preferable to the God of Love's. But this modification has the effect of enlarging the credibility of the Lover, in fact humanizes him a bit, as Chaucer does when, in the *Man of Law's Tale,* he gives Nicholas Trivet's iconically pure Dame Constance episodes of self-doubt and even an impulse toward suicide.

The Lover remains himself, and his identity as Guillaume's persona is untouched until, about halfway through the poem, the God of Love, addressing his followers immediately before assaulting the castle of Jealousy, points out that "Guillaume de Lorris," the lover at the heart of the matter, will not live to complete writing down the dream, and that a certain Jean Chopinel, equally a devotee of love, will do so. At this point, the verisimilitude which has persisted somehow for over ten thousand verses (though the going is not always easy) is irrevocably fractured. Later, just before the great battle between the forces of Love and Jealousy is to begin, the dreamer/narrator digresses at length in a distinctly authorial voice. But the most striking change in the Lover is an almost inevitable result of Jean's own particular conception of the poem, which introduces long dialectical discourses and confessions. These discursive episodes, which occupy most of Jean's eighteen thousand lines and constitute his chief structural method, largely dispel the space-time illusion thus far more or less sustained, shift the reader's attention and the center of gravity definitively away from the Lover and his endeavor to the drama of ideas which now surrounds him. The Lover sometimes sounds suspiciously like someone resembling Jean de Meun the dialectician, in such passages as the long one (15,861–16,218) in which he describes Nature and her works, discusses alchemy, and dilates on a good deal more before introducing Nature's "confession." When, therefore, the Lover's erotic quest finally regains center stage, at the end of the poem, the bizarre phallic metaphors with which he is shown to achieve his equally bizarre object—penile penetration of a rose—do not find us unprepared. The Lover of Guillaume's elegant and mimetic poem had long since faded out of existence, by a process comparable to the way Swift's shifting satiric imagination transmutes the iconicallly naive Gulliver of Book One into a series of quite different personae, all essentially speaking with Swiftian voices or with identifiable ironic variations. The difference between the Lover of the first half of the *Roman* (especially Guillaume's four thousand lines)

and that of the latter is symptomatic of the prevailing differences between Guillaume's personification allegory and Jean's.

* * * * * * * * * * *

The dream itself begins with the most sustained passage of purely
iconographic description in the entire *Roman*: the account of the ten
female personifications who are imaged on the outside of the wall surrounding the garden of *Deduit*. These figures, with conventional
iconographic attributes, are Hatred, Felony, Villainy, Covetousness,
Avarice, Envy, Sorrow, Old Age, Pope-Holiness, and Poverty. Lewis
and many other critics see these images as "those whom the garden
for ever excludes," representatives of modes of behavior and experience alien to the "courtly life" symbolized by the garden, from
which they turn away.[78] But this view may express a kind of delusion
(not necessarily limited to *Deduit* and his friends and descendants).
An alternative interpretation is offered by Fleming: "Though ten in
number, these abstractions are clearly based on the concept of the
seven capital vices and, within the ironic economy of the *Roman* as a
whole, form a part of the self-mocking trappings of the religion of carnal love."[79] Fleming's view appears to be supported by the Collins
gloss, which remarks: "The consequence of worldly *Deduit* is to dwell
with Villainy, Hate, Poverty, and the other images painted on the
wall of *Deduit*."[80]

Once he is admitted to the garden, the Lover encounters allegorical entities of three general kinds: personifications which are con-
genial to courtly life and love (or, if one prefers, the enterprise of
carnal love); personifications hostile to it; and the rose itself, not a
personification really but a pudendal emblem representing the young
girl whom the Lover comes to love—and especially that part of her
which he chiefly craves. The hostile personifications are few, and two
of them at least are decidedly disagreeable: *Dangier* and Foul Mouth.
These are abetted by the female personifications Shame, Fear, and
Jealousy. Of the hostile figures, only Reason, though opposed to Love
and in fact the "ideological center" of the opposition, is not in some
sense unpleasant. The explanation is that Reason, though the
mother of Shame, is not really of the same company as the others,
whom she transcends: she "looms down from her tower" at the dis-
tressed and frustrated lover, "comes down" to try to help him. The
garden of *Deduit* with its partisans and enemies of Love is not her

milieu. The others have existence only in it—they are in fact aspects of it; she has an independent existence, above them and apart from them.

Three things may be suggested about these hostile personifications. First of all, the "opposition party" is presented here from the perspective of the Lover and of those who support Love. The very shabbiness of these figures and their peevish, querulous talk are expressions of Love's disdain for them. They are not, then, in any sense "objective" icons, independent of parti pris, expressive of the permanent order of things, like their iconic ancestors of both persuasions in the *Psychomachia* (and like Reason here). They are, rather, an expression of the world as the Lover and his kind see it—a bit like the facetious expressionistic map of the United States from the perspective of provincial New Yorkers, which Saul Steinberg created for a *New Yorker* cover in March 1976. In this now famous drawing, only a preposterously shrunken Midwest and South separate the metropolis from Las Vegas, Los Angeles, and Florida. (The rose too, as we have noted, in which woman is all pudendum, is an icon of the same "expressionistic" sort.)

Moreover, they represent quite diverse ontological orders. Reason may, of course, be regarded as the Lover's own rational faculty, which he resists and finally ignores; but she is perhaps primarily an archetypal figure, akin to such other great female personifications as the scriptural Wisdom and Boethian Philosophy. Foul Mouth, according to the Collins gloss, represents "mauuaiz renom"—bad reputation—and something like that he must be: bad reputation itself, or those who reveal lovers' behavior and are to that extent the agents of bad reputation.[81] *Dangier* is the most elusive of this group. In his admirable rendering, Dahlberg translated the name as "Resistance," but has more recently questioned this decision.[82] The Collins gloss is not as direct or explicit in defining *Dangier* as it is with regard to other figures: evidence, perhaps, that the glossator too had some doubts about it. He writes of "danger de perdre sa renommee" —danger of losing her reputation—and, as is almost always the case, provides a cogent exposition.[83] *Dangier* is thus a relatively abstract, but wholly real and identifiable, dimension of the situation in which the girl finds herself. He is not perhaps quite part of her own moral or psychological constitution, as Shame and Fear unmistakably are. He is rather part of the seduction situation as the girl sees it, or should see it, from a moral perspective; and to the degree that *Dangier* is "resistance" he represents the approved course of conduct for her. Jealousy, finally, is the leader of the "opposition" and a kind of chorus of the girl's suspicious relatives and friends.[84] These six hostile personifications, then, represent five distinctly different levels of abstraction, and this is surely one of the reasons why Guillaume's allegory is so much livelier and more problematic than that of Prudentius.

Another reason is that Guillaume's personifications are often a good deal more than personifications. Like other figures in the best of late medieval personification allegory—*Everyman*, for instance—*Dangier* and Foul Mouth take on something of an autonomous existence as mimetic, coherent "characters," only part of whose role—the most important part, to be sure—is encompassed by their allegorical identities. The relish with which the manuscript illustrators imaged these villainous types testifies to the effectiveness of Guillaume's mimesis. The extra-allegorical features of the two males among Guillaume's hostile company (the phenomenon can be seen to a smaller degree in the four females, as well) may evoke from us questions with reference to the allegory itself which provide a stimulating dash of uncertainty and asymmetry. Why, we wonder, must transcendent Reason consort, even by implication, with two such disagreeable personages? We are apt in such matters to long sometimes for Prudentian consistency, particularly when on the side of the angels. Guillaume's complexity of personification complicates the allegory and reinforces the need for our imaginative participation in the process of comprehending it.

When we turn to the far more numerous partisans of Love—the garden, after all, belongs to one of them—we find even more levels of abstraction, and even more extra-allegorical autonomy of characterization. The God of Love is Cupid, son of Venus, emblem and patron of erotic pleasure (though the Collins gloss interprets him, in a curiously modern way, as a projection of the Lover's own nature).[85] He is surrounded by personifications of certain salient aspects of the life of elegant leisure which encourage love, and which are also aspects of the lives and natures of the Lover and girl themselves: Idleness (the Ovidian gatekeeper of love, sine qua non to all the rest);[86] *Deduit* (Diversion), the owner and principal icon of the garden; Joy, Courtesy, Beauty, Wealth, Generosity, Youth, Openness, and Pity. The last two of these symbolize impulses peculiarly within the girl's nature. Besides the God of Love, there are three other male personifications: Sweet Looks, the God's handsome young squire; Fair Welcome, son of Courtesy; and Friend. The first of these would seem to be, like most of the other figures, a dimension of "courtly love" as well as of the lovers. The last represents perhaps, like the Lover himself, young men of a recognizable nature, class, and role (akin to Pandarus in Chaucer's *Troilus and Criseyde*).[87]

Fair Welcome is the oddest of the group, and in a way the most peculiar personification in the poem, representing as he does the young girl's accessibility, that part of her which her lover most directly encounters and which most directly encounters him. Fair Welcome is akin to Openness and Pity, those other dimensions or faculties of the girl which most conspicuously advance the Lover's cause. The Collins gloss identifies Fair Welcome entirely with the girl, but makes a subtle distinction: whereas the rose symbolizes *sa amoureuse*—i.e., the girl from the Lover's perspective—Fair Welcome is *la voluptueuse fille*, the same personage as she experiences herself.[88] In any event, the incongruity of this male personification leads to bizarre complications of gender in Fair Welcome's encounter with the Old Woman, who undertakes to share her female experience with Fair Welcome in the strangest "woman talk" in medieval literature. On the other hand, it is a condition of the imprisonment of Fair Welcome in Jealousy's tower, a central episode of the poem. Above all, it makes the Lover's association with him (her?) oddly bisexual, halfway between that of lovers and that of male companions—or, more accurately, perhaps, asexual, thus possibly symbolizing the essentially reflexive or narcissistic nature of the Lover's passion.

Fair Welcome, then, is an exception to the generally realistic texture of Guillaume's allegory, within the limits of his abstract conception; and even Fair Welcome is himself a coherent and consistent personification, apart from complexities of gender. Guillaume's principal figures, like the first and chief of them, the Lover, are all in some essential sense mimetic; and though they are not, nor were they meant to be, "round," "three-dimensional," or "realistic," neither are they mere walking abstractions, like the virtues and vices of Prudentius. All this is perhaps one way of saying that Guillaume's *Roman* is indeed what it claims to be, a romance. Its characters allow the reader some measure of emotional identification, and its allegory exists in tandem with a fleshed-out fable.

* * * * * * * * * * * *

It is precisely as characters in a romance that Jean's allegorical personifications differ from Guillaume's. Although Jean retains all of Guillaume's figures and adds dozens more, the poem ceases to be a romance, and the personifications "characters." Even the principal ones lack the vestigial verisimilitude of *Dangier* or Fair Welcome. Nor are they walking abstractions, for they do not even walk very much (though they occasionally fight). They mainly talk. Much of their talk is lively and has the ring of human speech. It is in the vigor of their talk, the dialectical vitality of their assertions, the narrative or dramatic force of their exempla and anecdotes, that Jean's Reason, Friend, False Seeming, and Old Woman have their life. Their relations to each other, and to the now equally abstract Lover, are of small concern to us; and, in any event, these relations are lost amidst the vast monologues.

These monologues differ greatly in structure: Reason delivers a fundamentally cogent, philosophical argument to the Lover why he should abandon the God of Love. Despite her exempla and digressions (which all actually articulate some part of her argument), she says the kind of things that Reason ought to be saying. Friend, her de facto opponent, presents a highly idiosyncratic, shifting statement, which sometimes seems rather incoherent—as might be thought fitting for an enemy of Reason; neither does it define a personality behind it. False Seeming, on the other hand, is distinctly single-minded in projecting the character of a quintessentially hypocritical, self-serving cleric; while the Old Woman's mélange of melancholy reflections and cynical advice based on her experiences in love is the most psychologically realistic of all the monologues, however odd it may sound as directed to the male personification of Fair Welcome.

All four figures (only the first two of which are continuations from Guillaume) have literary antecedents. They are intensely interesting icons, abstract conceptions in flesh, though they display varying degrees of mimetic realism. This is equally true of the two great personifications whom Jean introduces in the final sections of the poem, Nature and Genius. Like Reason, these are not abstractions of human types but philosophical conceptions of ancient pedigree, taken by Jean from the writings of Alanus de Insulis and other philosophical sources, and used by him as mouthpieces for the dialectical development of his conclusion.[89]

By the end of the *Roman*, it has become clear where Jean had been heading all along: away from the relatively straightforward expression of a few important ideas through the medium of allegorical romance, toward complex expression of many related ideas through the medium of a loosely dramatic monologue. In Jean's poem, the allegorical personifications are ultimately swallowed by their words.

5

Satire

The *Roman* is, of course, all about sex. Virtually the entire poem purports to be an elaborate erotic dream, and poem and dream end with an allegorical copulation. Being medieval, the poem is also about love, the all-embracing subject of most sophisticated poetry in the Middle Ages. Christian doctrine, said St. Augustine, quoting St. Paul, is epitomized in the injunction to love.[90] If love is the chief subject of Christian doctrine, it is not surprising to find it as well the chief subject of literature which came out of Christian courts in the high Middle Ages. The greatest masters of lyric, romance, narrative, allegory—the troubadours, Chrétien de Troyes, Wolfram von Eschenbach, Gottfried von Strassburg, Guillaume de Lorris and Jean de Meun, Dante, Boccaccio, Petrarch, Chaucer, the Pearl poet, and others—are concerned above all with love. As we have suggested earlier, the tremendous, illuminating novelty in all this for the unprepared and thoroughly departmentalized modern reader is the more or less Platonic assumption that all expressions of human desire are hierarchically related expressions of love, from the charitable love of God and neighbor through sanctified sexuality, friendship, the rational love of self and other created things, down to the irrational, self-destructive obsessions of carnal appetite and comparable manifestations of *cupiditas*.

How shall one assess the Lover's passion to copulate with "Rose"? This is obviously one of the basic questions which each critical reader of the *Roman* must ask. Reason's short speech in Guillaume's part defines his love pragmatically as a deplorable and painful folly. The very much longer discourse given to Reason by Jean develops a philo-

48

sophical case against it; and in the priest Genius's difficult discourse, the last of Jean's dialectical chapters, Christian distinctions emerge from an invidious comparison of the garden of *Deduit* with the park of the Lamb. The Collins gloss calls it (among other, similar things) *fol amour* and *amour desordonnee*, with Reason and Genius as authorities for so doing.[91] The "Robertsonian" critics—Fleming, Dahlberg, Robertson himself—agree.[92] Lewis, who usually approaches the *Roman* quite differently, concurs with them in this important matter:

> [Guillaume's story] ... is the story of a lover whose deepest convictions remained opposed to his love and who knew that he acted neither well nor wisely. By implication the author therefore condemns what he relates. If he had finished his poem, it would probably have closed with the familiar palinode. He gives to Reason exactly the function which she had in the *Lancelot*: to speak the truth and not to be heard.[93]

Gunn believes that Nature and Genius, like Reason, are "emanations of the Eternal Being," but, unlike her, support the Lover; and he finds the contradiction unreconciled.[94] Lecoy is perhaps representative of the majority of critics in giving less weight to Reason's objections and finding Guillaume as above all the exponent of a new, civilized way of life:

> Guillaume is, in fact, one of the most resolute champions of that "courtesy" which sought to give a new form to personal relationships and, more particularly, to the life of the feelings, in medieval society. His work proposes above all to show us in action the power of two fundamental points of this new code: unqualified, virtually religious respect for woman, and love as the principal or essential condition of all true worth and perfection.[95]

We have already touched on Andreas Capellanus's *De Amore*, that central document of the New Courtesy, and the lack of scholarly unanimity about its meaning. The division with respect to the *Roman* is almost exactly parallel: those who find Andreas satirical of *amour desordonnee* are usually disposed to regard Reason, in both parts of the *Roman*, as an authorial *raisonneur* whose position forms the intellectual and moral touchstone of the poem.

This issue is at the heart of any reading of the *Roman*, and its very scope precludes further discussion here, except for brief consideration of one related matter: the poem's use of classical mythological materials bearing traditional satiric meanings. The most important such use in Guillaume's section is the connection of the Fountain of Love, iconographic centerpiece of *Deduit's* garden, with the Ovidian legend of Narcissus and Echo. This fountain, says Guillaume, is where Narcissus died; and the "perilous mirror" at its bottom, in which the Lover sees for the first time that rosebud which he at once adores, is the very reflecting surface in which Narcissus conceived his fatal passion for himself. The Collins gloss regards Narcissus as a type of the Lover, and comments on the passage as follows:

> By Narcissus, who admires himself in the mirror, should be understood the foolish, proud, voluptuous young men who admire themselves in their false vanities, which intoxicate them, and plunge into the sorrowful, deceiving darkness of the false fountain, in which they are given to taking their voluptuousnesses, which flee them and lead them on to death. And afterward, they are washed in a water called Styx, as was Narcissus. This Styx is one of the bogs of hell, and represents suffering or sorrow.[96]

This traditional mythographic account of Narcissus reminds us that Guillaume, in associating the classical story with the garden of *Deduit* (and, especially, with the Lover), must have intended it to be more than merely decorative. In fact, the connection might arguably be taken, as Robertson was the first to note, as a rather covert endorsement of Reason's condemnation of the Lover.[97]

Jean's section of the poem contains many more mythological allusions, and several myths narrated at considerable length. Among these are the stories of Pygmalion and of his great-grandson Adonis. Each is closely related in one way or another to the Lover's enterprise, and it is therefore of interest that conventional mythographic tradition declared the one an irrational idolator and the other a lecher and sensualist.[98] A comprehensive study of the mythological materials in the *Roman* has yet to be written, though Robertson broke ground with his valuable researches. The rich notes in Langlois's edition and in Dahlberg's translation survey all the allusions as such; it remains for their conventional associations in the mythographical literature to be assembled. When this is done, we shall have a clearer view than at present of how these alleged "digressions" may actually help articulate the Lover's folly, and therefore constitute an important expression of the *Roman's* satire.

* * * * * * * * * * *

Much of the other satire in the *Roman*—and there is a great deal more, almost all in Jean's section—is not specifically about sex, but about diverse corruptions of love, in the large medieval sense considered earlier. An important instance of this is the corruption of ecclesiastical charity.

In the figure of False Seeming, Jean objectifies those ecclesiastical corruptions which were to draw satire from nearly all the chief European poets of the later Middle Ages: Dante, Boccaccio, Langland, and Chaucer, among others. (Chaucer's ecclesiastical satire was directly influenced by Jean's: see p. 82 below.) False Seeming is a type of the religious who is proud and worldly, avaricious, self-serving, cupidinous, and finally hypocritical: the wolf in sheep's clothing and an inversion of the proper religious life. Moreover, lacking even shame, he coolly declares himself to be just what he is. He is thus an iconic figure, more a personification of his special kind of evil than an imitation of a corrupt man. (His English progeny include Chaucer's Pardoner and Shakespeare's Iago.) When he explains to the companions of Love who he is, he sounds distanced, as though referring to himself as an abstraction:

Barons, hear my theme: he who wants to become acquainted with False Seeming must seek him in the world or in the cloister. I dwell in no place except these two, but more in one and less in the other. Briefly, I am lodged where I think that I am better hidden. The safest hiding place is under the most humble garment. The religious are very covert, the worldly more open. I do not want to blame or defame the religious calling, in whatever habit

one may find it. I shall not, as I may, blame the humble
and loyal religious life, although I do not love it. I have in
mind the false religious, the malicious criminals who want
to wear the habit but do not want to subdue their hearts.
[10,976–10,996]

False Seeming's long discourse (10,922–11,984) should be understood in the context of thirteenth-century reaction against corruption among the fraternal orders, the competition between secular and
regular clergy, as well perhaps as the hostility of humanist authors
toward certain friars' small regard for poetic *sententia*, for the capacity
of poetry to convey serious truths of religion and philosophy.[99] The
key figure in this reaction (False Seeming refers to him more than
once) was William of Saint-Amour (1202–72), rector of the University of Paris and an influential theologian. His hostility to the mendicant orders of friars led to his exile. These historical correlatives are
complex and still not altogether clear. What is certain, however, is
that in developing his ecclesiastical satire, Jean gives us a figure both
expressive of particular actualities of his own generation, and also
universal in reference, as universal as exploitativeness, hypocrisy, and
shamelessness. False Seeming is as easy to apprehend and to relish as
Tartuffe or Iago.

Inevitably, critics are not unanimous as to how all this may be
related to the central issue of the poem. Some are bound to take exception to Professor Dahlberg's assertion that "False Seeming's perversion of the prelatical functions is . . . a reflection of the perversion
of the Lover's reason."[100] In any case, it is undeniable that Jean's
ecclesiastical satire broadens the scope of the *Roman* and thickens its
texture.

* * * * * * * * * * * *

It was neither sexual nor clerical satire which mainly scandalized
Christine de Pisan at the end of the fourteenth century, more than a
century after the *Roman's* completion, and evoked that curious and
fascinating debate on the merits of the *Roman* which is known as the
Quarrel (see p. 63–67 below). Christine objected vigorously to the
poem for several reasons, but the chief of these was what she took to
be Jean's antifeminism.

The harshest expression of this occurs in the course of Friend's

discourse to the Lover. This discourse as a whole is contrived to encourage the Lover in his quest: Friend, like Chaucer's Placebo and
Pandarus, is nothing if not accommodating. However, it contains
ironies within ironies, and, as is Jean's wont, something like an ironic
authorial voice often replaces that of the iconic Friend. Certain
speeches, like the following one, require a critical tact more subtle
perhaps than that of Christine for their appreciation:

> Truly, however, women are nearly all eager to take
> and greedy to ravish and devour until nothing can remain
> to those who most proclaim themselves theirs, and who
> love them most loyally. Juvenal tells us as much when he
> relates of Hiberina that she would rather lose one of her
> eyes than be attached to one man, for she was of such hot
> matter that no one man could satisfy her. No woman will
> ever be so ardent nor her love so secure that she may not
> wish to torment and despoil her sweetheart. [8,251–8,266]

There is much more in the same vein. Such behavior, says the
Friend, is a consequence of our fall from the purity of the Golden
Age. He proceeds to show us at entertaining length how a modern
Jealous Husband might address his wife. The result is a totally
destructive picture of female manners and morals, replete with allusions to such antifeminist superstars as Juvenal and Theophrastus;
and though he ultimately tries to distance himself from this Jealous
Husband ("this mad jealous boor—may his flesh be fed to the
wolves"), the Friend seems in all this somewhat disingenuous.

Another scintillating (or shocking) outpouring of apparently mis-
ogynistic satire transpires when the Old Woman, guardian of the imprisoned Fair Welcome, instructs him in the cynical ways of women
in love. Her monologue occupies nearly a tenth of the entire poem,
and its attitude and substance may be indicated by the following
passage:

> Briefly, all men betray and deceive women; all are sen-
> sualists, taking their pleasure anywhere. Therefore we
> should deceive them in return, not fix our hearts on one.
> Any woman who does so is a fool; she should have several
> friends, and, if possible, act so as to delight them to the

point where they are driven to distraction. If she has no
graces, let her learn them. Let her be haughtier toward
those who, because of her hauteur, will take more trouble
to serve her in order to deserve love, but let her scheme to
take from those who make light of her love. [13,235–
13,248]

This advice is Ovidian and exploitative. Nothing could be less
idealistic, less "courtly," less gentle and genteel, less sentimental.
Christine de Pisan was sorely tried by such passages, though her an-
noyance may have come at least partly from her lack of comprehen-
sion of Jean's literary strategies.[101] Chaucer, for one, took over the
material and the strategies from Jean for his triumphant creation of
the Wife of Bath, and—despite Love's displeasure in the Prologue to
his *Legend of Good Women* (see p. 76–77 below)—does not appear on
this account to have lost his standing at court, or to have aroused the
ire of the English ladies.

There is, however, no consensus among critics as to exactly what
Jean was up to here: whether his antifeminism represents an ancient
deposit of monkish misogyny; whether it is rather to be explained as
scholarly coarseness, literary jeu d'esprit (a playful attempt to raise
the ghosts of Juvenal and Ovid), rough masculine fun; or whether
perhaps (keeping in mind the personages who speak it, and their
natures and motives in the poem) it is part of the encompassing satire
of love's corruptions and their consequences, which some think to be
the chief matter of the *Roman*.

* * * * * * * * * * * *

The most difficult part of the *Roman* to appreciate—both in itself
and in its relation to the rest of the poem—is undoubtedly the five-
thousand-line episode in which Nature and Genius intervene, ostensibly on the Lover's behalf, just before the denouement (15,861–
20,637). The main problems are three. Much of Nature's enormous
"confession" seems to have little if anything to do with the issues of
the poem. When Nature does ultimately take interest in the Lover's
cause, it is in support of human procreation, an altogether irrelevant
matter to the followers of the God of Love and to *Deduit*, in whose
garden there are no merry-go-rounds or day-care centers. And, finally, when Genius (Nature's priest and confessor) conveys to Love's

host Nature's "excommunication" of the enemies of procreation, he concludes his "sermon" with a call to Christian charity through an invidious comparison between *Deduit's* garden, the Lover's own emblematic locus, and its Christian counterpart, symbolic of salvation, the park of the Lamb.

Scholars have approached this problem in expectably diverse ways, and the literature is too extensive and complex to be more than touched upon here. Langlois felt that the entire Nature-Genius episode was inserted by Jean "simply for the instruction of the reader," i.e., as a vast authorial digression;[102] and in similar vein, René Louis, likewise ignoring dramatic and dialectical implications, regards Nature and Genius as providing an alternative set of symbols to those of Guillaume's garden.[103] Most critics, however, have addressed the problem more directly. Lecoy suggests that Nature's endorsement of the Lover's cause is only a ruse, designed to assure procreation.[104] He does not take up the role of Nature's and Genius's words themselves, though he does valuably discuss their backgrounds in Alanus and other authors. Lewis thought this part of the poem a botched attempt to draw mystical parallels between human sexuality and divine love:

> It was the misfortune of Jean de Meun to have read and remembered everything; and nothing that he remembered could be kept out of his poem. Mystical ideas were present to his mind along with naturalistic ideas; from his natural treatment of sex he reverts ... to the mystical parallel of human and divine love which he had hinted at in the speech of Reason. This final attempt to "do something" with courtly love is made, oddly and clumsily enough, through the mouth of Genius; not that justifications, both subtle and pleasing, cannot be found, but that Jean has not found them.[105]

Gunn, however, saw the doctrines of Nature and Genius as, dialectically, the highest and last stage of the *Roman's* developing analysis of love, and their intervention as a dramatic exhortation to the followers of Love to rise above their meaner instincts:

The poet makes it evident that the doctrine taught by

Nature and Genius is by no means on the same plane with
those set forth by the preceding doctors of love. It has a
universality, a finality which the doctrines of the
others—excepting Reason—do not possess. Nature—in
spite of the dialectic that fills her discourse—and Genius,
her deputy, do not argue; they promulgate their doctrine
as the all-encompassing and all-binding truth. They appear appropriately, therefore, after the hero and the
heroine have passed through the preliminary stages of
desire and of education in the meaning of love.[106]

Some important scholarship of the past twenty years has taken a
quite different approach, regarding the personifications and doctrines
of Nature and Genius as themselves less than normative. Robertson
asserts, for instance, that Genius, Nature's confessor, is not really a
Christian priest at all, though he sometimes talks like one, but rather
represents natural inclination, "the inclination of created things to
act naturally."[107]

Neither Nature nor Genius is responsible for this result,
over which they have no control. The responsibility rests
with Cupid and Venus, with desire and pleasure, to which
man voluntarily subjects himself as the lover did at the
beginning of the poem. The end of the poem is thus simply
an elaborate allegorical account of what Raison says much
earlier about the nature and function of desire and
pleasure. Nature is innocent, but man, through his erring
will, abuses her, making the laws of Nature suit his own
cupidinous ends.[108]

Rosemond Tuve sees what she calls the "ersatz . . . religion" of
Nature and Genius as an elaborate and subtle satire, in which Genius
is "a blandly condescending male" and Nature "a poor faulty female,
not overbright."[109] Neither is what he or she purports to be. They
share the disorder of their erotic surroundings, and, in particular,
Genius's pastoral-sounding homily is disfigured by all sorts of error
and heterodoxy. John Fleming, in the most detailed and provocative
exposition of this general point of view, assesses the matter thus:

56

The action of the final chapter of the *Roman* runs its course
without reference to Reason, and the necessary hierarchies
are neatly inverted. Nature does not use Venus; Venus
uses Nature. . . . That Jean should on the one hand hold
the goddess Natura in the highest respect, making her the
vehicle of much conventional knowledge and wisdom concerning sublunary matters, and on the other expose her as
a slightly ridiculous figure of fun reveals no confusion of
poetic design or philosophic formulation. As always, Jean
depends upon his readers to bring to the poem a set of fairly rigorous commonplace theological concepts against
which his ironies can play. . . . There are . . . many things
about which Nature can know nothing whatsoever, and
the adduction of "natural" solutions to questions which
demand supernatural ones gives rise to the comedy of the
Roman. . . . With specific regard to sexual behavior,
Nature's advice to man is no different from that which she
gives to animals. She urges heterosexual intercourse to the
end that the species may be preserved.[110]

We have here one of those intensely interesting questions of
implication and tone which provide part of the *Roman's* peculiar intellectual challenge. The careful reader will wish to make his own
survey of critical assessments as he listens to Nature and Genius for
himself.

He may also want to look into Jean's immediate literary source
for these two figures, the *De Planctu Naturae* of Alanus de Insulis
(Alan of Lille).[111] This influential work of the mid-twelfth century,
much admired throughout the later Middle Ages, is a philosophical
satire, composed—like Boethius's *Consolation*—in alternating sections
of verse and prose. Nature's complaint comes to the narrator in a
trance: of all her created things, only man violates her laws. This contrast between disobedient man and the rest of creation forms precisely the burden of Nature's "confession" in the *Roman*, which is undoubtedly modelled after Alanus's book. Homosexuality is the first
such violation which Nature deplores, but is only one of several kinds
of irrational sensuality that displease her. She proceeds to survey
other kinds of nonsexual behavior which she also regards as un-
natural: gluttony, avarice, arrogance, and the like. Finally, Genius

comes on the scene to read out his sentence of excommunication for those who have sinned against Nature.

We must notice that in Alanus, Nature and Genius are normative; Nature acknowledges that her jurisdiction is restricted to the realm of the created, and that "supernatural" matters are beyond her scope; and she is not single-mindedly preoccupied with replenishment of the species (although procreation and the "naturalness" of heterosexual marriage and generation do receive much of her attention). The *De Planctu Naturae* is not, however, despite its great interest and influence, a ripe work, and its thematic development is less clear than in such mature productions of Alanus as the *Anticlaudianus*.[112] Nevertheless, it seems safe to say that the principal complaints which Nature makes against man are that by sinning, he behaves "unnaturally," and, with specific regard to sexuality, that he is given to gross sensuality (of which homosexuality, which precludes procreation, seems to her the most conspicuous example).

Alanus's satire, then, is entirely consonant with traditional moral philosophy and with Christian doctrine. Nature and Genius of the *De Planctu Naturae* would be natural allies of Reason in the *Roman*, not antagonists. Clearly, therefore, these figures have undergone a sea change in transit from Alanus to the *Roman*, where they are apparent advocates of the cause which Reason condemns. Careful reading of these last sections of the poem, however, may persuade us that their advocacy is more apparent than real; that heterosexual union and procreation are what they approve, not *fol amour*— indeed, that Genius's ultimate condemnation of the garden of *Deduit* assures us of this; but that the dreamer/narrator, and the barons of Love, certainly *believe* that they have this distinguished endorsement. If so, it would be neither the first time that we have found the Lover's perspective shaping the appearances of things in this garden (see p. 43 above), nor the first time that Jean would be seen exhibiting (like Chaucer after him) a taste for parody.

6

The Poem's Reception

The survival of 250 or more manuscripts of the *Roman*, and the frequency with which the poem was printed during the fifteenth and sixteenth centuries, are ample testimony to its fame. As Langlois noted:

> The success of the *Roman de la Rose* was immediate and considerable, and lasted, without interruption, until the middle of the sixteenth century. . . . Its influence on literature established itself from the thirteenth century; in the fourteenth, borrowings, imitations, quotations multiplied to the extent that a simple listing of them would be tiresome, and a volume would hardly suffice to show the extent of the influence which Guillaume and Jean exerted upon subsequent literature.[113]

That volume has yet to be written, and we shall attempt here only a general survey.

Within the century or so after its completion, the *Roman* had appeared in at least two Italian and two Dutch adaptations, in addition to the Middle English *Romaunt*.[114] Both Italian texts are usually dated c. 1300, and mark the beginning of a definable influence on Italian verse of the fourteenth century. (Langlois rejects, however, Benedetto's claim that the *Roman* also influenced certain thirteenth-century Italian poets, such as Brunetto Latini.)[115] One of the Italian versions, *Il Fiore*, may have been written by a Tuscan called Durante. In it, the *Roman* is reduced to 232 sonnets; the rose becomes a "flower"; all descriptive, moral, and philosophical passages are omitted, and only the erotic material and the satire upon mendicant friars is retained. The other Italian poem, *Il Detto d'Amore*, was, according to Langlois, "directly inspired by the *Roman*, and includes no idea not to be found in Guillaume and Jean, especially in the work of the first." Of the Dutch versions, one was by Einric van Aken, and was completed before 1317, possibly somewhat earlier. The *Roman* appears not to have been translated in Spain, though it was hardly unknown there. It had to wait until 1839 for its first German version.[116]

In France itself, of course, the poem's influence was most pronounced. As early as the 1290s, Gui de Mori's adaptation appeared, and other thirteenth-century poems also bear the *Roman's* mark: among them the *Dieu d'Amours*, the *Dit de la Rose*, the "Carmen de Rosa" in *Carmina Burana*, Rutebeuf's *Voie de Paradis*, the *Roman de la Poire*, certain *chansons* of Thibaut de Champagne, and possibly the *Tournoiement Antecrist* of Huon de Méri. In the fourteenth century, Guillaume de Deguilleville's *Pelerinage de la Vie Humaine* (1330–35, second version written in 1355) both reveals in its own composition the influence of the *Roman* and also takes a critical attitude toward it, when Venus declares that Jean de Meun is really one of her men.[117] The most prominent poet of the latter part of the century, Guillaume de Machaut, was deeply influenced by the *Roman*:

> The longer poems of Machaut display an interest of the kind we might expect in exemplary materials. . . . But Machaut is much more important as a continuator of the allegorical devices of the *Roman de la Rose*, which he not only used, but adapted to suit his own purposes. He does not make intensive use of conventional iconographic descriptions, although good examples of the technique are furnished by the garden in "Le Dit de l'Alerion," and the fountain in "La Fonteinne Amoureuse." But he does use Jean de Meun's personified abstractions. The God of Love, Raison, and other familiar figures appear once more. . . . The personified abstractions are for the most part very gracious and courteous beings, cultivated and good-natured ladies and gentlemen, who have more "personality" than their predecessors in the *Roman*. Their attractiveness is actually not difficult to account for, since

Machaut customarily prefers to use Love and his followers
to show the characteristics of reasonable love rather than
to mock the failings of the kind of foolish love attacked by
Jean de Meun.[118]

Machaut himself exerted a powerful influence on such other
poets of the period as Froissart, Deschamps, and Oton de Grandson,
and thus transmitted to them the style and techniques he had
learned from the *Roman*.[119] In England, Chaucer, of course, is preeminent
among the poets who learned part of their craft from Guillaume
and Jean (as well as from Machaut), and Gower is another. In the
next century, Lydgate would join the company. These names by no
means exhaust the *Roman's* influence on French and English literature
of the fourteenth and early fifteenth centuries. The subject, as
we have noted already, remains to be thoroughly examined. They do,
however, give us some sense of its importance.

* * * * * * * * * * *

One of the most interesting products of the *Roman's* influence at
this time is the *Echecs Amoureux* (Chess of Love), attributed to the late
fourteenth century.[120] This poem has not been edited or published,
and, unfortunately, we are likely never to have a good edition of it,
for its only complete manuscript was seriously damaged at Dresden
during the Second World War.[121] The poem was sufficiently important
in its day to have been translated a few years after its appearance
by John Lydgate, as *Reason and Sensuality* (c. 1408). Its author was an
admirer and careful student of the *Roman*, and his poem develops the
situation of a young man walking through an allegorical garden of
love where he is given diverse kinds of advice with diverse moral implications:
some good, some bad.[122]

At least as interesting to students of the *Roman* as the *Echecs*
itself, however, is a prose gloss upon it which appears in five MSS in
the Bibliothèque Nationale, and which Professor Fleming, whose discussion
of it is essential, calls "a fascinating document, a major
achievement of late medieval humanism, which . . . discusses the
'sens allégorique' of the Garden of *Deduit* in precisely the way Robertson's
analysis of other literary gardens would lead us to suspect it
might."[123] This *Echecs* gloss, that is to say, illuminates not only its
own poem but the *Roman* as well. Fleming describes and assesses its

contents as follows:

> Like John the Scot, in his tropological analysis of the
> Garden of Eden, [the glossator] thinks of the world of
> human nature as one large garden. Within this there are
> three smaller gardens, as it were, belonging to Pallas, Juno,
> and Venus; and representing the three modes of life. He
> discusses all three gardens at some length, but it is to the
> garden of Venus that he directs his most penetrating ex-
> egesis. Venus' garden is called the Garden of *Deduit*, and
> its doorkeeper is Oiseuse. We are once again in familiar
> territory, and he says as much: this garden of Venus is the
> same garden written of in the *Roman de la Rose.* "Venus is
> not forgotten, for she has a gracious and pleasing garden
> where all those who seek the delights and vanities of the
> world can amuse and enjoy themselves. Oiseuse keeps the
> gate of this garden, which is the real Garden of Delight of
> which we would speak."

All of this is to say that the Garden of *Deduit* is a post-
lapsarian Eden, a specific and accessible image pregnant
with rich possibilities of interpretation. Plurality of meanings is a commonplace of medieval scriptural interpretation. . . . Such a device is employed by the exegete of the
Echecs, who now considers the Garden of *Deduit* itself as
the world. . . . "Thus the whole garden is like the world,
even more so the Garden of *Deduit* of which we are speaking." Here there are many wonderful and beautiful things,
yet they are transitory and mutable. Flowers wither, day
turns to night, and so forth. "For the comforts and
pleasures of the world—the joys, loves, honors, wealth,
and all sorts of worldly prosperity which one enjoys in
it—are all vanity, transitory things, accompanied by difficult labors and pain, intermingled with sorrow, as has
been said many times before, and as Fortune has so often
shown."[124]

The *Echecs Amoureux* and its gloss demonstrate, then, once more
what we can readily learn from reading the works of Machaut,
Chaucer, and their contemporaries: that by the latter half of the four-

teenth century, the *Roman de la Rose* had provided western European poetry with an allegorical locus, a set of allegorical personifications, and an archetypal fable through which the period might project its abiding interest in the varieties of love and their relation to the inherited values of humanist Christian culture.

* * * * * * * * * * *

We have already observed that as early as the mid-fourteenth century, hostility to the *Roman* had revealed itself in Deguilleville's *Pelerinage de la Vie Humaine*, in which Jean de Meun is said to be himself a follower rather than a satirizer of the carnal Venus. Hostility of a different sort appeared at the very end of the century, in a well-publicized epistolary exchange between certain of the poem's admirers (Jean de Montreuil, Gontier Col, Pierre Col) and detractors (Christine de Pisan, Jean Gerson). Known ever since as "the Quarrel"—the *débat* or *querelle*—on the *Roman de la Rose*, this episode provides a fascinating, if still somewhat clouded, glimpse into French intellectual life c. 1400, and an index of how deeply the *Roman* was able to stir sophisticated readers of contrary dispositions.[125] Students of the poem are especially interested in the letters of the Quarrel as the earliest examples of sustained "literary criticism" addressed to the *Roman*.

The first document of the Quarrel is usually said to be Christine's *Epistre au Dieu d'Amours* (1399), a poem in which women are defended against the slanderous attacks on their character ascribed to such defamers as Ovid and Jean de Meun. (This poem was printed in the early sixteenth century as *Le Contre Romant de la Rose, nommé le Gratia Dei*.)[126] Christine de Pisan, Venetian born, lived most of her life in France (1363–c. 1440), and became the first Frenchwoman to support herself by her pen.[127] She was a prolific and talented poet, an early feminist, and a vigorous and individual personality. In her delightful letters deploring and refuting the *Roman*, she sounds at once high-minded and feline, humble and aggressive, deferential to distinguished gentlemen but merciless toward their errors, pious, self-effacing, and very clever. Along with her resentment of Jean de Meun's supposed misogyny and hostility to marriage, she repeatedly and lengthily condemns his use of gross terms for the male generative organs.

There is no definitive canon of documents in the Quarrel.

Charles Ward counted fourteen, Langlois fifteen; more recently, Eric Hicks has included twenty-four, Joseph L. Baird and John R. Kane twenty-two, and Peter Potansky twenty-nine.[128] Some are in French, some in Latin. All were apparently written between May 1399 and the end of 1402.

Christine's ally in opposition to the *Roman* was Jean Gerson (1362–1428), one of the great theologians of his age and chancellor of the University of Paris. Gerson found the poem so immoral and dangerous that he urged its burning. In his *Treatise* against it—composed, interestingly, in the mode of the dream vision—he has Chastity draw up eight articles in condemnation of the *Roman*, and, more specifically, of the Lover, whom he holds responsible for all the contents of the poem: thus, the Lover has persecuted Chastity and associated with "an accursed Old Woman worse than the devil, who teaches, shows, exhorts all young virgins to sell their bodies . . ."; he condemns marriage and reviles all women; he castigates young men who take up the religious life; he uses impure and lecherous language; he slanders Reason; he speaks of holy things with foul words; "he promises Paradise, glory, and reward to all men and women who perform the works of the flesh, even outside marriage"; "in his own person, he uses holy and sacred words to name the dishonorable parts of the body and impure and shameful sins. . . ."[129]

The dream ends with Lady Theological Eloquence, the advocate, urging the court of Christian Justice to ban the work:

> May such a book therefore be put aside and exterminated without any use in the future, especially in those parts in which he employs disreputable and prohibited characters, such as the accursed Old Woman, who ought to be judged to the punishment of the pillory; and Venus, that is, Lechery, which is mortal sin; and the Foolish Lover, who ought not to be allowed to perform foolishness for his own pleasure.[130]

Although the *Roman's* detractors, like Chastity in her indictment, generally fail to distinguish between its authors' satirical personae and the authors themselves, or between the authorial narrator and the Lover of his dream, their case is somewhat less simplistic than these excerpts suggest, and has even attracted some modest sympathy from a few modern scholars, although the defenders are (naturally) thought by most readers to have the better part of the debate. Grover Furr, for instance, asserts that Christine de Pisan and Jean Gerson well understood that the *Roman* could be thought immoral only in a literal sense, and that it is in fact an allegorical satire; but believing that contemporary readers would not recognize this, they considered it dangerous even so.[131] Yet the matter is considerably more complex. Although most commentators take the debate very seriously, some, such as Rosemond Tuve, urge us to give greater attention to its "*jeu d'esprit* quality."[132] Some of the recent scholarship, including Professor Furr's excellent dissertation, seeks to understand the Quarrel in the context of developing French humanism, and with respect to rivalry among religious and intellectual groups of the time. More investigation must be accomplished before we can adequately gauge the intention and tone of these intriguing documents, and the precise kinds of seriousness (and playfulness) that they embody.

The *Roman's* defenders were no less distinguished than its detractors, and were in fact among the most important humanists of France. Jean de Montreuil was provost of Lille and sometime secretary to the dukes of Berry, Burgundy, and Orleans, to the dauphin, and to King Charles VI. Gontier Col was first secretary and notary to the king; his brother Pierre was likewise a royal secretary, as well as canon of Paris and Tournay.[133] One of their principal arguments, though certainly not their language, might well be used by modern critics to refute the detractors: when Jean de Montreuil, quoting Cicero, avers that Christine sounds like a "Greek whore who dared to criticize the great philosopher Theophrastus," his discourse has the undeniable ring of another age.[134] Besides such *ad feminam* invective, the defenders praise Jean de Meun elaborately as a wise, pious, and orthodox philosopher. Gontier Col writes thus to Christine:

> Woman of high and exalted understanding, worthy of honor and great esteem, I have heard say from many notable clerks that among your other studies and virtuous and praiseworthy works, as I understand by their remarks, you have recently written a kind of invective against the book of the *Rose* composed by my master, teacher, and

friend, the lamented Master Jean de Meun, true Catholic, worthy master, and, in his time, doctor of holy theology, a most profound and excellent philosopher, knowing all that to human understanding is knowable, whose glory and fame lives and will live in the ages to come among understanding men, elevated in his merits, by the grace of God, and by the work of Nature.[135]

But the heart of the defence appears in Pierre Col's long letter to Christine of June-September 1402, in which he invokes the now familiar concept of literary persona to account for, and excuse, those pages of Jean's which had given her and her ally Jean Gerson such offense:

> I say that Master Jean de Meun in his book introduced characters, and made each character speak according to his nature, that is, the Jealous Man as a jealous man, the Old Woman as an old woman, and similarly with the others. And it is wrongheaded to say that the author believes women to be evil as the Jealous Man, in accordance with his character, declares. This is clearly not true of the author. He merely recites what any jealous man says about women invariably, and Meun does this in order to demonstrate and correct the enormous irrationality and disordered passion of jealous men.[136]

The letters of the Quarrel give us a vivid look at several distinctly superior minds at work, and probably also at play; and the apparent oddness of much of what they are up to is a salutary reminder of the great difference between the literary culture of 1400 and that of our own day. Above all, perhaps, two things ultimately emerge through all the rhetorical grapeshot of these documents. For one, we have—in such letters as that of Pierre Col quoted above (and printed in part, together with Christine's response, on pp. 183–202 below)—the first literary analysis of the *Roman*, or it may be of any medieval narrative poem, that a modern reader, once he has penetrated the incrustation of leisurely insult, encomium, and other rhetorical embellishment which the age demanded, can immediately recognize as such. And, finally, we have unmistakable evidence of the sort of esteem in which the *Roman* and its authors were held by some of their late-fourteenth century admirers—who regarded it as a work of high moral seriousness, and its principal author as an important philosopher and Christian thinker—as well as the earnestness with which it was approached by its detractors, who evidently saw in it the potential for great harm.

Gerson himself was constrained to acknowledge Jean de Meun's genius: "In loquentia Gallica non habet similem."[137] In the year 1400, the *Roman de la Rose* was a poem to be reckoned with.

7

After the Quarrel

The *Roman* remained widely read and imitated throughout the fifteenth century. Writers praised or blamed it according to their intellectual disposition and literary orientation. As Langlois has noted, the many writings of this period pro or contra women invariably cite Jean de Meun. Martin Le Franc's *Champion des Dames* (1441) has a chapter called "Contre maistre Jehan de Meun, que les amoureux ensieuvent, et incidentement de son vilain langage," thus following in the path marked out by Christine de Pisan. Others did the same.[138] However, François Villon (1431—c. 1463), the only great poet produced by either France or England during the literary depression of these decades, was deeply influenced by the *Roman*, as Silvio Baridon has described:

> It is impossible to summarize briefly . . . the extent and depth of the influence which Jean de Meun exerted on Villon. It may be said that Villon knew the *Roman* as did few of his contemporaries, that he read and reread it until he had it imprinted on his memory. From this came a series of allusions which we find in his work, even when he is unaware of them. Indeed, the frequent imprecision of his recollections proves that he was quoting from memory. The influence of the *Roman* on Villon, as Louis Thuasne has shown, occurs in two forms, one general and the other particular. The first consists of common ideas on love, death, and fortune; of satire against monks and women; of concern for the passing of time, the vanity of riches,

power, beauty. . . . The second consists of the expression of similar ideas "through the particular phraseology in which they are expressed, the choice of words used." It is a question for Villon here of a direct and continuous influence of the *Roman*, such as we shall not see again with respect to any of the other great authors.[139]

As we have seen, the *Roman* had scarcely been completed before adaptations began to appear in French as well as in other languages. There were more in the fifteenth century: first, a French prose version, which is still unpublished, noted by Langlois in two MSS, B.N. fr. 1462 and Chantilly 744.[140] The second is by Jean Molinet, and was published in three editions between 1500 and 1521. Molinet's version must arrest our attention, both because of its evident success, and because the outlandish interpretation which he attached to it is evidence that by the end of the fifteenth century, as Fleming has observed, many readers were forgetting how to read medieval allegory.[141]

* * * * * * * * * * *

This history of the *Roman de la Rose* in the sixteenth century, indeed, is a striking instance both of the enthusiasm with which Christian allegory was still received and also of the dangers which could beset allegorists whose understanding of the traditional mode, or whose tact in deploying it, was not equal to their enthusiasm. Some readers may see in the immoderate extravaganzas of Molinet, and later of Clément Marot, the impending decadence itself of Christian allegory.

What cannot be doubted is that there was a great appetite for the *Roman* between 1480 and 1538, when twenty-one printed editions appeared. One must, therefore, wonder what was in the minds of those who read the Burgundian *rhétoriqueur* Molinet's prose version. Did they really believe the curious things that Molinet says about the poem's meaning? Though not printed until 1500, this book may have been composed as early as 1483, and it must be one of the oddest productions of its time, and its title one of the silliest:[142]

Cest le romant de la rose
Moralisie cler et net

Translate de rime en prose
Par vostre humble molinet[143]

In a rambling, effusive prologue, Molinet distinguishes three
kinds of love: divine, natural, and foolish. His description of this
third kind has a certain windy charm:

> Foolish love is vain pleasure, frequent cogitation, a blazing
> and inextinguishable fire, insatiable ambition, incredible
> deception, diabolical illusion, of rage the bitter portion, of
> true repose the destruction, of carnal music the invention,
> of gifts habituation, of words multiplication, of foolishness
> accumulation, of honor retrogradation, of sense annihila-
> tion, of famine the expansion, of health retardation, of
> good manners corruption, of vices the generation, of praise
> the suppression, of poverty repletion, of purse evacuation,
> of fraudulent images the profusion, of natural color the
> mutation, of light privation, of strength diminution, of
> spirit perturbation, of bodily members dessication, of life
> abbreviation, of human body perdition, and of the soul
> damnation.

Putting aside his humility, Molinet nourishes the wish to "turn and
convert . . . viciousness to virtue, physical to spiritual, the worldly to
the holy, and above all to moralize the poem."[144]

Each section in his version is followed by a *moralité*, and the
moralités are condensed and summarized at the beginning in a *table*.
Although Molinet acknowledges that the *Roman* is about *fol amour*,
his allegorizations treat the episodes of the poem *in bono*, as representations of Christian history and doctrine, with no evident concern
for coherence or the intentions of Guillaume and Jean. Thus, the
Lover is as if animated by diverse kinds of divine love. The river at
the beginning of the dream represents baptism. The Lover's homage
to the God of Love is as if to a religious superior. His ultimate conquest of the rose represents the cutting down by Joseph of Arimathea
of Christ's body from the cross. All this farrago has of course no accurate relation whatever to the poem itself, nor to any other known
interpretation of it. Bourdillon's verdict on Molinet's allegorizing is
harsh but essentially accurate: "cheap, far-fetched, and unconvinc-

ing."[145] Wishing to convert viciousness to virtue, Molinet succeeds merely in converting a great poem into a travesty. And in his zeal for morality, allegory, and rhetoric, he manages to subvert all three.

* * * * * * * * * * * *

The four editions of the poet Clément Marot's recension of the *Roman de la Rose* (1526, 1529, 1531, and 1538) survive in many copies, and were evidently much in demand. A modernized version in verse (a hurried potboiler, according to Gaston Paris), it was produced by Marot in 1526 during his imprisonment for heresy, which perhaps accounts for the absence of his name from the editions.[146] Marot's allegorism is less ambitious than Molinet's, being confined to a three-page "Preface to the Reader" (*Preambule au liure*) which is largely given to asserting and developing general principles of allegory. His analysis of the rose itself constitutes his chief application of these principles. With conventional medieval scriptural interpretation in mind, he elicits a fourfold interpretation *in bono*. Here is a fair example of his method: "I should say, first of all, that the Rose which the Lover so much desires represents the condition of wisdom, which is most appropriate to the Rose by virtue of that flower's merits, sweetnesses, and odors. . . ." Besides "the condition of wisdom," the rose signifies "the state of grace," "the glorious Virgin Mary," and

> the infinite sovereign good and glory of eternal beatitude, which, as true lovers of its sweetness and delights which are perpetual, we can obtain by avoiding the vices which impede us, and receiving aid from the virtues which will introduce us to the gardener of infinite joy and the rose-bush of perfection and glory, which is the beatific vision of the essence of God.[147]

Modern readers are likely to agree that Marot's interpretation, though more modest in scope than Molinet's, is not more acceptable as a scheme for reading the *Roman*. Both allegorizations are manifest betrayals of the poem's substance and tone. We are confronted, then, with the apparent paradox that during these decades of the *Roman's* ultimate fame—its *gerbe finale*, as Baridon called it—the great poem was often encumbered by these (to us) grossly inappropriate readings, classic examples of what Rosemond Tuve called "imposed allegory."[148] Surveying this literary landscape, Professor Fleming concludes that by 1500 the *Roman* "was no longer clearly understood."[149] Even allowing for the possibility that delight in their own allegorical wit, ingenuity, and rhetoric at least partly deflected Molinet and Marot from concern with what the *Roman* really is about, we must admit that their editions appear to give substance to Fleming's assertion.

* * * * * * * * * * * *

However, the early sixteenth-century gloss in the Collins MS, to which we have already referred (see p. 15 above), shows that in some circles, at least, the *Roman* still received more accurate readings.[150] This gloss contains no references to patristic literature, and only a handful to religious texts of any sort, yet it is both Christian and humanist in spirit and letter. Most of its mythological explications are adapted from Colard Mansion's Ovidian compendium, *Bible des Poetes*, an influential work which transmitted to the sixteenth century the *Ovidius Moralizatus* of Pierre Bersuire (Berchorius), a scholarly fourteenth-century Benedictine.[151] Its prevailing freedom from the pedantries which might suggest an academic or ecclesiastical provenance indicates that the learned, humanistic, sometimes eloquent glossator, of rather conservative and orthodox disposition, may have prepared this MS for the library of a cultivated nobleman of literary taste and traditional values.

Perceiving the *Roman's* protagonist as an emblematic young man under the deleterious influence of fleshly lust or disordered love, deaf to the strictures of Reason or of God, and gaining at last a Pyrrhic victory, the glossator provides dozens of diverse insights which rarely seem false to the spirit and intention of the great work which they purport to explain. The rose is, of course, "his beloved." Fair Welcome represents the same personage from her own perspective: "the voluptuous maiden." The God of Love is sometimes a projection of the "voluptuous young man" himself, sometimes a hypostatization of "fleshly concupiscence," whose arrows are "temptations of the flesh." Friend represents "fleshly delight," and the barons of the God of Love symbolize "all the vices by which one falls into voluptuous love." Foul Mouth is "bad reputation" or "those whose speech reveals foolish love." False Seeming and Constrained Abstinence represent "those who are religious in appearance." Nature is "a divine power given to things through which they give birth to their own kind."

Genius is given both a general identification—"the god of nature and of pleasure"—and a specific, for "in disordered love" Genius "is the means of fulfilling libidinous love." Within the frame of this allegorical structure, the glossator provides a reading which is as authentic and coherent as the contemporary printed commentaries of Molinet and Marot are arbitrary and artificial. Authenticity apart, one wonders whether the Collins glossator, with his moral and behavioral satire, or the printed commentators, with their *in bono* idealism, more accurately represent the way the *Roman* was likely to be understood during these early decades of the sixteenth century.

* * * * * * * * * * *

All the major French authors of the sixteenth century and many of the lesser ones admired the *Roman*, and, as Baridon and others have shown, its influence is often visible in their work.[152] Clément Marot knew the poem thoroughly, of course. Aside from his modernization, echoes of it appear throughout his oeuvre.[153] Marot's contemporary, Rabelais, also had an exact knowledge of the *Roman*, and he drew on it when forming his own style and composing his own great work. According to Baridon:

> The *Roman*, by virtue of certain of its general characteristics—its satire, learning, philosophical reflection, realism as graceful as it is cynical—inevitably attracted the curiosity and interest of Rabelais. His work became in the sixteenth century what the *Roman* had been in the thirteenth: "The Bible *par excellence* of free thinkers, and each of these two works embodies that political, religious, and philosophical satire of which France has the most distinguished and durable examples."[154]

But when we turn to the *Pléiade* masters of the second half of the century, Ronsard and DuBellay, we find the *Roman* more a respected monument of the older poetry than a creative force in their own work. The style and substance of literature was changing, and the *Roman* had evidently become old-fashioned. Thus, DuBellay, in his *Deffense*, praises it as a classic but manages to sound condescending:

Of all the old French poets, only Guillaume de Lorris and

Jean de Meun are worthy to be read, not so much because modern writers would wish to imitate them as because we can find there a first image of the French language, venerable for its antiquity.[155]

Ronsard, too, who as a child had relished the *Roman*, and whose mature works seem to have certain points of contact with it, apparently regarded it as something marmoreal and rather obscure: it is better, he wrote in his preface to the *Franciade*, "to write commentaries on the *Roman de la Rose* than to toy with some Latin grammar which has outlived its time."[156]

The sixteenth century, then, was a watershed in the fortunes of the *Roman*. At its beginning, as we have seen, the poem was being issued in multiple editions and modernizations, was much read and discussed, and was still a living masterpiece. By the end of the century, it was largely ignored, and would remain so, except for eccentric readers here and there who discovered and rejoiced in it during the eclipse of the centuries of light.

With the revival of interest in things medieval—that ripple which appears in the middle of the eighteenth century and becomes a mighty tidal wave by the nineteenth—the *Roman* was rediscovered, along with other great creations of its age. In 1735, two centuries after the last of the "early editions," the poem was brought back into print by an antiquarian abbé; and between Méon's first scholarly edition, which came out on the eve of Waterloo, and Langlois's great critical text, which began publication exactly a century later, as the *belle époque* was collapsing into the Great War, the *Roman de la Rose* assumed its present exalted status as a consummate medieval masterpiece, "the most popular and influential of all French poems in the Middle Ages, which set a fashion in courtly poetry for two centuries in western Europe."[157] Beyond that, it is a work which can still excite a reader's imagination and intellect, once he clears away the impediments which changing language and culture must impose, and begins to hear this exquisite and funny story of man's idealism and foolishness, of his most powerful and durable instincts and his no less powerful and durable aspiration to transcend them.

8

Chaucer, the *Roman*, and the *Romaunt*

Of all the medieval poets whose works provide evidence that they read the *Roman de la Rose*, none used the poem with more conspicuous success than Chaucer.[158] Writing a century and more after Jean de Meun, the great English master seems to have absorbed the *Roman* into his very bones, translating at least part of it, and filling his own work, from the dream visions to the *Canterbury Tales*, with things he had learned from the *Roman*. If, as has been reasonably suggested, the ancient poet to whom Chaucer owes most is Ovid, one may safely claim that the "moderns" who most profoundly influenced him were the authors of the *Roman de la Rose*.[159] This being so, devotees of Chaucer have long maintained a special interest in the *Roman*, and Chaucerians have contributed notably to our understanding of it.

The Middle English version known as the *Romaunt of the Rose* is one of the earliest extant translations of the *Roman*. It exists without ascription in a unique MS of the early fifteenth century, in the Hunterian Museum at Glasgow, and a slightly different text was first printed in Thynne's edition of Chaucer's works (1532). The *Romaunt* is fragmentary: it covers less than a third of the *Roman*, and is not consecutive. Our MS itself is incomplete, lacking eleven leaves, and it is corrupt in many lines. Skeat, Chaucer's great nineteenth-century editor, accepting the findings of the contemporary German philologists Lindner and Kaluza, declared that the *Romaunt* actually consists of three fragments, *A*, *B*, and *C*, each of which he ascribed, on linguistic evidence, to a different translator. Only fragment *A*, he wrote, "appears to be a real portion of Chaucer's own translation."[160]

Robinson agreed, though with somewhat less assurance: "If there is no definite evidence in favor of Chaucer's authorship, there is also no conclusive reason for rejecting it."[161] The most recent editor of the *Romaunt*, Ronald Sutherland, along with modern Chaucerians generally, accepts the view that Chaucer is *probably* responsible for fragment A (equivalent to lines 1–1668 in the Lecoy edition), but certainly not for the rest of the *Romaunt*.[162]

Sutherland's is the most elaborate recent study of the provenance of the *Romaunt*. It concludes in part that fragments B and C are the work of a northern author, and that a reviser joined the three pieces, eliminating many of the northernisms in the latter fragments. His book should be consulted, along with the discussions of Skeat and of Robinson, by readers interested in the textual history of the *Romaunt* and especially in such matters as the relation of the Glasgow MS to the Thynne text and to Langlois's classification of the *Roman* MSS. For studying the *Romaunt* and the *Roman* together, one may use Skeat's text, which gives the French of fragment A (only) from Méon's edition; or, better, Sutherland's volume, which prints in parallel columns the *Romaunt* and Langlois's text of the *Roman* for all three fragments.

Whatever may have been Chaucer's role in making our extant *Romaunt of the Rose*, we have his own word for it that he "translated the Romauns of the Rose," for the God of Love so accuses him in the prologue to *The Legend of Good Women*:

> Thow art my mortal fo and me werreyest,
> And of myne olde servauntes thow mysseyest,
> And hynderest hem with thy translacyoun,
> And lettest folk to han devocyoun
> To serven me, and holdest it folye
> To truste on me. Thow mayst it nat denye,
> For in pleyn text, it nedeth nat to glose,
> Thow hast translated the Romauns of the Rose,
> That is an heresye ageyns my lawe,
> And makest wise folk fro me withdrawe;
> And thynkest in thy wit, that is ful col,
> That he nys but a verray propre fol
> That loveth paramours, to harde and hote.[G 248–260][163]

In this most interesting passage—written, we may suppose, in the early 1380s, about the time of *Troilus and Criseyde* but just before the *Canterbury Tales*—Chaucer both anticipates the epistolary Quarrel which was to erupt a few years later, and appears to share the God of Love's characterization of the *Roman* as a satire upon *fol amour*.[164] With respect to this latter point, one wonders how much of the poem, and which parts, he actually translated. It seems hardly likely that he ever translated all of it, though that possibility cannot of course be excluded. However, as we have seen, the only translation we have that appears probably, or even possibly, from his hand, is the very opening: Guillaume's allegorical account of the Lover's entrance into the garden of *Deduit* and his seizure with infatuation for a rosebud. We may suppose, then, that Chaucer's translation once included the subsequent dialogue with Reason, at the beginning of Jean's section, in which appears the first explicit satire upon the Lover's enterprise. It is here, and in such later parts as the Jealous Husband's speech as imagined by Friend, that the *Roman* reaches its depths of "heretical" satire, and it was these passages, rather than Guillaume's romantic allegory, that one might expect to have agitated the God of Love and drawn from him the description of the poem quoted above. Unless, of course, the God of Love saw more in Guillaume's lines than romance—saw in them, in fact, what the Collins glossator would see in them (see pp. 72–73 above), an allegorical anticipation of the same condemnation of *fol amour* which Reason was to advance doctrinally, and the Old Woman was to objectify dramatically in the ironic effusions of her undisciplined tongue.

It is, of course, also possible—so obnoxious was the *Roman de la Rose* to the God of Love!—that *any* connection with the accursed poem was too much, and even Chaucer's innocent dabbling with the relatively harmless verses of fragment A would have caused offense. But this is speculation, and dangerously close, perhaps, to being idle. All that is indisputable in the matter is that Chaucer made some kind of translation of the *Roman*; that he later allowed the God of Love to characterize the poem as hostile to the cause of those who love "paramours, to harde and hote"; and that the only text we have which may be his translation, or part of it, is fragment A of the *Romaunt*, which is Guillaume's allegorical account of the onset of sexual passion.

* * * * * * * * * * *

It is, in any case, this opening section of the poem which most powerfully influenced Chaucer's own early poetry, both directly and by way of such fourteenth-century French poets as Machaut, Deschamps, and Grandson, whose styles had themselves been formed by the *Roman*.[165] For instance, three of Chaucer's youthful "complaint" poems—*The Complaint unto Pity*, *A Complaint to his Lady*, and *The Complaint of Venus*—contain the clear mark of the *Roman*. In the first of these, a frustrated lover expresses his plight by reference to a world crammed with abstract personifications much like those of Guillaume, and including some of the same: Pite, Love, Cruelte, Bounte, Beaute, Lust, Jolyte, Assured Maner, Youthe, Honeste, Wisdom, Estaat, Drede, Governaunce, Gentilesse, Courtesye, Trouthe, Desir. In *A Complaint to his Lady*, the lady at issue is characterized in terms of a similar set of abstractions: Bountee, Sadnesse, Beautee, Pleseaunce, Faire Rewthelees, Good Aventure. *The Complaint of Venus*, which is a series of connected ballades, translated (as Chaucer tells us in the poem) from the works of Oton de Grandson, "flour of hem that make in Fraunce," juxtaposes in true *Roman* style the contending figures of Love and Jelosie. No doubt Chaucer would inevitably have associated the genre of the amorous complaint with the *Roman de la Rose*, crucial passages of which participate in that genre; and the *Roman* would in turn have suggested the mode of personification allegory. The lyric poems of Chaucer bear the stamp of the *Roman* in other, subtler and more comprehensive ways, as well, leaving us in little doubt as to the large role which the French poem played in Chaucer's early imaginative life.

All these poems are referred to at the end of that passage in the Prologue to the *Legend of Good Women* in which Alceste, "the worthyeste queene," seeks to exculpate Chaucer from the God of Love's accusation:

> Whil he was yong, he kepte youre estat;
> I not wher he be now a renegat.
> But wel I wot, with that he can endyte
> He hath maked lewed folk delyte
> To serven yow, in preysynge of your name.
> He made the bok that highte the Hous of Fame,
> And ek the Deth of Blaunche the Duchesse,

And the Parlement of Foules, as I gesse,
And al the love of Palamon and Arcite
Of Thebes, thogh the storye is knowen lite;
And many an ympne for your halydayes,
That highten balades, roundeles, vyrelayes. [G 400–411]

What is particularly striking about this partial inventory of Chaucer's early work is that virtually all the poems mentioned, the dream visions as well as the "ballades," though entered in Chaucer's credit column with the God of Love, are in varying degrees literary progeny of that wicked *Roman de la Rose* whose baneful influence we have observed the God so deploring. The single exception—an early version of the *Knight's Tale* of Palamon and Arcite—is a product of Chaucer's excursions in Boccaccian romance, though the place and circumstances of the heroes' imprisonment—"a tour, in angwissh and in wo"—may nevertheless reflect the fate of Fair Welcome in the *Roman*; and the two poems share a satirical impulse with respect to the disastrously "harde and hote" love of paramours.

The explanation of this paradox is not far to seek. The *Roman* is, as we have seen, a thoroughly ironic work: all the satire so objectionable to Love is comprehended in an enormous dream-monologue which purports to commemorate a successful *affaire* of the narrator's and to provide others with the "art" of having their own. This kind of irony, which Professor Robertson has shown to be an essential feature of medieval style and a direct consequence of medieval thought, was one of the things the *Roman* bequeathed to such later poets as Chaucer, along with its personification allegory and other devices of expression and form, chief of them of course the dream- or love-vision itself.[166] In it, perspective is all. The exquisite God of Love, like some critics old and new, may be expected to appreciate everything about a poem except its meaning. If he is really prepared to believe that the *House of Fame*, the *Book of the Duchess*, and the *Parliament of Fowls* serve his cause and praise his name (as Alceste, who should know, avers), why indeed should he not be a bit hazy about the *Roman de la Rose*? We poor mortals, whom these poems were chiefly contrived to please and instruct, may hope to know better if we listen or read with sufficient attention.

The literary consequences of this approach—the elusiveness of

meaning, the shifting of perspectives, the conjunction of playful sur-
faces with serious contents, of *ernest* with *game*—are noteworthy
features of all these dream-vision poems which Chaucer wrote under
the influence of the *Roman*; and of course they are features of the
latest of the group, the *Legend of Good Women*, in which the inventory appears. In this latter poem, the underlying situation is quite different from that of the *Roman*. The narrator/dreamer is not a be-
mused young lover but rather a reflective and circumspect poet—a
persona of Chaucer himself—whose affection for flowers is probably
genuine. The dream vision is merely a playful introduction to what
was to be the chief matter of the poem, the "legends" of "good
women." But no one now cares very much about these legends
themselves, and Chaucer in fact never completed his collection of
them. Perhaps the conception was faulty, or perhaps his interest in it
flagged. The Prologue, at any rate, is what readers have always found
delectable. In this Prologue, the *Roman*'s extended colloquy between
the Lover and the God of Love is adapted to Chaucer's own pur-
poses with great skill. The episode in Guillaume is itself an ironic
variation of the Boethian literary topos, ultimately scriptural, in
which a troubled mortal confronts a personification of transcendent
wisdom, from whom the mortal may, or may not, learn something
about himself. This topos, or motif, appears without irony in a
number of medieval poems, including some of the greatest: the *Divine
Comedy*, *Piers Plowman*, and *Pearl*, to cite three. In Guillaume,
however, the student is only too willing and the teacher only too per-
suasive. In Chaucer's *Legend*, the ironies which color the meeting between suppliant and God of Love are perhaps more subtle still, and
there is more jeu d'esprit and good humor, though less intellectual
complexity. In both poetic confrontations, however, nothing is quite
what it purports to be, no one quite what he claims to be or perhaps
thinks he is. And in the *Legend of Good Women*, this pervasive irony
extends to the "legends" themselves, whose chief interest for us lies in
the sometimes complex and funny ways in which the ladies who are
commemorated there firmly decline to be ticketed in our imaginations with the rubric "good women." The conception, imperfect and
fragmentary as its actualization may be, is one of Chaucer's most
charming and profound, and it came, directly or indirectly, from his
encounter with the *Roman*.

The three earlier experiments in dream vision reveal equally well the originality with which Chaucer could adapt *Roman* materials, refracted through the prism of intervening French poetry, for his own diverse ends. In the *Book of the Duchess*, Chaucer complicates the genre by providing a psychological motive for the dream in the form of an Ovidian tale which his dreamer reads before falling asleep; and only when the "man in blak" appears and preempts the dreamer's attention do we recognize that the dreamer himself is not to be the unrivalled protagonist of the poem. There is little personification allegory here, but enough to assure us that both the dreamer and the man in black are second cousins to Guillaume's Lover: both of them (the man in black more directly) are at some point characterized by "ydelnesse"; elsewhere, the lady White is defined with respect to her connection with "Trouthe hymself." In the *House of Fame*—like the *Legend of Good Women*, a long fragment—Chaucer's use of Guillaume's mode of dream vision is most daring, though least successful, and his startling attempt to graft it onto a Dantean epic leaves too many formal and thematic issues unresolved. The merit of the poem is in its imaginative and expressive parts, not its ungainly whole. One of the most striking of these parts is the emblematic literary iconography in the description of the temple of Venus (Book One). The poem's kinship with the *Roman* is relatively oblique but unmistakable.

The *Parliament of Fowls* is Chaucer's finest achievement in the genre of love vision, and a poem deeply inspired on nearly every level by the *Roman* and its imitations (as well as by Alanus de Insulis, Boccaccio, and others), though here again Chaucer does not give us a mere imitation of the archetypal work, but develops original modifications of his materials. As he did in the *Book of the Duchess*, Chaucer provides a literary stimulus for his dreamer's dream—this time, Macrobius's famous commentary on the *Somnium Scipionis*, which Guillaume cites at the very beginning of the *Roman*. After the narrator/dreamer's rather leisurely summary of this work, which, he says, he has been reading before falling asleep, he tells us that Africanus himself appeared in the dream and led him to a walled park—a fascinating iconographic reconstitution of elements of Guillaume's garden of *Deduit* together with motifs from Dante and elsewhere. Inside this *locus amoenus* we find "Cupid, oure lord," surrounded by a large company of *Roman*-style personifications: Plesaunce, Aray, Lust, Courteysie, Delyt, Gentilesse, Beute, Youthe,

Foolhardynesse, Flaterye, Desyr, and many more. Women are dancing about a "temple of bras," over which Venus and Priapus preside.
The iconography is more intense, less elegant than Guillaume's, and
the satirical thrust more immediately perceptible. But here again, as
in the two earlier vision poems, Chaucer departs from the relatively
classical structure of the *Roman* and develops one which is more
modular and Gothic, in which there is surprising juxtaposition of
scenes and even of ontological levels, and in which "meaning" hangs
upon symbolic iconography and structural parallels. In the *Parliament*
we soon pass away from these emblems of human love to "another
part of the garden," where Lady Nature is presiding over the mating
of the birds—it is St. Valentine's day—and this episode is to provide
the chief matter of the poem.

These early works of Chaucer's reveal both the impression which
the *Roman* made upon his mind, and also the brilliant resourcefulness
with which he adapted the French poem. Chaucer's modifications
are all in the direction of structural complexity. None of his dreamer/
narrators is the archetypal *fol amoureux* of the *Roman*, who requires
and receives no "characterization" outside his enormous dream.
Chaucer's dreamers, on the other hand, all define themselves at some
length, and each is different from the others. What they have in common at the start is chiefly a certain lack of harmony in their relation
to Love, the implications of which are given to the reader to consider.
Their dreams are trailed by enigmas and obscurities, and the poems
from which these dreams flash out have, finally, something of the surreal vagueness of the dreamworld itself.

* * * * * * * * * * * *

More fruitful still, perhaps, was the lesson which Chaucer was to
learn from certain pages in Jean de Meun's continuation of the
Roman. The *Canterbury Tales* contains many evidences of this influence, which has yet to be studied in its full scope. Two of Jean's
figures, however, above all, left their unforgettable mark on the *Tales*:
False Seeming and the Old Woman.

The first of these, Jean's brilliant satirical portrait of the hypocritical, worldly, and unashamed cleric, is reflected first in Chaucer's
portraits of the Monk, Friar, and Pardoner in the General Prologue,
but chiefly in the great *Pardoner's Prologue* and *Tale*. Fansler has considered the relation between False Seeming and the Pardoner and

Friar:

On reading the *Pardoner's Prologue*, we are immediately struck with many resemblances it bears to Faux-Semblant's self-revelation. Like the harangue in the French poem, what the Pardoner has to say takes the form of a confession, and the relation of his personal experiences, impudent, intimate, disgusting, is not a whit overdrawn, as Jusserand says. The Friar makes no confession; but Chaucer makes one for him and attributes to him some of the traits that Faux-Semblant so shamefully boasts are his own.

To be more specific: Faux-Semblant says that he loves good dishes and wine, and that although he preaches poverty, his bags overflow with coin, and he never makes friends with any poor man. For "poor man" Chaucer substitutes "lazars." The Frere knew all the taverns and inn-keepers, had no acquaintance with lepers, but dealt with the rich, with merchants. Like Faux-Semblant, too, he did not go about as a poor clerk in thread-bare coat, "But he was lyk a maister or a pope." . . . But how closely this precious pair was associated together in the mind of Chaucer may be indicated, perhaps, by the fact that the poet divided one of Faux-Semblant's couplets between them: "En aquerre est toute m'entente, / Miex vaut mes porchas que ma rente." The Pardoner says of himself: "For my entente is nat but for to winne," and Chaucer says of the Frere: "His purchas was wel bettre than his rente," while the Frere himself (through Chaucer) puts a similar expression into the mouth of the fiend: "My purchase is th'effect of al my rente."[167]

Similarly, the Wife of Bath's great confessional reverie was much influenced by Jean's Old Woman and Jealous Husband, who provided Chaucer with his basic character and much of the style and substance of the ironically antifeminist diatribes which she associates with her husbands. Chaucer used other literary materials as well in devising this consummate figure; and, of course, the Wife is, finally, a thoroughly original creation; but it will not diminish our admiration for Chaucer's genius, nor our acknowledgement of the diversity of his sources, to assert that the Wife of Bath is quite simply inconceivable without the antecedent conceptions of Jean de Meun in the *Roman*. These two figures—the Pardoner and Alice of Bath—are at the summit of Chaucer's art of characterization in the *Canterbury Tales*. The notable variety of scholarly interpretations testifies to their vitality. Like Jean's False Seeming and Old Woman, Chaucer's characters are endowed with the dramatic conviction of their verisimilitude, as well as with the philosophical spaciousness of their allegory. But Chaucer's modifications, again, tend toward complexity. How can the Pardoner be a "eunuch" in view of his libertinism, and vice versa? Is the Wife of Bath "good" (though no better than she should be), or "bad" (though endearing), or neither, because not an imitation of a real person or type at all? In conjunction, Chaucer and the authors of the *Roman* provide a distinguished example of how great art, fertilizing the mind of a master, can issue into a yet richer and more intricate perfection.

Two

Mapping the Garden

The *Roman de la Rose* is very long and it is crowded with "characters" and episodes of the most diverse kinds. As we have remarked, its authors—Jean de Meun in particular—have sometimes been taxed with a too luxuriant digressiveness, a lack of architectonic skill. To be sure, Jean does not display the structural decorum of Dante. But neither does anyone else except Dante. Guillaume and Jean were, after all, writing a romance, and medieval romances are nothing if not episodic, copious, and rather unpredictable. The *Roman* has, however, like other great Gothic structures, an inner, thematic and dialectical order, which justifies every episode and every "digression." But perceiving this order requires a careful overview of the poem, a detailed sense of its development.

In any event, a visitor to the garden of *Deduit*—especially one who has not been there often, or recently—may be forgiven for losing his way amidst such rich but dense growths of allegory and dialectic. The materials in chapters nine and ten are intended to serve him as a map. The first of the two Analytical Outlines divides the poem into four primary sections, of unequal length but based on narrative and thematic development; the second divides these sections into constituent episodes and dialectical elements. The Narrative Summary, which is keyed to the outlines, summarizes and paraphrases the major contents of the poem.

The first sets of line numbers in the outlines refer to the edition of Lecoy, those in parentheses to that of Langlois (as well as to the translations of Dahlberg and of Robbins).

9

Analytical Outlines

[Outline of primary sections:]

Prologue: The dreamer introduces his dream. 1–44 (1–44)

   I: The young man becomes a vassal of the God of Love.
45–4,190 (45–4,220) [Jean de Meun's part of the poem begins
with 4,029 (4,059).]

  II: The discourse of Reason to the young man.
4,191–7,200 (4,221–7,230)

  III: The discourse of Friend to the young man.
7,201–9,972 (7,231–10,002)

  IV: The conquest of the rose.
9,973–21,750 (10,003–21,780)

[Detailed outline:]

Prologue: The dreamer introduces his dream. 1–44 (1–44)

   I: The young man becomes a vassal of the God of Love.
45–4,190 (45–4,220)

    A. He sees and enters the garden of *Deduit*.
45–688 (45–690)

    B. He describes the contents of the garden.
689–1,612 (691–1,614)

    C. He falls in love with a rose.
1,613–1,878 (1,615–1,880)

D. He becomes a vassal of the God of Love, and receives his commandments.
1,879–2,762 (1,881–2,778)
E. He is unable to approach the rose.
2,763–2,934 (2,779–2,950)
F. In despair, he receives advice from Reason and Friend.
2,935–3,338 (2,951–3,356)
G. The intervention of Venus enables him to kiss the rose.
3,339–3,492 (3,357–3,510)
H. Angered by this, Jealousy erects a fortress around the roses, and a tower in which to imprison Fair Welcome.
3,493–3,908 (3,511–3,936)
I. The young man despairs, but remains faithful to his amorous quest.
3,909–4,190 (3,937–4,220)

II: The discourse of Reason to the young man.
4,191–7,200 (4,221–7,230)

A. Reason analyzes the young man's problem.
4,191–4,598 (4,221–4,628)
B. She explains the nature of friendship, fortune, and wealth.
4,599–5,428 (4,629–5,458)
C. She discusses justice.
5,429–5,666 (5,459–5,696)
D. She urges him to abandon the God of Love and Fortune, and to follow her.
5,667–6,870 (5,697–6,900)
E. He rejects her proposal, and criticizes her use of indecorous language; she explains his error in this matter, and departs.
6,871–7,200 (6,901–7,230)

III: The discourse of Friend to the young man.
7,201–9,972 (7,231–10,002)

A. Friend advises the young man how to outwit his enemies.
7,201–7,764 (7,231–7,794)
B. He explains the importance of wealth to a lover's quest, and describes his own impoverishment.
7,765–8,226 (7,795–8,256)
C. The corruption of love since the Golden Age.

8,227–8,424 (8,257–8,454)

D. How a modern Jealous Husband might address his wife.
8,425–9,330 (8,455–9,360)

E. More about the Jealous Husband, and the bad effect of domination upon marriage.
9,331–9,462 (9,361–9,492)

F. More about the Golden Age, and the decline which has followed it.
9,463–9,648 (9,493–9,678)

G. Some rules for a lover to follow.
9,649–9,972 (9,679–10,002)

IV: The conquest of the rose.
9,973–21,750 (10,003–21,780)

A. The young man, though pleased with Friend's advice, is still frustrated in his quest, and is rejected by Wealth.
9,973–10,237 (10,003–10,267)

B. He mollifies Foul Mouth, and receives a promise of help from the God of Love.
10,238–10,408 (10,268–10,438)

C. Love assembles his forces, including False Seeming.
10,409–10,921 (10,439–10,951)

D. The discourse of False Seeming to the company of Love.
10,922–11,984 (10,952–12,014)

E. The assault begins; False Seeming kills Foul Mouth.
11,985–12,350 (12,015–12,380)

F. Love's forces capture the Old Woman, guardian of Fair Welcome, and induce her to give her ward the young man's gift.
12,351–12,709 (12,381–12,739)

G. The discourse of the Old Woman to Fair Welcome.
12,710–14,516 (12,740–14,546)

H. With the help of the Old Woman and Fair Welcome, the young man is admitted to the fortress and approaches the rose, but he is repulsed by *Dangier*, Fear, and Shame.
14,517–15,104 (14,547–15,134)

I. The "author" digresses, and defends his poem against charges of obscurity, indecorous language, and ecclesiastical satire.
15,105–15,272 (15,135–15,302)

J. The forces of Love are defeated, and Love calls upon his mother, Venus, for help.
    15,273–15,860 (15,303–15,890)
K. Nature enters the conflict.
    15,861–16,292 (15,891–16,322)
L. Genius's discourse to Nature.
    16,293–16,698 (16,323–16,728)
M. The "confession" of Nature to Genius.

1. God's creation of the world.
    16,699–16,918 (16,729–16,948)

2. The effects of celestial bodies upon the earth and its inhabitants.
    16,919–17,070 (16,949–17,100)

3. Necessity and free will.
    17,071–17,844 (17,101–17,874)

4. The weather.
    17,845–17,999 (17,875–18,029)

5. Illusions, phantoms, and dreams.
    18,000–18,504 (18,030–18,534)

6. Comets do not announce the death of kings.
    18,505–18,558 (18,535–18,588)

7. True nobility is the result of virtue.
    18,559–18,866 (18,589–18,896)

8. More on comets and other incorruptible celestial bodies.
    18,867–18,936 (18,897–18,966)

9. Of all God's corruptible creation beneath the sphere of the moon, only man ignores Nature's laws, especially the law of procreation.
    18,937–19,304 (18,967–19,334)

10. Nature sends Genius to the God of Love.
    19,305–19,375 (19,335–19,405)

N. Genius's sermon to the host of Love.

1. Genius is welcomed by Love and Venus.
    19,376–19,474 (19,406–19,504)

2. Genius excommunicates the enemies of procreation, and encourages the others to procreate.
    19,475–19,808 (19,505–19,838)

3. Genius urges his hearers to live virtuously, so as to enter the beautiful park of the Lamb.
   19,809–20,006 (19,839–20,036)
4. Saturn's castration and the end of the Golden Age.
   20,007–20,236 (20,037–20,266)
5. Genius contrasts the park of the Lamb with the garden of *Deduit*.
   20,237–20,637 (20,267–20,667)

O. Venus shoots a firebrand at the tower, and routs the enemies of Love.
   20,638–21,315 (20,668–21,345)

P. The young man finally has his pleasure with the rose; the dreamer awakes.
   21,316–21,750 (21,346–21,780)

10

Narrative Summary

Prologue: *The dreamer introduces his dream.*

Contrary to what is often claimed, some dreams are apt to signify the good and evil in our lives. I shall tell you a dream which I experienced in my twentieth year, when dominated by Love, and which later came true. Love commands me to make a poem of it, which should be called *Romance of the Rose*. It contains the whole art of love. May she for whom I have written it accept it with grace—she who deserves to be called Rose.

I: *The young man becomes a vassal of the God of Love.*

A. *He sees and enters the garden of "Deduit."*

I became aware that it was spring—the month of May, the season of love—five years ago or more. I arose, dressed, and went outside to enjoy the freshness of the morning. I came to a river, and, walking along its bank, I arrived before a square garden, surrounded by a high, crenellated wall. On the wall were sculpted and painted certain images: Hatred, Felony, Villainy, Covetousness, Avarice, Envy, Sadness, Old Age, Pope-Holiness, and Poverty.

I wanted to enter this pleasant garden. Walking alongside the wall, I found a little door, at which I knocked. It was opened by a lovely young girl called Idleness, a friend of *Deduit*, the owner of the garden. At her invitation, I entered this earthly paradise, and was enchanted by the songs of innumerable birds.

B. *He describes the contents of the garden.*

After taking a few steps, I met *Deduit* himself and his friends. A lady called Joy was singing to a group of beautiful people, who then

93

proceeded to dance. A lady named Courtesy invited me to join the entertainment. *Deduit* and his sweetheart Joy were both splendidly clothed; the God of Love was even more richly attired, and wore a chaplet of roses. At his side was a young man, Sweet Looks, watching the carols and holding his master's two bows and ten arrows. One bow was black and of coarse, knotty wood, the other finely made and ornamented. Of the arrows, five were of gold, and named Beauty, Simplicity, Openness, Company, and Fair Seeming; the other five, black, were Pride, Villainy, Shame, Despair, and New Thought. These two sets of arrows evidently corresponded to the two bows. Among the dancers, I noticed Beauty, Wealth (accompanied by her friend, a handsome young man), Generosity (of the lineage of Alexander, and holding by her hand a knight of the lineage of King Arthur), Openness (accompanied also by her friend, who seemed worthy to be the son of Windsor's lord), Courtesy, Idleness, and finally Youth, who embraced and kissed a companion of her own age (about twelve years) without inhibition.

When the dance was finished, I strolled through the garden, admiring the trees, animals, fountains, and flowers. I finally arrived at a fountain beneath a pine tree, which bore an inscription declaring that this was the fountain where Narcissus had died. [Story of Narcissus and Echo.] With some trepidation, I approached the fountain and looked inside. I saw at the bottom two crystal stones, which had the marvelous property of reflecting in minute detail the contents of the garden. This was the perilous mirror in which Narcissus had admired himself, and no one can look in it without falling literally madly in love, for it is here that Cupid, son of Venus, sowed the seed of love and set his traps for young people. Thus it is called the Fountain of Love. If I had known its powers, I would never have approached it.

C. *He falls in love with a rose.*

I saw in this mirror some rosebushes, and was seized with a mad desire for one particular bud. The God of Love shot an arrow—Beauty—at me, striking me in the eye and lodging in my heart. This wound made my desire for the rose even more intense. Then Love sent at me the arrows of Simplicity, Courtesy, and Company, each of them going to my heart, which was now burning fiercely. Finally, he launched Fair Seeming, which bore an ointment designed to relieve the pain of my wound, but not to cure it.

94

D. *He becomes a vassal of the God of Love, and receives his commandments.*

The God of Love made me his vassal, and told me his commandments: avoid villainy; avoid slander; be friendly and polite to everyone; avoid all coarseness of language; respect women, and, above all, defend them against slanderers; avoid pride, which is sinful; take care with your appearance, and dress as elegantly as your means allow; be clean; always be happy and joyous; learn to use your natural gifts; finally, avoid avarice and the reputation of miserliness. Remember, too, that a lover must think always of love, must leave his heart in one place only, and must give it away, not merely lend it. But attending to these rules does not preclude suffering or frustration.

I was upset by these prospects, and wondered how I could endure them. Love told me that I would have help: first of all, from Hope, but also from Sweet Thought, Sweet Talk, and Sweet Looks. Having given me this advice, Love disappeared.

E. *He is unable to approach the rose.*

I then wondered if I ought to tear away the hedge to approach my rose. Fair Welcome, son of Courtesy, now appeared, and encouraged me to proceed, even opening a passage through the thorns for me. But the rose was guarded by a base churl, *Dangier*, who was hiding beneath the leaves, and was aided in his disagreeable work by Foul Mouth, Shame, and Fear. Of these four guardians, Shame, daughter of Reason and Misdeeds, was certainly the most worthy. She had been sent by her mother at the request of Chastity, mistress of the roses and buds, who, when attacked by Venus, needed help. For the same reason, Jealousy had called on Fear. When, then, I summoned up enough courage to ask Fair Welcome to cut the bud for me, Fair Welcome firmly refused. *Dangier* then leapt up at Fair Welcome, and strongly reproached him for bringing me so near the roses. Fair Welcome fled, and I was obliged to retreat.

F. *In despair, he receives advice from Reason and Friend.*

I despaired. My suffering attracted the attention of noble Reason, who now descended from her high tower and tried to persuade me to abandon my amorous quest. She said that Idleness was a fool and her company dangerous, and that my pursuit would bring me great sorrow. But I refused to abandon Love. Recalling his advice to me, I determined to seek a Friend whose loyalty I could trust. I found such a Friend, and he restored my courage, advising me to

95

establish a friendly relationship with *Dangier*. I was finally able once more to approach the rose.

G. *The intervention of Venus enables him to kiss the rose.*

The rosebud was now larger than before, though not yet fully opened. I asked Fair Welcome if I might kiss it, but he refused, for fear of Chastity. Venus now appeared, armed with a flaming torch, and induced Fair Welcome to change his mind. I then enjoyed a sweet kiss (but since that time I have suffered much trouble and pain).

H. *Angered by this, Jealousy erects a fortress around the roses, and a tower in which to imprison Fair Welcome.*

Foul Mouth spread the news. Jealousy learned it and showered Fair Welcome with reproaches. Fair Welcome now fled, as did I. Jealousy decided to erect a walled fortress about the roses, and a tower in its midst where Fair Welcome would be imprisoned. Shame and Fear now reproached *Dangier* for his negligence, and he promised to be a more effective defender in the future.

I was in despair, and cursed Foul Mouth, the source of my trouble. But Jealousy proceeded to execute her project. She constructed a strong castle, with a central tower, and four gates opening in each direction, to be guarded by *Dangier*, Shame, Fear, and Foul Mouth. As for Fair Welcome, he was to be imprisoned in the tower under the surveillance of an Old Woman who would surely be hard to fool, for she knew all the "old dance," having once led a riotous youth.

I. *The young man despairs, but remains faithful to his amorous quest.*

I was now deep in despair, and thought of Fortune and her wheel. I had not lost my confidence in Fair Welcome, whose body only was in prison; but I hoped that he would not suffer from his misadventure, and would not too readily believe the lies that would be said about me.

[*End of Guillaume de Lorris's part of the poem.*]

Only Hope could now sustain me; but Hope is sometimes deceiving, and I was tempted to return to Reason, whose discourse I had ignored. Yet I did not wish to betray Fair Welcome, nor, above all, the God of Love, to whom I had sworn homage. I decided to persevere in my amorous quest.

II: *The discourse of Reason to the young man.*

A. *Reason analyzes the young man's problem.*

However, Reason heard my complaints, and returned to try to persuade me to follow the path of wisdom. She first of all offered a description of love in a series of antitheses. I told her that this was not helpful. She then explained that love is a sickness of thought which occurs between two persons of different sex, and which arises from a passion provoked by the undisciplined contemplation of the loved one. This love leads to the desire for carnal union and the pleasures which come therefrom. But, added Reason, the only legitimate aim of love is procreation and the maintenance of the species. Whoever makes its pleasures his chief object becomes a slave to that chief vice, voluptuousness, source of all evils. Naturally, there is no question of love, or even pleasure, in the case of those who sell themselves, like beasts, and it is surprising that there are men who want such women. This does not, however, mean that women should not receive gifts, especially if the woman reciprocates them. But love dominated by extravagance and covetousness is deplorable. Good love must be born of a true heart. With pleasure as my single object, I was wasting myself. I should banish this love from my heart.

B. *She explains the nature of friendship, fortune, and wealth.*

I was not moved by Reason's argument; but she had put me in a dilemma: I must either love or hate. I chose to love. But I wanted Reason to tell me about a kind of love unknown to me to which she had alluded, and which she seemed to approve. In fact, she said, there are several kinds of love. True friendship is one, free of all self-interest, characterized by virtue and generosity, unmoved by Fortune. In this connection, one should observe that adverse fortune is more profitable than favorable fortune, since it allows us to recognize our true riches, that is, the constancy of our friends. Moreover, it is not really wealth which makes us wealthy, but rather the contentment of sufficiency. The rich become slaves to their wealth, laboring to accumulate it, fearing to lose it, and leaving it only reluctantly when they must die. The true nature of wealth is to circulate, without interest. Fortune's gifts are always insecure; only those goods which we possess in ourselves cannot be taken away. All others should be scorned and renounced.

Then Reason asked me why I had accused her of urging me to hate. I answered that it was because she had advised me to despise my lord, and, moreover, had preached a kind of love so austere and rare that I could never attain it. She replied that it could be either my fault or someone else's that friendship was impossible for me to achieve. But there is another, closely related love which I should strive for: the love of all persons, not just individual ones. I could express this love by doing to others as I would like them to do to me. No one should live without this love.

C. *She discusses justice.*

She continued: It is, in fact, the forgetfulness of this love, which comes from charity, that has made judges necessary. But love is much greater than justice. Love itself is capable of establishing peace and concord; but even the most excellent justice would still eventually need love in order to temper its inevitable harshness. Moreover, the officers who adminster justice are too often dishonest and violent, exploiting those whom they ought to be protecting. As an example of this violence, Reason told me the story (from Livy) of Appius and Virginia.

D. *She urges him to abandon the God of Love and Fortune, and to follow her.*

I now commented on a coarse word which Reason had uttered, and she promised to respond a bit later to the reproach. For now, she insisted that opposing extravagant love was not the same as advocating hate. She had already spoken of the love called friendship and of the love called charity; she now said a few words about the love of parents for their children, a love without special merit because it is common to all nature, even though those who lack it are considered culpable.

She proceeded to explain that if I wished to love, I should take her, Reason, as a friend, and I would then know all manner of happiness and success. If I were loyal to her, she would be my servant. But I must abandon this Love, and scorn Fortune, for her power is only illusory. Besides, she is notoriously capricious, and her gifts have no relation to virtue or justice. When she makes a man rich or powerful, she does not thereby make him good. Power used wickedly is not really power, for evil has no real existence, but is merely the absence of good. A wicked man, then, is not properly a man. Why does Fortune have the power to confer great honor upon wicked men? Because the punishment which a criminal receives is more cruel and exemplary the higher the elevation from which he falls. If I accepted Reason's law, there would be no man more truly powerful than I, and I would be immune to the blows of fate, which cannot, in any case, be avoided.

E. *He rejects her proposal, and criticizes her use of indecorous language; she explains his error in this matter, and departs.*

But I summarily repulsed Reason's proposal. I could not betray the master to whom I had promised fidelity, nor was I interested in Socratic wisdom. Nevertheless, before leaving Reason, I wished to say again that I was astonished at her shameful utterance of such coarse words as "testicles." Reason smiled and replied that using the proper names of good things was not sinful, and that God had, anyway, left the choice of names to her discretion. Women might use whatever paraphrases they preferred, but Reason liked the names themselves. Besides, literal language as used by poets often contains hidden meanings.

I replied that I hoped someday to study poetry, and that I now felt that she had justified her use of objectionable language. As for me, if I was a fool, it was my own misfortune. I remained determined not to renounce Love. Reason then departed.

III: *The discourse of Friend to the young man.*

A. *Friend advises the young man how to outwit his enemies.*

Friend appeared at that very moment, and urged me to serve Love loyally. I should not approach the castle where Fair Welcome was imprisoned, but rather glance discreetly from a distance. I must be very genial to Foul Mouth and fool him: it is not sinful to trick a trickster. I should also trick the Old Woman and Jealousy, by assuming a false air of friendliness and kindness. As for the other warders (*Dangier*, Shame, Fear), if I were able to approach them, I should give them moderate gifts, or else promise to do so (whether I kept the promise or not). Bribing them while pretending innocence, and being persistent in my enterprise, would serve my cause. But I must lose no time, for many rivals would surely turn up. I should be discreet and approach the guardians only when they were in good humor. Finally, if the opportunity should arise, I must not hesitate to pluck the rose, whatever the guardians might say, so long as I felt in my heart that they really consented. A little violence in this case need not displease them, and would show them in fact that I was manly. Some persons like to be forced. Naturally, I should not use violence against sincere resistance. And as for Fair Welcome, I should agree with everything he might do and say.

B. *He explains the importance of wealth to a lover's quest, and describes his own impoverishment.*

I was surprised to hear this lesson in hypocrisy and deceit, and would have liked to defy Foul Mouth before deceiving him, but Friend discouraged me. He told me, however, of a way to reach the castle quickly, not accessible to poor people: the road Give-Too-Much, laid down by Foolish Generosity. One scarcely enters it before all the defenses of the fortress crumble. But Friend, being impoverished, could not take me there. Only Wealth could do this—but Poverty would bring me back. Poverty should be avoided; Friend had been ruined by her, and thus lost his own friends. Death itself would not break the bond of affection between Friend and me, but Poverty is worse than Death, because its effects are prolonged.

I then accepted my circumstances and renounced the way of Give-Too-Much, determining to be satisfied with giving small gifts. Friend assured me that if I followed his advice, I should ultimately pluck the rose.

C. *The corruption of love since the Golden Age.*

Thus far, Friend's speech had explained to me how to conquer my beloved. But once this conquest was accomplished, I must know how to retain her, a task as hard as the conquest itself, for most women are simply eager to fleece their lovers. Formerly it was different. During the Golden Age, when men knew nothing of tyranny or property, love also was unfettered and carefree. People then knew that love and lordship have never gone together.

D. *How a modern Jealous Husband might address his wife.*

Today, however, when a husband wishes to exercise the rights which he thinks he has over the body of his wife and over her goods, the result is contention.

The husband might say: You are nothing but a gadabout, and you think only of pleasure. When I go off on a business trip, you dress up richly, and have the nerve to pretend that it is for love of *me*! And what of the long conversations which you have privately with this young man who comes running at your whistle? Must I beat you and chain you to the house to restore you to your duties? It must have been the devil who told me to marry you. There are certainly no Penelopes or Lucreces today. And what a strange custom we follow at the moment of marriage: no one buys a horse without examining it thoroughly, whereas we take a woman on the basis of her charm merely. But once the marriage has been solemnized, the real nature of the woman reveals itself, and I know no man who does not then regret his entanglement. We hear of virtuous women, but most women are bad, and destroy one's soul and body.

Certainly (the husband might continue) I should have been better off hanging than marrying so elegant a woman. Your costly, cumbrous gowns, of which you are so proud, only hamper me when I wish to approach you, and all your manners and delicacies prove only one thing, that you hardly value my affection. Besides, when we are in bed, you have to undress anyway. What good, then, are all these adornments? Moreover, there is no worse enemy of Chastity than Beauty, who has always succeeded in having on her side the chambermaid of Chastity, Ugliness. (Far from opposing her mistress, Ugliness ought to protect and aid her.) Consequently, every woman who wishes to be beautiful thereby declares war on Chastity: the craze has reached even cloisters and abbeys. And what I say of women is true also of certain men. But I am not one of these. My coat of coarse fabric and lamb's fur protects me as well as a richer fabric could, and I would be squandering my money if I bought *you* delicate and precious dresses. That would permit you to go out and flaunt yourself all the time, and it would make you lose the respect which you owe to God and to me. Even at night, when you are in bed by my side, I may not approach you; you are surly, you complain, you claim to be sick. But I ask if you treat your gallants the same way! Your body should be given to dogs and wolves! How can you scorn me, I who dress and feed you? How can you abandon yourself to these ribalds who flatter you, but who—among themselves—dishonor you and say only the most infamous things of you? For you can be sure that what pleases them about you is not your person, but the wealth of jewels and ornaments which I gave you. And tell me who gave you the dress which you wore the other day! Your mother, if I am to believe *you*, who wished to spare me expense. I would ask that old whore about it, but the trouble would be wasted. Mother and

101

daughter are as one.

E. *More about the Jealous Husband, and the bad effect of*
   domination upon marriage.

From words, the Jealous Husband would proceed to deeds,
beating his wife unmercifully; and the neighbors, hearing the noise,
would hasten to separate the two. It is quite evident that such conduct does not restore love to the relationship. And if the wife
pretends to be reconciled, the husband still has to fear her anger and
vengeance. Husband and wife ought to be equals, united by the law
of marriage. Any attempt by one to dominate kills love in the other.
Love can live only in a free heart: that is why love so often dies when
lovers marry.

F. *More about the Golden Age, and the decline which has*
   followed it.

The ancients lived in liberty, without bonds of servitude.
They would not have abandoned their freedom for all the gold in
Araby or Friesland. People were satisfied with what they had, wealth
was equally divided, peace reigned, love united men. But one day
Fraud appeared, followed by Sin and Misfortune (who can never
have enough of anything); then Pride, Covetousness, Avarice, and
Envy, as well as all the other vices. Then Poverty, hitherto unknown
among men, came up from hell and brought with her her son,
Larceny, who knows his way to the gibbet. Men, as if led astray by an
evil spell, abandoned their former way of life. They became false,
established property, divided the land, set up boundaries, fought
with one another. To enforce order, men chose someone to be their
leader. But he alone was incapable of restraining the robbers, and it
was decided to give him helpers. And this was the origin of kings and
princes. Thus, men learned to work precious metals, and then iron
for forging arms; then they learned to erect castles and fortresses for
sheltering these treasures which the wealthy amassed, and which
they feared might be stolen; but they nevertheless lost their peace of
mind.

G. *Some rules for a lover to follow.*

The lover, then, who wants to keep his mistress must follow
certain rules of conduct. He must study arts and sciences; he must
never reproach his beloved for wishing to leave him; if, by chance, he
surprises her in an unfaithful act, he should pretend not to have seen

anything; he must never open her letters; he must allow her always to come and go as she pleases; he must be careful not to believe evil things which may be said about her; he must utter no reproach for her faults, and above all he must not beat her, but rather allow himself to be beaten by her.

If on occasion the lover wishes to allow himself an infidelity, without on that account losing his first love, he must see that the gifts which he gives to his new conquest are not known to the old; he must also avoid assignations in the same places; in case he is suspected, he must deny everything, and appease his beloved's anger with warm caresses. And if he is obliged to admit what he has done, he should explain that he has committed his crime under duress and unwillingly.

He must never boast of his good fortune; if his beloved is ill, he must stay near her and vow to make a pilgrimage; and he should not prohibit her from eating, but he should give her only soft and tender things. He must also pretend to have dreamt of her. This is how one should regulate his conduct, if he wishes to keep the love of his friend, for women are fickle. Virtuous women are, naturally, exempt, but there are hardly any of these. All women, moreover, enjoy hearing their beauty praised, and should be flattered. The ugliest one will believe it. Finally, women hate to receive advice, and always think they know best. If I were to follow these counsels, Friend concluded, I would long enjoy my love affairs.

IV: *The conquest of the rose.*

    A. *The young man, though pleased with Friend's advice, is still frustrated in his quest, and is rejected by Wealth.*

Friend's words pleased me, much more than Reason's had done. Moreover, Sweet Thought and Sweet Talk now appeared again, but they could not bring with them Sweet Looks. I walked away; following the advice I had just received, I regretfully left the immediate vicinity of the castle where Fair Welcome was imprisoned. But I remained preoccupied with finding a way to achieve the success I craved.

Walking near a fountain, I now met Wealth, who was guarding the entrance to the road Give-Too-Much. She refused to allow me on it because I was not one of her friends. But she said that no wise man envies them that privilege, for if Give-Too-Much is itself a pleasant and joyous road, it leads to Poverty; and even if I were to go that way, I might still fail to conquer the castle, though I would be sure to meet Hunger. I should have done better, she said, to have heeded Reason.

    B. *He mollifies Foul Mouth, and receives a promise of help from the God of Love.*

    I now remembered that Friend had advised me to obtain the good will of my enemies, especially Foul Mouth, through hypocritical kindness. I proceeded to do this; my penance lasted a long time. Finally Love, judging that I had been thoroughly tested, appeared to me one day and asked if I had observed all his commandments. Though I responded modestly, he recognized my fidelity, despite a momentary temptation by Reason, and he promised me his help in the conquest of the castle.

    C. *Love assembles his forces, including False Seeming.*

    To this end he convoked his followers: Idleness, Nobility of Heart, Wealth, Openness, Pity, Generosity, Boldness, Honor, and many others: all of them persons with noble sentiments. Among this company slipped Constrained Abstinence and her inseparable companion, False Seeming. The presence, in religious garb, of this last, son of Fraud and Hypocrisy, disturbed Love a bit. But Constrained Abstinence defended his coming.

    Love then explained to the host his intention of attacking the castle Jealousy had built, which had caused him much grief. This castle was strong and the task would be hard. Ovid and other allies were dead; they could have aided the lover, Guillaume de Lorris, in his quest. Guillaume would begin a poem in praise of Love, which would be completed after his death by Jean de Meun.

    The forces of Love retired to deliberate. Wealth could not be counted upon, because of her scorn for me. False Seeming and Constrained Abstinence would attack Foul Mouth; Delight and Skillful Concealment would attack Shame; Boldness and Security would attack Fear; Openness and Pity would attack *Dangier*; and Courtesy and Generosity would take care of the Old Woman. But without the help of Venus, mother of Love, the campaign would be in doubt. Love said that his mother would intervene when she saw fit. Love then swore a solemn oath of vengeance upon Wealth, who refused her aid: he would ruin all her favorites. The poor were better lovers, anyway.

But False Seeming, who was there, did not dare come forward, for he was not sure how Love felt about him. Love then said that False Seeming was accepted among us, but asked him to talk about himself.

D. *The discourse of False Seeming to the company of Love.*

False Seeming said that he could be found among both secular and religious men, but was more apt to be among the religious, for he could hide best beneath their humble garments. He was referring, of course, to false religious: those who preach humility but are full of pride, who preach poverty but chase after wealth. Secular life does not necessarily entail the loss of the soul, nor religious life its salvation. The wolf is particularly dangerous when clothed in sheepskin, as we see in today's Church.

False Seeming would help us in all circumstances, if we accepted him and his friend, Lady Constrained Abstinence, among us. He was traitor, thief, perjurer, able to assume diverse appearances: a man for all seasons. He could also wear women's clothes, and become prioress, nun, or abbess. He took only the chaff of religion, and left the fruit. His conduct had little to do with his words. Love remarked that he looked like a holy hermit.

Certainly (he replied), but I am a hypocrite. I preach abstinence, but I love to eat and drink. I preach poverty, but I accumulate wealth. Besides, though I feign poverty, I have only disdain for the poor, who are no good to *me!* My concern is for the rich, from whom I can expect handsome gifts. And I can always say, in my defence, that the rich, having more occasions to sin than the poor, have also more need of my counsel—which is, however, false, for Solomon tells us that the state of destitution is as perilous for the soul as that of abundance.

As for the practise of begging, it is quite certain that there is no authority for it in the examples of Jesus Christ and the apostles, who never begged. Every man who can should earn his living by labor; and prayer does not exempt him from this obligation. It is true that God instructed the just to give their goods to the poor and to follow him; but he did not mean by this that the just should become beggars. We have on this matter the witness of St. Paul, who also recommends labor. It is possible, indeed, to give all one's time to prayer, if one wishes; one can then enter an order furnished with its own property, such as the white monks, black monks, canons regular, Hospitallers, or Templars. The problem of mendicancy has been much discussed lately, and the cases where this mendicancy is allowable have been fixed. See the opinion of Master William of Saint-Amour, who was banished from the kingdom, victim of my mother Hypocrisy. I must say that Master William had had the courage to write a book in which he exposed her life, and tried to deny me mendicancy and oblige me to work. *Me* work! I prefer to look religious and cover my tricks with the mantle of sham piety.

Love was shocked, and asked if he feared God. Certainly not (answered False Seeming). The fear of God leads to poverty; wealth and honors go to usurers, cheats, and despoilers of the people. I heap up the goods of Fortune, I build palaces, I satisfy all my desires. I am everywhere; I confess emperors, kings, dukes, barons, counts, and also women of all conditions, provided that they are rich and powerful. I persuade them that their own priests are merely animals. (And yet religious hypocrites are not hard to unmask: see Matt. 23.) And we have still other weapons: we ruin our opponents with calumny; we boast loudly; we interfere everywhere. That is why we have left deserts and woods, and now lodge in towns and castles.

We are servants of Antichrist, lambs in appearance, devouring wolves in our hearts, and wish to dominate the world. All manner of felons and criminals will find grace before justice, if they can enrich us and gratify us with their gifts. Otherwise, their punishment will be even heavier than they deserve. And things would have got still worse, when, in 1255, a diabolical book entitled *The Everlasting Gospel* appeared, which claimed to be inspired by the Holy Spirit and which purported to surpass the four biblical gospels as the sun surpasses the moon, or as the kernel surpasses the husk. But the University, guardian of Christianity, lifted its head and wanted to have the book censured. Those who had published it, incapable of defending its monstrosities, withdrew it: a shame, for acceptance of this book would have increased my power.

Be that as it may, Fraud, my father, is emperor of the world; my mother Hypocrisy is empress. We reign by deceiving nearly everyone about our true nature. Those who know what we are do not dare oppose us. God, certainly, will punish them for their cowardice, but no matter, if our reputation for virtue assures us power. It is to Beguines, with their pale faces, that princes ought to confide the government of their lands; and it is with them that I align myself to exercise my frauds.

Of course, I do not claim that one should scorn every man who wears the garb of poverty; but one should scrutinize his sincerity. As for you, Love, I don't dare lie to you, for I think that you would not let yourself be tricked. Otherwise, I would certainly have treated you like the others. As it is, you will have to take your chances with me and with my friend, Constrained Abstinence.

E. *The assault begins; False Seeming kills Foul Mouth.*

The forces of Love then prepared to assault the castle. False Seeming and Constrained Abstinence were to attack Foul Mouth, and disguised themselves as pilgrims, False Seeming taking care to furnish himself with a razor named Cut-Throat, which he slipped into his sleeve. The two traitors went to find Foul Mouth and asked him for hospitality; they also wished, if it would not annoy their host, to offer him a sermon. Foul Mouth, deceived by the pious appearance of his visitors, agreed. Constrained Abstinence, speaking first, berated him for heaping calumny on the young man. Foul Mouth protested that he had believed, as he had been told, that the young man had kissed the rose. False Seeming asserted that the young man was innocent, and urged Foul Mouth to confess, claiming that he was a better confessor than any parish priest. Foul Mouth then knelt, but False Seeming seized his throat, strangled him, cut his tongue out with the razor, and threw the body in a ditch. He finally got through the undefended gate and put to death all the Norman mercenaries, fast asleep after their habitual drunkenness.

F. *Love's forces capture the Old Woman, guardian of Fair Welcome, and induce her to give her ward the young man's gift.*

Courtesy and Generosity now rejoined False Seeming and Constrained Abstinence, and all four seized the Old Woman, guardian of Fair Welcome, who was not eager to be beaten. She was told that she must persuade Fair Welcome to accept a chaplet of flowers which the lover had sent him, and she must arrange a meeting between the two. The lover would promise to behave himself, and she would receive some jewels for her trouble. She agreed, fearing only the indiscreet chattering of Foul Mouth. But when she saw him lying dead in the ditch, she had no further hesitation, and promised all that was asked. (False Seeming remarked that the lovers could have evaded her vigilance, in any case; and I reflected that I had indeed planned such evasion if the Old Woman had been difficult.)

She returned to Fair Welcome, and asked why he was so sad. He was uneasy, he said, over her long absence, and he inquired where she had been. The Old Woman explained that she had been charged with giving him a chaplet from a young man whom she had met and who seemed quite amorous. But Fair Welcome was still distrustful. Who could this young man be? Then the Old Woman, after having assured him that it was a young lover calumniated by Foul Mouth, heartily praised the discretion and nobility of the youth whose interests she had taken in hand. But Fair Welcome was not yet reassured, and hesitated to accept the chaplet. What would we tell Jealousy if she asked where it had come from? The Old Woman replied that it could be attributed to *her*. Then, without further resistance, Fair Welcome accepted the lover's gift. And the Old Woman proceeded to give him some advice.

G. *The discourse of the Old Woman to Fair Welcome.*

I am old (she said) and you are young. Listen to my advice; it will be useful. I was once pretty, and attracted many lovers. But when I had learned all about love, my prime was already passed, and lovers fled my door. Now I can only teach you what I myself learned too late. If I had kept my youth, how I would take vengeance on all the young good-for-nothings who now mock me! But alas! I have only memories left. A young woman who leads a joyous life does not waste her time, especially if she thinks about acquiring enough for her expenses. Then I came here, where your guardianship was given to me. My intention has not been to initiate you to love, but rather to tell you what I would have done, in case you ever wish to try.

You must remember always to sell your heart to the highest bidder—ignore fidelity—and open your hands to receive. Swear to every rich lover that he is your favorite. Oaths of love are meaningless, and all men are faithless sensualists. String along several, and distract them with longing. To achieve this, false hair, cosmetics, and unguents are useful. Exploit your natural advantages, hide your imperfections. Keep your hands gloved if they are not clean. As for the chamber of Venus, meticulous cleanliness is necessary. Stockings and shoes should hide ugly feet. If your breath is foul, turn your face away. When you laugh, keep your mouth closed (especially if your teeth are crooked). The same applies to the art of crying. Behavior at table is also very important; above all, avoid getting drunk or falling asleep there. Finally, a woman should seize the proper moment— youth—to savor the joys of love: it should not be allowed to slip away.

A woman should not shut herself in at home; she should go out and be admired—but only when properly dressed and adorned. Let her then set her snares for all men. But she must not make two appointments for the same hour. Let her shun poor men, travelers from abroad (unless very rich), and those who are too elegant and self-satisfied. Naturally, one should never rely on promises without money. And one should keep the lover uncertain, giving in to him only gradually and reluctantly. He will then be more grateful.

She must squeeze her lover dry, with the help of her servants, sister, or mother. If she thinks he is tiring of giving gifts, she will ask for a loan (with no intention of paying). She should also complain continually about the alleged dangers to which their love exposes her, and she should pretend jealousy, which will please her lover. For women are naturally free (despite marriage), and always seek to recover their lost liberty. Nature's impulses can never be banished, and, though the law forbids us to follow our natural appetite and tries to make us faithful to a single partner, we ignore this law whenever we can.

When she is to make love, a woman should be sure that the room is in shadow, so that none of her physical blemishes, or her body filth, may be visible. The pleasure of love ought to come to both jointly; they must sail into port together. If she has no pleasure at all, she should disguise the fact. If they are at the gentleman's establishment, it is useful to make him wait awhile and to simulate fear. In case of rigorous surveillance by a jealous husband, she can get him drunk with wine, or feed him soporific herbs. Or she can pretend to have some illness which requires a visit to the public baths, where she can easily meet her lover. In fact, it is impossible to guard a woman who does not guard herself.

Generosity is not a female quality, and a woman should give her lover small cheap gifts, not a valuable one. (Every wise man will scorn the gifts of a woman, for they are merely deceitful.) But you, dear boy, should try to acquire the finest gifts for yourself, in order to provide for your future, when you will no longer be young. Alas! I gave away all the gifts I received to my lovers, especially one; but he beat me for my trouble. And a day came when the gifts ceased to arrive, and he became a poor beggar, and I, with no resources or husband, came here. Learn from my example.

H. *With the help of the Old Woman and Fair Welcome, the young man is admitted to the fortress and approaches the rose, but he is repulsed by "Dangier," Fear, and Shame.*

This discourse was heard willingly by Fair Welcome, and it diminished his fear of the Old Woman. It seemed to him that if not for Jealousy and her gatekeepers, the castle would have been easy to take. Foul Mouth was dead, and even some members of his own party hated his slanderous tongue. He thanked the Old Woman for her solicitude, and told her that he was ignorant of love and did not wish to learn about it. He was quite indifferent to his suitor; but since he had accepted the gift, he was disposed to receive the young man, on condition that Jealousy not be suspicious. The Old Woman said to fear nothing, and asked me for a gift, which I insincerely promised her.

At the castle's rear gate I found Love and his company, including the vile False Seeming and his lady, pregnant with Antichrist. I found also Sweet Looks, who led me directly to Fair Welcome and the rose. I was on the verge of touching the flower which I so desired, when *Dangier*, hidden till then in a corner, rushed to bar the way. Fear and Shame now came, and all three scolded me, ordering me to leave the garden. They subdued Fair Welcome and locked him up. I begged, for my own punishment, to be put in the same prison, but this request was, naturally, rejected. I then protested against the unjust imprisonment of Fair Welcome, but my enemies replied harshly and prepared to eject me from the garden. I called softly for a little help from my friends: Love's troops were alerted, and prepared for battle.

I. *The "author" digresses, and defends his poem against charges of obscurity, indecorous language, and ecclesiastical satire.*

Loyal lovers, listen carefully, so that the God of Love may help you. Hear the dogs yelping for the rabbit—the same rabbit which you pursue—and the ferret which must make him leap into the net. If you understand my words, you will have a useful Art of Love. On the other hand, any obscure passages will become clear when I interpret the dream. But first I must defend myself against wicked accusations of bawdy language. If it should be true, however, that there are shameful passages, I beg your indulgence, and I ask you to reply to my critics that the very subject matter of this work required such language. And if you, worthy ladies, find here any remarks too brutal for feminine manners, I beg you not to blame me. My sole aim is to teach; I seek only to reproduce what knowledgeable old authors have said. The object of poetry is to give profit and delight. And I protest that my intention in depicting False Seeming has never been to attack anyone who sincerely follows the holy rules of a religious order; I aim only at hypocrites, secular or cloistered. And if anyone claims that he was injured by my blows, he can avoid such wounds by avoiding hypocrisy. I have not said anything that lacks the authority of experience or reason; and if I say anything to which the Church can object, I am prepared to change it.

J. *The forces of Love are defeated, and Love calls upon his mother, Venus, for help.*

The first encounter now took place. It was between *Dangier* and Openness. Brutal *Dangier* knocked down the noble lady and prepared to subject her to a sad fate, when Pity arrived and sprayed *Dangier* with her tears. *Dangier* then felt his combative power dissolve. Shame reminded him of his duties, however, and drew her own sword against Pity, but she was then attacked by Delight. The attack was vain, for Delight was beaten to the ground by Shame's blows. At this moment appeared Skillful Concealment, who struck Shame and dazed her. Then Fear, usually a coward, rose angrily and cut down Skillful Concealment, only to find herself at grips with Boldness, against whom she easily prevailed. Now Security arose, and engaged Fear in hand-to-hand combat. The fighting became general, but the troops of Love got the worst of it, and their chief had to ask for a truce, which permitted him to call on his mother, Venus.

The messengers of Love arrived at Mount Cytherea, residence of the goddess, who, in the company of Adonis, was resting after the hunt. She used this respite to give her young friend some advice—advice which he ignored, for Adonis was to be slain by a boar. (This shows that we should always believe what our sweethearts tell us; and if they swear to us that they are entirely ours, we should believe them as we do the Paternoster. If Reason tries to intervene, ignore her.) When Venus learned of Love's trouble, she decided to fly at once to his aid, and swore to destroy the castle of Jealousy. From the moment of her arrival, Venus swore that she would destroy

111

Chastity in the hearts of all women, despite Jealousy, and she invited her son to swear the same for men. Both took their oath before the entire army.

    K. *Nature enters the conflict.*

    At this moment, Nature, who has charge of the things beneath the heavens, entered her smithy. She was very busy there, forging the individuals destined to perpetuate the species. Nature is always at Death's heel. Though Death will hunt us all down eventually, she cannot destroy the species. So long as one individual remains, the common form will remain. Nature, then, at her forge, guards against Death and Corruption, and labors without respite to renew individuals by new generation. And Art uses Nature's work for her models, though imperfectly. Art can also learn enough of alchemy to color all metals, but cannot transmute species. However, this does not mean that alchemy is not a true art. Whatever may be the case with species, individuals can indeed be made to change from one form, or species, to another. Thus, glassblowers turn fern into glass; the same might be done with metals, if we knew how to refine them properly.

    But Nature, though absorbed in her task, carried sorrow in her heart over a deed which she repented, and would gladly have abandoned her work if she had had her master's authorization. (Great Nature defies description by philosophers, or representation by artists; only God, who created her, fully grasps her.) When Nature heard the oath pronounced by Venus and Love, she felt much better, though still tormented by her single fault. She summoned her chaplain, Genius, in order to confess.

    L. *Genius's discourse to Nature.*

    It is true (Genius said) that women are easily angered, changeable, and prone to wrath and spite. Their vices are innumerable. Unhappy is the man who confides to them what should be secret! And in the intimacy of the bed, they know how to worm secrets from their husbands. The wretched man ends by giving way, then regretting it, but too late. One should tell men to protect themselves. Naturally, this does not mean that all relations with women must be avoided, if only for having children. Honor them; dress them; hand over to them the keeping of your house, if they are capable of it; let them exercise their trade, if they have one—but they should not be allowed to assume authority over men: that is a counsel of Scripture itself. And those who have sweethearts should be good companions to them, but should hold their tongues and scorn confidences of the pillow.

M. *The "confession" of Nature to Genius.*

1. *God's creation of the world.*

God (said Nature, kneeling and weeping) created the world by a free act of his will and with the sole intention of manifesting his goodness. He gave charge of it to me, putting in my hands the beautiful golden chain which binds the four elements. As I am servant and vicar of God, they must obey my laws, especially that which asserts that the essential forms of the universe maintain and perpetuate themselves, despite the decay of individuals. In general, the world respects this rule: all but a single creature.

I do not complain of heaven, the firmament of fixed stars, which accomplishes its regular revolution in thirty-six thousand years. This heaven is invisible to us, but reason demonstrates its existence. Nor do I complain of the seven planets; these properly fulfill their role, passing successively through their twelve houses (the signs of the zodiac) and remaining there the appointed time.

2. *The effects of celestial bodies upon the earth and its inhabitants.*

Planetary movement produces a harmony which is the cause of concord in our music. The planets also influence the accidents and substances of things here in the sublunary world; specifically, the combination and equilibrium of the four elements: cold, hot, dry, moist. But this equilibrium, which is the condition of life, is unstable; little by little, heat sucks up moisture, according to an inevitable law, until the moment when death intervenes. However, many men perish unnecessarily before the term fixed by this natural process; and these premature deaths, about which I can do nothing, keep me from leading men to the term of life which I have established. (Empedocles and Origen are examples.)

But natural inclination can be resisted, and Reason can help us reverse wicked inclination. The celestial bodies have, certainly, great power, but they can do nothing contrary to Reason.

3. *Necessity and free will.*

It is difficult to explain to lay people how predestination and divine foreknowledge can be reconciled with free will. But this reconciliation exists; otherwise, good lives would not merit recompense,

113

nor wicked lives punishment. God certainly knows in advance all events; his knowledge cannot be imperfect: to say so would be contrary to Reason. Consequently, one may claim, all human will can lead only to inevitable action, and there is no liberty.

But this argument, with its appearance of proof, leads us to the problem of good and evil and of divine justice. If one accepts it, piety and prayer lose their value. God ought to acquit criminals and treat the virtuous and the hypocrites equally. Yet it cannot be doubted that God is just and good. He cannot fail to recompense or punish each according to his merits; one cannot, therefore, believe in the absolute necessity of destiny.

But there is another argument in favor of necessity: if anyone foresaw and announced in advance an event which in fact occurred, but which had been only possible, not necessary, and which might *not* have occurred, he would have declared a true thing; but he would at the same time have declared a necessary thing, truth and necessity being two interchangeable logical concepts (that is, all which is true is necessary, and vice versa). Thus, the event would fall under the category of necessity. But, in fact, the person in question would have said a true thing but *not* a necessary one, since it was a question only of a *possible* event. The necessity of which we are speaking is only conditional necessity, not simple necessity, so this reasoning is worthless which claims that a true event is also inevitably a necessary event. And to say that God knows events precisely *because* they will occur is to make his foreknowledge depend on the events themselves, and thus compromise his omniscience. Other notions, too, have been advanced.

In fact, God knows infallibly what will be the decisions of free will; but this foreknowledge does not impose any constraint on men. It has its source only in the omnipotence of divine knowledge. And it has nothing in common with any kind of necessity. It cannot be said that things happen because God knows them in advance; nor can it be said that God knows them because they must occur. God sees the entire course of things as in a present, under his eyes (even what concerns the most distant future). He sees, in particular, where souls will go after death. This is what is called predestination. Be that as it may, the order of the world which is wished by God cannot fail to be realized. The celestial bodies will always exert their influence on individuals, and the hearts of men will always be characterized, according to their natural tendency, by idleness and self-indulgence, virtue or vice. But the free will is so powerful that it can modify these celestial influences in some measure. As reasonable creatures, we are responsible for our own follies.

4. *The weather.*

However (continued Nature), I must return to my subject, the celestial bodies, and the accuracy with which they fulfill their task. It is they who stir up the winds and provoke storms and tempests, which sometimes knock down steeples or uproot trees. Then the good weather returns and the air smiles again.

5. *Illusions, phantoms, and dreams.*

In Alhazen's treatise on optics can be found the explanation of certain astonishing properties of mirrors. For example, there are magnifying mirrors which make small objects large. There are also mirrors which diminish the objects and make them appear far off, others which start a fire by reflection of the sun's rays, others still which deform or reverse or multiply images, yet others which make phantoms appear, sometimes even between the mirror and the eye of the spectator.

Too much undisciplined thinking, extreme melancholy, or irrational fear can awake phantoms in the imagination. Even excessive meditations of devotion can engender in the spirit the delusory images of objects meditated upon. Whereas some dreamers, such as Scipio, can see spiritual substances in their actuality, others think that what they see is outside themselves, although it is in fact inside themselves.

6. *Comets do not announce the death of kings.*

The heavens also have the power to engender comets. Ordinary people believe that these comets announce the death of princes, but that is an error. Their influence is felt by the poor as well as by the powerful. Moreover, kings are not wealthier than petty people. It is contentment which brings wealth, and poverty is the fruit of covetousness.

7. *True nobility is the result of virtue.*

Nobility itself is only a specious value. At their birth, all men are alike and equal as men. It is capricious Fortune who introduces the differences. True nobility comes from the heart, intelligence, and virtue. Those who imagine that they have inherited it from their parents are deceived; wealth alone can be inherited. Birth imposes the obligation to follow in the noble ways of one's parents in order to confirm oneself in their nobility.

8. *More on comets and other incorruptible celestial bodies.*

Celestial influences also make the stars appear to be dragons or flying sparks which fall from the heavens, as fools think. But nothing can fall from the heavens, for the skies are incorruptible and nothing could damage them. It is the heavenly bodies, too, which cause changes of season, snow and hail, and those eclipses which arouse such terror in the ignorant. It is they which, through the intermediary of the winds, raise tempests at sea, then bring calm (I do not speak here of those which are caused solely by the moon). The heavenly bodies always accomplish their duty well.

9. *Of all God's corruptible creation beneath the sphere of the moon, only man ignores Nature's laws, especially the law of procreation.*

I do not complain either of the elements, whose combinations end by dissolution, since everything in the universe beneath the sphere of the moon is subject to corruption. I do not complain of the plants, nor of the birds or fish, nor of other creatures. All these obey my laws, and, most particularly, the law of reproduction, which joins the male and female for the sake of procreation. Only man refuses to follow the rule.

10. *Nature sends Genius to the God of Love.*

Go, Genius (she concluded), find Love, Venus, and all their company, and bring them my greetings—except for hypocritical False Seeming and his friend. Tell Love that I send you to excommunicate all his enemies, and that I excuse all the sins of those who take the trouble to love and multiply the species.

N. *Genius's sermon to the host of Love.*

1. *Genius is welcomed by Love and Venus.*

Genius then drafted, under the dictation of Nature, the pardon and judgment which he had to proclaim. He absolved Nature and enjoined her to get back to her forge and resume her work; then he flew to the camp of Love, from which False Seeming had already disappeared and which Constrained Abstinence was preparing to leave. The arrival of Genius brought joy to everyone's heart.

2. *Genius excommunicates the enemies of procreation, and encourages the others to procreate.*

In the name of Nature (he began), vicar and constable of the

eternal emperor, let those traitors be excommunicated and condemned without delay, who scorn the work by which is assured the
endurance of the world. Let paradise be given, however, to those who
strive to love well and lawfully. Work vigorously, seize the handles of
your plow, drive the plowshare deeply into the straight furrow. Imitate your parents, to whom you owe your life.

3. *Genius urges his hearers to live virtuously, so as to enter
   the beautiful park of the Lamb.*

In the name of heaven, my lords, avoid the vices of which
Dame Nature has given me a list (you will find it in the *Roman de la
Rose*). At the same time, you will avoid hell. Lead a good life, practise
loyal love, confess yourselves, invoke God. If you follow the lessons of
this sermon, you will enter the lovely park where the son of the virgin
ewe leads his flock with him. One experiences there an eternal present, which is an eternal spring, warmed by a sun which never sets.
The weather is even more beautiful than it was under the reign of
Saturn, at the time of the Golden Age.

4. *Saturn's castration and the end of the Golden Age.*

This Saturn was castrated by his son Jupiter, who wanted to
secure power. He thereby ended the happiness of the Golden Age,
and brought in the successive ages of silver, brass, and iron, in the
course of which men became worse and worse—thus pleasing the infernal gods, who are jealous of living men.

5. *Genius contrasts the park of the Lamb with the garden of
   "Deduit."*

The lovely park of the Lamb is as much better than the
garden of *Deduit* as truth is better than fiction. The latter offered on
its outside certain ugly images; the former is surrounded by the very
universe itself. All the joy and beauty of the one were only illusion:
Death was there, waiting for its prey. In the park, however, an eternal
felicity reigns, which cannot be described. In one is the perilous fountain of Narcissus, which sickens those who admire themselves there;
in the other is the fountain of life itself.

O. *Venus shoots a firebrand at the tower, and routs the enemies of
   Love.*

It was decided now to assault the tower. When Shame and
Fear refused Venus's invitation to surrender, she announced that all
the roses in the garden would be given to whoever wanted them,
clerks or laymen, religious or secular—secretly or openly. (Those with

other tastes would naturally pass up the roses, God confound them!) Then Venus held her bow and aimed her brand at a little aperture hidden in the tower, which Nature had placed on the front, between two pillars. Within was a fragrant sanctuary, covered by a priceless cloth. (The image was even more beautiful than that of Pygmalion.) The flaming arrow struck and set fire to the castle; *Dangier* fled, followed by Fear and Shame, and Fair Welcome was rescued by Courtesy, Pity, and Openness, who urged him now to admit the lover.

P. *The young man finally has his pleasure with the rose; the dreamer awakes.*

Like a good pilgrim, I now headed toward the aperture, the goal of my pilgrimage. I took my sack and staff, but with great effort, for the staff was stiff and strong. I had also the two hammers which Nature forged for me. I tried to penetrate the aperture with my staff, but there was a barrier there. Eventually I penetrated, with some difficulty: no one had been there before. Finally I seized the rose. (Some seeds which I had scattered there made the rosebush expand.) Thus I had achieved my quest, with gratitude to the God of Love, Venus, and their army, but none to Reason, Wealth, or my enemies such as Jealousy. It was soon day, and I awoke.

THREE

Personifications and Allusions

The glossaries in chapters eleven and twelve should help the reader of the *Roman* to identify and sort out its multitude of names, and to move freely from the often manifold English versions to the Old French originals. For example: depending on which text or translation one reads, the garden in which the poem mainly occurs is said to belong to *Deduit, Deduiz,* Diversion, Mirth, or Delight. The relevant entry and cross-references in the Glossary of Personifications will quickly show that these names all belong to the same figure, and will provide a brief account of who he is.

The Glossary of Allusions indexes references in the poem to scriptural and apocryphal writings; classical myths; ancient and medieval literature, history, and general culture; and other diverse classes of persons and places. Each name is accompanied by a brief identification, and, where possible, an indication of its specific role in the *Roman.* Apart from its intended utility as a reference tool, this glossary may suggest something of the contents of that thirteenth-century intellectual world which Guillaume and Jean distilled into their poem.

We have not included here all the allusions, as Langlois more or less does in his valuable "Table des Noms Propres" (5:331–46), but only those which might for any reason puzzle the modern reader. Thus, we omit very familiar mythological names (Venus, Neptune) and geographical locations (France, Jerusalem), well-known persons (Plato, Aristotle), and common religious names (St. Mary, Judas), including names of the deity. In addition, we have omitted a few proper names (such as *Agnès*) which are of no intrinsic importance and have not, in any case, been identified by scholars, as well as a small number of self-explaining allusions which offer no problems. However, familiar names with unfamiliar French forms (such as *Moÿsi* and *Pharisien*) are included, together, of course, with all other allusions which the modern student or reader may not recognize but

121

needs to if he is to understand the poem.

The Glossary of Personifications is mainly devoted to those personified abstractions which are the "characters" of the *Roman*. Here we have sought completeness, and have tried to include all the psychological, moral, and other sorts of figures which (or who) give the *Roman* its special poetic texture. In addition, there are a few allegorical abstractions such as *Amistiez* (Friendship) whose personification is perhaps doubtful but which are structurally akin to unmistakable personifications, as well as a somewhat larger number of oddments such as *Coupe Gorge* (Cut-Throat), a razor; *Refus* (Refusal), a forest; and various allegorical arrows, swords, gifts, and the like. The main object of this glossary is to aid the reader in keeping track of these very numerous and diverse allegorical flowers in Guillaume's and Jean's garden, whose dazzling profusion (like the comparably copious dramatis personae in a Tolstoy novel) can entail a measure of confusion—particularly inasmuch as many of these allegorical figures have two or more meanings to be distinguished and identified. Here, too, a survey of the entire glossary may help the reader to grasp the sometimes elusive shape of the poem's allegorical vision.

One or two entries—e.g., *Nuiz* (Night)—appeared to be at home in both glossaries, and have been so classified. It seemed more important to be inclusive than discriminating, if choice were necessary. Thus, for instance, the Glossary of Personifications contains both those massive allegorical figures whose importance dominates and pervades the poem, such as *Resson* (Reason), *Amis* (Friend), and *Nature*, as well as a large host of lesser figures, such as *Soffisance* (Sufficiency), who have, by contrast, mere walk-on roles. The glossary does not usually attempt to distinguish between the major figures and the marginal ones, but seeks only to provide the necessary tools for the reader, who will be able to make such discriminations for himself.

These glossaries should enable him to identify virtually any allusion or allegorical figure in the original French text, in the Chaucerian *Romaunt of the Rose*, or in the English translations of Ellis, Robbins, and Dahlberg. Elaborate cross-referencing will (it is hoped) make it a simple matter to connect the Old French names, printed in italic, with their English versions, printed in roman, and vice versa. Given the vagaries of medieval scribal practise, it seemed unnecessarily confusing to show all the variant spellings of the names as they appear in Lecoy's text, upon which the glossaries are based. Nevertheless, we have sometimes included a few such variants, usually from Lecoy's edition but occasionally from Langlois's, where there seemed any chance of obscurity. When significant variants occur in the *Romaunt*, they appear in the glossary entries immediately after the French forms. (Certain names from the *Romaunt*, however, have no equivalent in the Old French text or in its modern translations, because the *Romaunt* used "apocryphal" French materials which did not get into the standard texts of the *Roman*; these names will therefore stand alone, in their own glossary entries.) Last, in many of the entries, are the modern English versions—specifically, such versions as are not identical or nearly identical with French or *Romaunt* forms. (When they are, we have not usually included them at all.)

Two final matters. When the *Roman* asserts or implies the gender of an allegorical personification, we have indicated it. Absence of gender identification in the glossary means that there is none in the poem. Each glossary entry is followed by the line number of its first appearance in the Lecoy text, and, where relevant, in F. N. Robinson's text of the *Romaunt* in the revised edition of his *Chaucer*. Multiple numbers, of course, refer to multiple meanings or usages of a name in the poem.

11

Glossary of Personifications

Abonde, Abundance: see *Habonde*

Abstinaunce: see *Attenance*. [*Romaunt* 5,848]

Abstinence-Streyned: see *Contreinte Atenence*. [*Romaunt* 6,341]

Age: see *Vielleice*

Amanz, Amaunt: Lover, the protagonist and narrator of the poem. In the rubrics and titles of the MSS, he is regularly identified thus, though never in the text itself, where his connection with the class of lovers is, however, often implied.

Amis, Ami: Friend, the adviser and confidant of the narrator. [3,093]

Amistiez: Friendship, one of the kinds of love delineated by Reason. [4,655]

Amors, Amours: sexual passion personified; the God of Love. [22]

Art: a feminine personification; she imitates Nature. [15,987]

Atenance Contreinte: see *Contreinte Atenence*

Attenance, Astenance: Abstinence, the same as *Contreinte Atenence* (q.v.). [10,690]

Avarice: one of the feminine personifications on the wall surrounding the garden of *Deduit*. [197]

Baraz, Barat: Fraud (Deceit, Falsehood, Guile); father of False Seeming. [5,125]

Beaute: see *Biautez* [*Romaunt* 952]

Beauty: see *Biautez*

Bel Acueil: Fair Welcome (Fair Welcoming), son of Courtesy.

Though personified as a young man, Fair Welcome eventually becomes identified with the young lady symbolized by the Rose. [2,776]

Bel Samblant: Fair Seeming, last of the five golden arrows of the God of Love. [949]

Bialacoil: see **Bel Acueil.** [*Romaunt* 2,984]

Biau Samblant, Biaus Semblanz: see **Bel Samblant**

Biautez, Biaute: Beauty, first and most important of the five golden arrows of the God of Love. [938]

Beauty personified as a lady; companion of the God of Love. [992]

Bien Celer: Skillful Concealment, a masculine personification, one of the barons of the God of Love. [10,428]

Boldness: see **Hardement**

Cajolery: see **Chuerie**

Chance: see **Male Aventure**

Chasteez, Chasteé, Chastaé: Chastity, a feminine personification. [2,830]

Chastite: see **Chasteez.** [*Romaunt* 3,043]

Cheance: Fall (Misfortune) personified. [6,539]

Chuerie: Cajolery (Flattery), a forest where Openness obtained the lance she uses against *Dangier*. [15,298]

Compaignie: Company (Companionship), the fourth of the five golden arrows of the God of Love. [944]

One of the barons of the God of Love. [10,424]

Constrained Abstinence: see **Contreinte Atenence**

Contempt of Death: see **Despit de Mort**

Contreinte Atenence: Constrained Abstinence (Forced Abstinence, Feigned Abstinence), a feminine personification; one of the barons of the God of Love. [10,428]

She is pregnant with Antichrist by False Seeming. [14,713]

Corrupcion: Corruption personified. [15,977]

Cortoisie, Curtesie: Courtesy, a feminine personification; mother of Fair Welcome. [778; *Romaunt* 796]

Third golden arrow of the God of Love (although, in an earlier account, this arrow is said to be Openness). [1,765]

One of the barons of the God of Love. [10,423].

Coupe Gorge: Cut-Throat, the razor of False Seeming. [12,066]

Covetousness: see *Covoitise*

Covoitise, Coveitise: Covetousness, one of the feminine personifications on the wall surrounding the garden of *Deduit*. [169; *Romaunt* 181]

Crime: see *Pechiez*

Cuers Failliz, Queurs Failliz: Faint Heart, father of Larceny. [9,517]

Cut-Throat: see *Coupe Gorge*

Dangier, Daunger: Resistance (Danger), guard of the rosebushes; masculine personification of female modesty, corresponding to Ovid's *Pudor* (*Amores* I.ii.32). [2,811; *Romaunt* 3,018]

Deceit: see *Baraz*

Deduit, Deduiz: Diversion (Mirth, Delight), a masculine personification; owner of the garden in which the poem is set. See **Oiseuse**. [588]

Delight: see *Deduit*

Delit, Deliz: masculine personification of delight or pleasure. [4,440]
    One of the barons of the God of Love. [10,424]

Desesperance: Despair (Wanhope), fourth of the five black arrows of the God of Love. [967]

Despit de Mort: Contempt of Death (Scorner of Death, Death Scorner), the shield of Boldness. [15,510]

Deth: see **Mort.** [*Romaunt* 4,992]

Distresse: a "senatour," or companion, of Elde. [*Romaunt* 4,997]

Diversion: see *Deduit*

Douleur: Suffering (Grief), imprisoner and tormentor—together with Labor—of Age. [4,493]

Doute de Male Renomee: Fear of a Bad Reputation (Fear of Evil Name, Fear of Ill Renown), shield belonging to Shame. [15,436]

Douz Palers, Douz Parler: Sweet Talk (Sweet Speech, Soft Speech), masculine personification; one of the God of Love's four gifts to the Lover. [2,657]

Douz Pensers: Sweet Thought (Gentle Thought), masculine personification; one of the God of Love's four gifts to the Lover. [2,631]

Douz Regart: Sweet Looks (Sweet Sight, Soft Looks), a masculine companion of the God of Love, and keeper of his bows. [906]

Personification of the seeing of one's beloved: one of the God of Love's four gifts to the Lover. [2,702]

Drede: see *Peor*. [*Romaunt* 3,958]

Droiz, Dreiz: Right (Law) personified. [5,361]

Duenna: see *Vielle*

Elde: see *Vielleice*. [*Romaunt* 349]

Eneur: see *Honor*

Envie: Envy, one of the feminine personifications on the wall surrounding the garden of *Deduit*. [235]

Esperance: Hope, a feminine personification, one of the God of Love's four gifts to the Lover. [2,601]

Evil Hap: see *Male Aventure*

Evil Tongue: see *Male Bouche*

Fain: Hunger (Famine), feminine personification; chambermaid of Poverty. [10,110]

Faint Heart: see *Cuers Failliz*

Fair Seeming: see *Bel Samblant*

Faire-Semblaunt: see *Bel Samblant*. [*Romaunt* 963]

Fair-Welcomyng: see *Bel Acueil*. [*Romaunt* 5,856]

Faith: see *Foiz*

Faithlessness: see *Noviaus Pensers*

Fall: see *Cheance*

False Seeming: see *Fausemblant*

Falsehood: see *Baraz*

Fals-Semblant: see *Fausemblant*. [*Romaunt* 5,848]

Famine: see *Fain*

Fausemblant: False Seeming, a masculine personification; companion of Constrained Abstinence; son of Fraud and Hypocrisy; type of the hypocrite or deceiver. See *Traïson*. [10,429]

Faynt Distresse: the "scrippe," or satchel, of Abstinaunce. [*Romaunt* 7,403]

Fear: see *Peor*

Fear of a Bad Reputation: see *Doute de Male Renomee*

Fear of Ostentation: see *Soupeçon d'Amboufissemant*

Feigned Abstinence: see *Contreinte Atenence*

Felonie: Felony, or Evil Inclination; one of the feminine personifications on the wall surrounding the garden of *Deduit*. [155]

Flattery: see *Chuerie*

Foiz, Feiz: Faith (Good Faith) personified. [5,361]

Fole Largece: Foolish Generosity (Mad Largess), personification of prodigality; maker of the road Give-Too-Much, the most direct way to the castle in which Fair Welcome is imprisoned. [7,867]

Foly: Folly personified. [*Romaunt* 3,235]

Foolish Generosity: see *Fole Largece*

Forced Abstinence: see *Contreinte Atenence*

Forfez, Forfaiz: Transgression personified. [5,523]

Fortune: feminine personification, whose turning wheel symbolizes the instability of mundane prosperity and adversity; mother of Gentility. [3,953]

Foul Mouth: see *Male Bouche*

Franchise: Openness (Independence), the third golden arrow of the God of Love. (But cf. *Cortoisie*.) [942]
> Feminine personification of good-natured acquiescence. [1,189]
> One of the barons of the God of Love. [10,422]

Fraud: see *Baraz*

Friend, Freend: see *Amis*. [*Romaunt* 3,346]

Friendship: see *Amistiez*

Gaiety: see *Jolivetez*

Generosity: see *Largesce*

Genius: a "priest," confessor of Nature. [4,314]

Gentility: see *Gentillece*

Gentillece: Gentility (Nobility) personified; daughter of Fortune. [6,538]

Gile: see *Baraz*. [*Romaunt* 6,112]

Give-Too-Much: see *Trop Doner*

Gladnesse: see *Leesce*. [*Romaunt* 746]

God of Love: see *Amors*. [*Romaunt* 878]

Good Faith: see *Foiz*

Good-Hope: see *Esperance*. [*Romaunt* 2,941]

Grief: see *Douleur*

Gronyng: an "herbergeour," or provider of lodgings; associated with Elde. [*Romaunt* 5,000]

Grucchyng: an "herbergeour," or provider of lodgings; associated with Elde. [*Romaunt* 5,000]

Habonde, Dame: Lady Abundance (Dame Habundia), a sorceress and night rider. [18,397]

Haine: Hatred, one of the feminine personifications on the wall surrounding the garden of *Deduit*. [139]

Hardement: Boldness (Hardihood, Courage) personified, one of the barons of the God of Love. [10,423]

Hardynesse: see **Hardement**. [*Romaunt* 5,861]

Hate: see **Haine**. [*Romaunt* 147]

Hide Close: see **Bien Celer**

Hidewell: see **Bien Celer**

Honor: one of the barons of the God of Love. [10,423]

Honte: Shame, third of the five black arrows of the God of Love. [966]

    Daughter of Reason. [2,820]

    Cousin of Fear, companion of *Dangier*. [3,630]

Hope: see **Esperance**. [*Romaunt* 2,803]

Humilitez: Humility, one of the barons of the God of Love. [10,427]

Hypocrisy: see **Papelardie**

Idleness: see **Oiseuse**

Independence: see **Franchise**

Infortune: Misfortune, the absence and contrary of Fortune. [*Romaunt* 5,493]

Ipocrisy: *see* **Ypocrisie**. [*Romaunt* 6,112]

Ire: a "senatour," or companion, of Elde. [*Romaunt* 4,997]

Jalous, Li: the Jealous Husband whose behavior and speech are described by Friend. [9,335]

Jalousie, Jelousy: Jealousy, a feminine personification, who arranges for the erection of a castle in which Fair Welcome is imprisoned. [2,844; *Romaunt* 3,820]

Joinece, Jeunece: feminine personification of Youth; one of the barons of the God of Love. [1,258]

Jolivetez, Jolietez: Gaiety personified; one of the barons of the God of Love. [10,426]

Joustice: Justice personified. [5,365]

Joy: see **Leesce**

Knavery: see *Larrecin*
Kynde: see *Nature, Dame*. [*Romaunt* 1,699]

Labour: see *Travaill*. [*Romaunt* 4,994]
Larceny: see *Larrecin*
Largesce, **Largesse:** a feminine personification of Generosity.
   [1,125; *Romaunt* 1,150]
      One of the barons of the God of Love. [10,422]
Larrecin: Larceny (Knavery, Theft), son of Poverty and Faint Heart.
   [9,512]
Law: see *Droiz*
Lecherie, **Leccherie:** feminine personification of Lechery. [3,585;
   Romaunt 3,911]
Ledeur, Laideur: feminine personification of Ugliness; chamber-
   maid and antagonist of Chastity. [8,944]
Leesce: feminine personification of Joy (Jollity, Gladness). [728]
Love: see *Amors*. [*Romaunt* 22]
Lover: see *Amanz*
Luxure: see *Lecherie*

Mad Largess: see *Fole Largece*
Male Aventure: Misfortune (Chance, Evil Hap) personified. [9,499]
Male Bouche: Foul Mouth (Evil Tongue) personified, companion of
   Dangier. [2,819]
Malencoly: a "senatour," or companion, of Elde. [*Romaunt* 4,998]
Malice: a feminine personification. [5,534]
Maufez: Misdeeds, father of Shame. [2,825]
Mesfaiz: see *Maufez*
Mirth, Myrthe: see *Deduit*. [*Romaunt* 601]
Misdeeds: see *Maufez*
Misfortune: see *Cheance*.
Mort: masculine personification of Death. [4,490]

Nature, Dame: a feminine personification. [1,431]
Newe-Thought: see *Noviaus Pensers*. [*Romaunt* 982]
Night: see *Nuiz*
Nobility: see *Gentillece*
Nobility of Heart: see *Noblece de Queur*
Noblece de Queur, Noblece de Cueur: Nobility of Heart (Noble

Heart) personified, one of the barons of the God of Love. [10,421]

Noviaus Pensers: New Thought (Faithlessness), fifth and last of the black arrows of the God of Love. [968]

Nuiz, Nuit: feminine personification of Night; wife of Acheron, mother of the Furies. [16,896]

Oiseuse: feminine personification of Idleness, gatekeeper of the garden of *Deduit*. [580]

A principal baron of the God of Love. [10,419]

Old Age: see **Vielleice**

Old Woman: see **Vielle**

Openness: see **Franchise**

Orguelz: feminine personification of Pride; first of the five black arrows of the God of Love. [961]

Pacience: Patience personified, one of the barons of the God of Love. [10,427]

Papelardie: Pope-Holiness (Hypocrisy), a feminine personification, one of the images on the wall surrounding the garden of *Deduit*. [407]

Peccune: Riches (Wealth), a feminine personification. [5,175]

Pechiez: Sin (Crime) personified. [9,499]

Peor: a feminine personification of Fear; a companion of *Dangier* and cousin of Shame. [2,820]

Peyne: a "senatour," or companion, of Elde. [*Romaunt* 4,997]

Pitié, Pitiez, Pite: feminine personification of Pity. [3,233; *Romaunt* 3,501]

One of the barons of the God of Love. [10,422]

Poope-Holy: see **Papelardie.** [*Romaunt* 415]

Povreté, Poverte: feminine personification of Poverty, one of the images on the wall surrounding the garden of *Deduit*. [440; *Romaunt* 450]

Pride: see **Orguelz.** [*Romaunt* 975]

Queurs Failliz: see **Cuers Failliz**

Reason: see **Resson**

Refus, Bois de: Wood of Refusal, the forest where *Dangier* has obtained his mace. [15,287]

Resistance: see *Dangier*

Resson, Raison, Resoun: feminine personification of Reason; mother of Shame. [2,824; *Romaunt* 3,034]

Richece, Richesse: Wealth (Riches), a feminine personification. [1,017; *Romaunt* 1,033]

> One of the barons of the God of Love. [10,421]

Right: see *Droiz*

Sadness: see *Tritesce*

Scorner of Death: see *Despit de Mort*

Security: see *Seürté*

Semblant: Seeming, a masculine personification. [12,089]

Seürté: Security (Assurance), a feminine personification, one of the barons of the God of Love. [10,425]

Shame: see *Honte*. [*Romaunt* 980]

Sikernesse: see *Seürté*. [*Romaunt* 5,862]

Simpleice, Symplesse: Simplicity, second of the golden arrows of the God of Love; the one which wounds the most. [940; *Romaunt* 954]

> One of the God of Love's barons. [10,424]

Simplicity: see *Simpleice*

Sin: see *Pechiez*

Skillful Concealment: see *Bien Celer*

Soffisance, Soufisance: personification of Sufficiency (i.e., contentment with what one has). [9,500]

Sorowe: see *Tritesce*. [*Romaunt* 301]

Soupeçon d'Amboufissemant: Suspicion of Ostentation (Fear of Ostentation), the sword of Fear. [15,488]

Speche: see *Douz Palers*. [*Romaunt* 2,836]

Streyned-Abstinaunce: see *Contreinte Atenence*. [*Romaunt* 7,323]

Suffering: see *Douleur*

Suspicion of Ostentation: see *Soupeçon d'Amboufissemant*

Sweet Sight: see *Douz Regart*

Swete-Lokyng: see *Douz Regart*. [*Romaunt* 920]

Swete-Speche, Swete-Spekyng: see *Douz Palers*. [*Romaunt* 2,825]

Swete-Thought, Swete-Thenkyng: see *Douz Pensers*. [*Romaunt* 2,793]

Syknesse: a "senatour," or companion, of Elde. [*Romaunt* 4,997]

Tens: Time, a masculine personification. [361]
Thefte: see *Larrecin.* [*Romaunt* 7,401]
Thought: see *Douz Pensers.* [*Romaunt* 2,804]
Time: see *Tens*
To-Moche-Yevyng: see *Trop Doner.* [*Romaunt* 5,837]
Too-Great-Giving: see *Trop Doner*
Traïson: Treason or betrayal, the substance of False Seeming's crutch. [12,062]
Transgression: see *Forfez*
Travaill: Labor, imprisoner and tormentor—together with Suffering —of Age. [4,493]
Travauz: see *Travaill*
Treason: see *Traïson.* [*Romaunt* 7,415]
Trespas: see *Maufez.* [*Romaunt* 3,033]
Tritesce: Sorrow (Sadness), a feminine personification, one of the images on the wall surrounding the garden of *Deduit.* [292]
Trop Doner: Give-Too-Much (Too-Great-Giving), the most direct road leading to the castle in which Fair Welcome is immured. [7,866]

Ugliness: see *Ledeur*

Vielle, La: the Old Woman (Duenna, Old Whore), embodiment of the cupidinous love of material things or *visibilia.* [10,697]
Vielleice: Old Age, a feminine personification, one of the images on the wall surrounding the garden of *Deduit.* [339]
Vilanie, Vilanye: Villainy, a feminine personification, one of the images on the wall surrounding the garden of *Deduit.* [156; *Romaunt* 166]
   One of the black arrows of the God of Love. [963]

Wanhope: see *Desesperance.* [*Romaunt* 981]
Wealth: see *Richece*
Wel-Heelynge: see *Bien Celer.* [*Romaunt* 5,857]
Woo: see *Douleur.* [*Romaunt* 4,995]
Wykked-Tonge: see *Male Bouche.* [*Romaunt* 3,027]

Ydelnesse: see *Oiseuse*. [*Romaunt* 593]

Youth: see *Joinece*. [*Romaunt* 1,282]

Ypocrisie: Hypocrisy, mother of False Seeming; she caused William of Saint-Amour to be exiled. [10,439; 11,477]

12

Glossary of Allusions

Absalon, Absalom: third son of King David, and the handsomest man in all Israel (2 Sam. [Douay version, 2 Kings] 14:25). A type of beauty, and, in certain medieval iconographic traditions, of vainglory. [13,840]

Acheron: husband of Night. In mythology, a river of hell. [16,899]

Adan, Adans: Adam, the first man. [11,344]

Adonys: Adonis, favorite of Venus, slain by a wild boar; son of King Cynaras and his daughter Myrrha. According to one medieval tradition, Adonis's hunt of the boar is emblematic of the carnal pursuits of Venus; according to another, it represents the hunt of charity. [15,647; 21,172]

Aeacus: see *Eachus*

Albumasar, Albumazar: celebrated Arab astronomer of the ninth century. According to Nature, he predicted the birth of the Virgin Mother. [19,147]

Alcipiadés, Alcibiades: Athenian general, favorite student of Socrates; brilliant but unprincipled. Said by the Jealous Husband to be physically handsome but spiritually ugly. [8,913]

Algus: Arab mathematician (Al-Khwarizmi) of the ninth century, whose work helped transmit decimal calculation and algebra to Europe. [12,760]

Alhacem, Alhazen: Arab physician and mathematician of the eleventh century; author of *Observations*, an influential treatise on optics. [18,004]

Alletho, Alecto: one of the three Furies, who pursue and punish men for peculiarly inhumane crimes. The others are Megaera and Tisiphone. [19,805]

Almageste: *Almagest*, the great work of Ptolemy, Greek astronomer of the second century, containing his astronomical and trigonometrical systems. [7,010]

Amanz, Sainz; Saint Amand: St. Amandus, seventh-century Merovingian ascetic, bishop, and missionary to Flanders. [14,116]

Amphion de Thebes: son of Jupiter and Antiope, whose marvellous playing of the lyre caused stones to move of their own accord and form the wall about Thebes. [20,999]

Amyas: in *Romaunt*, a scribal mistake for "Miauz" (q.v.). [*Romaunt* 3,826]

Annius, Ennius: Ennius, early Roman poet (239–169 B.C.). [18,701]

Apelles: Greek painter of fourth century B.C. [16,149]

Apolin, Apollo: classical deity who was believed to speak to men through the oracle at Delphi. [5,828]

Appius: lecherous judge who tried to gain access to the maiden Virginia (daughter of Virginius) by corrupting justice. The story from Livy's *Annals* (I.iii.44–58) was also used by Boccaccio, Gower, and Chaucer (*Physician's Tale*). [5,559]

Argentuell, Argenteuil: site near Paris of convent where Heloise assumed her religious vows. [8,765]

Argus: in mythology, the possessor of a hundred eyes. [14,353]

Arnold, Saint: see **Hernoul, Saint**

Arrabe, Araby: a region fabled for its gold; "gold of Araby" is a very common expression in the *chansons de geste*. [9,468]

Arraz, Arras: Arras, city of Artois in northern France. [1,214; *Romaunt* 1,234]

Artais: see **Roberz d'Artais**

Atalus, Athalus: king of Pergamum in Asia Minor, died 197 B.C.; according to John of Salisbury, the inventor of chess. [6,661]

Atropos: one of the three *Parcae*, or Fates: mythological emblems of human mortality, imaged as three spinning sisters. Cloto, who presides at birth, holds the spindle; Lachesis draws out the thread of destiny; Atropos cuts it off. [10,341]

Augustyns: Augustinians, one of the orders of friars. [*Romaunt* 7,459]

Aureole, Aureolus: *Liber de Nuptiis*, a lost work ascribed to the Greek philosopher Theophrastus, who died c. 287 B.C. The work was regarded as antifeminist. St. Jerome preserved part of it in his

Contra Jovinianum. [8,537]

Austyn: St. Augustine of Hippo (354–430). The book referred to is *De Opere Monachorum.* [*Romaunt* 6,583]

Avicenne, Avicenna: celebrated Arabian physician and philosopher (980–1037). [15,931]

Bachus, Bacchus: god of vineyards, viniculture, and intoxication. [17,921]

Balenuz, Balenus: supposed author of treatises on magic. His identity, and even his existence, are uncertain. [14,369]

Barré: the "barred" or Carmelite order of friars, so called because of the appearance of their habit. [12,105]

Beguins, Bygyne, Beguines: a semi-conventual religious community of women. In the thirteenth and fourteenth centuries, they came under the influence of the friars, were accused of various extravagant heresies, and were increasingly in bad odor. [11,908; *Romaunt* 7,366]

Belidienes: the fifty daughters of Danaus, son of Belus—the Danaïdes—who were punished for murdering their husbands, by being obliged ceaselessly to pour water into a bottomless cask. [19,273]

Belin, Dam: popular name for a sheep; from the *Roman de Renart.* [11,093]

Benoait, Saint; Benoit: St. Benedict (c. 480–543), founder of Benedictine monasticism. [14,707]

Bïere: an old name for the forest of Fontainebleau. [15,299]

Bise: Boreas, personification of the cold north wind. [5,912]

Blake: Black, or Benedictine, monks. [*Romaunt* 6,695]

Boece, Boethius: the philosopher Boethius (c. 470–525), author of the *Consolation of Philosophy.* [5,007]

Boreas: see *Bise*

Bucholiques: Virgil's *Eclogues* or *Bucolics.* According to a famous tradition, the Fourth Eclogue prophesies the coming of Christ. [19,139]

Burgoyne: Burgundy. [*Romaunt* 554]

Cacus: see *Chacus*

Cadmus: legendary founder of Thebes, and bringer of the Phoenician alphabet to Greece. He slew a dragon who had devoured his companions, and sowed the dragon's teeth. [19,706]

Calabre, Calabria: region of extreme southern Italy, where the poet Ennius (see **Annius**) was thought to have been given beautiful gardens by his contemporaries. [18,700]

Caribdis, Charybdis: legendary whirlpool in the Strait of Messina, between Italy and Sicily, feared by sailors. [4,273]

Carmes: Carmelite order of friars. See **Barré.** [*Romaunt* 7,460]

Cartage, Quartage: Carthage, north African city founded by Phoenicians in the seventh century B.C. [5,348]

Catillus, Catullus: Roman poet of love (c. 84–c. 47 B.C.). [10,492]

Caÿn, Caïn: eldest son of Adam and Eve, murderer of his brother Abel. [18,003]

Cerberus: three-headed dog, which guards the entrance to Hades. [19,778]

Cerdagne: see **Sardaigne**

Ceres: see **Tritholemus.** [10,153]

Cesariens: Caesars. [6,434]

Chacus, Cacus: a giant, son of Vulcan, who stole Hercules' cattle and was finally slain by Hercules. Cf. *Aeneid* VII. [15,543]

Chanouns Regulers: members of certain orders which observe a rule, as distinguished from secular canons. [*Romaunt* 6,694]

Charle, Charles: Charlemagne (742–814), king of the Franks and restorer of the Western Empire. [1,426]

Charles, Challes: Charles, count of Anjou and Provence, king of Naples and Sicily (1226–85). [6,610]

Chaton: "Dionysius Cato," the supposed author of the *Disticha*, a collection of moral sayings from the third or fourth century A.D., which had a great reputation in the Middle Ages. He was erroneously associated with Cato the Elder (234–149 B.C.), the Roman statesman. [7,023]

Cicero: see **Tulles**

Cipioun, Kyng: see **Scypion**

Citheron: Cytherea, or Cythera, an island off the southern coast of Greece, home of Venus; near the place where she arose from the sea. [15,631]

Claudïens: Claudian, Latin poet of the fourth century, last of the classic poets. [6,325]

Cloto: see **Atropos.** [19,738]

Confiteor: the prayer of confession. [10,366]

Confort, de: the *Consolation of Philosophy* of Boethius (q.v.). [5,007]

Constantin: Constantine, a celebrated physician, born at Carthage in the eleventh century. [15,931]

Constantinoble: Constantinople. [20,780]

Cordeliers, Cordyleres: Franciscan order of friars, so called from the cord or rope worn about their waists. [12,105; *Romaunt* 7,459]

Cornuaille, Cornewaile: Cornwall. [3,882; *Romaunt* 4,250]

Corradin: Conradin, Manfred's nephew, decapitated by Charles of Anjou. [6,626]

Cresus: Croesus, rich king of Lydia, victim of Fortune. [6,459]

Cupido: Cupid, son of Venus. [1,586]

Cybelé: Cybele, an earth goddess associated with orgiastic rites. [17,921]

Cynaras: king of Paphos, who was deceived into begetting Adonis on his daughter Myrrha. [21,157]

Cypris, Dame: Venus. [21,198]

Cyrcé: Circe, a magician and emblem of rampant sensuality (see *Odyssey* X). She transformed Ulysses' companions into swine, but could not ultimately keep Ulysses with her. [14,376]

Daire: Darius Codomannus, the last king of Persia (336–330 B.C.), conquered by Alexander the Great. A victim of Fortune. [6,743]

Dallida: Dalila, deceiver and betrayer of Samson. [9,176]

Dedalus: Daedalus, a type of the skillful craftsman. According to the myth, he made wings for himself and his son Icarus. [5,196]

Deïaneira: Dejanira, who caused the death of her friend Hercules by giving him a poisonous shirt. [9,165]

Demophon: Demophoön, son of Theseus, and king of Athens. He abandoned Phyllis (see **Phillis**). [13,182]

Denis, Saint; Saint Denise: apostle to the Gauls, first bishop of Paris (third century). Also: celebrated abbey near Paris, location of sepulchres of French kings. [8,657]

Destinees: the Fates or *Parcae*. See **Atropos**. [10,157]

Deucalion: mythical king of Phthia in Thessaly, a Greek Noah: when Zeus determined to destroy the degenerate race of men, Deucalion and his wife Pyrrha were saved on account of their piety. [17,568]

Dorys: Doris, mother of the Nereids, or sea nymphs. [9,481]

Doʐe Cesariens: *The Twelve Caesars* by Suetonius (c. 69– c. 141), an important collection of anecdotal biographies of the early Roman emperors. [6,426]

Dream of Scipio: see **Macrobes**

Dydo, Dido: queen of Carthage. Abandoned by Aeneas, she killed herself (*Aeneid* IV). [13,145]

Dyogenés: Diogenes (413–323 B.C.), Greek philosopher who was indifferent to the vicissitudes of Fortune. [5,839]

Eachus, Eacus: Aeacus, one of the three judges of hell, sons of Jupiter. The others are Rhadamanthus and Minos. [19,825]

Echo, Equo: a nymph in love with Narcissus; she died of grief because her love was not returned. [1,442]

Egite: Egypt. [17,631]

Elanches: the *De Sophisticis Elenchis*, a logical treatise by Aristotle, devoted to the means of convincing an adversary, apart from the truth of the thesis being sustained. [11,031]

Empedoclés: Greek philosopher (fifth century B.C.) who leapt into the mouth of Mount Etna in Sicily, in order to demonstrate his disdain of the fear of death. [17,009]

Enee: Aeneas, eponymous hero of Virgil's *Aeneid*, who abandoned Dido (see **Dydo**). [13,144]

Ennius: see **Annius**

Eolus: Aeolus, god of the winds. [17,976]

Eraclitus: Heraclitus (576–480 B.C.), Greek philosopher indifferent to the vicissitudes of Fortune. [5,839]

Ernoul: see **Hernoul, Saint**

Escoce: Scotland. [10,124]

Esmiens: Amiens, formerly capital of Picardy, in northern France. [10,054]

Eson: Aeson, the old father of Jason. The magician Medea rejuvenated him in order to endear herself to Jason. See Ovid, *Metamorphoses* VII. [13,219]

Ester: Easter. [*Romaunt* 6,435]

Esvangile Pardurable: *The Everlasting Gospel*, or *Evangelium Eternum*, of Joachim of Flora, published in 1254 by the Franciscan Gerard de Borgo San Donnino. The attack on this work, now lost, was led by William of Saint-Amour (see **Guillaume de Saint Amor**) and the secular masters, and it was condemned in 1255 by

Pope Alexander IV. [11,772]

Ethna: see **Empedoclés.** [17,015]

Euclidés: Euclid, celebrated Greek geometrician, who taught at Alexandria c. 306–283 B.C. [16,141]

Foiz, Sainte; Feiz: St. Foy (St. Faith), a virgin and martyr, who died c. 287. [12,567]

Fontaine d'Amors, Fonteine Perilleuse: the Fountain of Love in the garden of *Deduit.* See **Narcisus.** [1,595]

Forseneries: the three Furies, euphemistically called "Eumenides," or Well-meaning Goddesses. See **Alletho.** [16,906]

Frere Menour: Franciscan friar. [*Romaunt* 6,338]

Frise: Friesland, a province in the Low Countries. Also Phrygia, an ancient country in central Asia Minor. [8,445; 9,468; *Romaunt* 1,093]

Furies: see **Forseneries**

Galian: Galen, celebrated Greek physician of the second century A.D. [15,929]

Gallus: Latin poet (66–26 B.C.), author of lost *Elegies.* [10,492]

Ganelon: betrayer of Roland at Roncesvalles (*Chanson de Roland*); a type of the traitor. [7,836]

Ganz, Gaunt: Ghent. [562; *Romaunt* 574]

Gauvains, Gaugain, Gaweyn, Gawain: a knight of King Arthur's court, model of prowess and courtesy. [2,081; *Romaunt* 2,209]

Georgiques: Virgil's *Georgics,* a didactic poem on tillage, cultivation, and the breeding of animals. [20,085]

Germain, Saint: bishop of Paris, sixth century. [14,224]

Gibbe: a common English name for a tomcat. Cf. **Tiberz, Dam.** [*Romaunt* 6,204]

Gile, Saint: St. Giles (possibly of the eighth century) was one of the most popular medieval saints, the patron of cripples, beggars, and blacksmiths. [13,699]

Golden Verses: see **Vers Dorez.** [*Romaunt* 5,650]

Greve, La; Grieve: Place de Grève, a central square of Paris, now Place de l'Hôtel-de-Ville. The execution of criminals once took place there. [5,019]

Guillaume de Saint Amor: William of Saint-Amour, influential French theologian of the thirteenth century, rector of the University of Paris. He was an adversary of the mendicant friars, who caused him to be exiled. [11,476]

Guindesores: Windsor, site of a palatial residence of the English monarchs. [1,226]

Hecuba: wife of King Priam of Troy. A victim of Fortune: she lost nineteen children, and witnessed the killing of her husband. [6,739]

Heleine: Helen, the beautiful inamorata of Paris, whose abduction of her led to the Trojan War. [13,198]

Heloÿs: Heloise, prioress of the Paraclete (see *Paraclit*) and mistress of Abelard. [8,730]

Heraclitus: see *Eraclitus*

Herculés: legendary hero, demigod of Roman mythology; a type of masculine force subdued by a woman. See *Deïaneira, Sanson.* [9,153]

Hernoul, Saint; Ernoul; Arnold: traditional patron of betrayed husbands. [9,101]

Hiberine, Iberine: Hiberina, a Roman woman of insatiable sexuality, mentioned by Juvenal (VI. 53). [8,258]

Hippocrates: see *Ypocras*

Homer: see *Omer*

Homer, Seint: see *Omer, Seint*

Horace: see *Orace*

Hospitelers: see *Ospital.* [*Romaunt* 6,693]

Hôtel-Dieu: see *Ostel Dieu*

Huchaÿn: Huchain, uncle of Alhazen. See *Alhacem.* [18,004]

Hymeneüs: Hymen, god of marriage, son of Apollo. [20,986]

Icarus: see *Dedalus*

Io: see *Yo*

Iole: see *Yolé*

Isengrin, Sire: Sir Isegrym, a personification of the wolf; from the *Roman de Renart.* [11,095]

Ixion: see *Yxion*

Jacobins: a Dominican friar. [11,170]

Jason: heroic sailor who obtained the Golden Fleece; lover of Medea, whom he abandoned. [9,475]

Juliens, Saint: St. Julian the Hospitaller, the subject of many legends in the Middle Ages. [8,804]

Justinians: the Emperor Justinian (483–565), compiler of the definitive codification of Roman law. [11,315]

Juvenaus: Juvenal (c. 60–c. 140), Roman satirical poet. [8,257]

Keu, Key: Sir Kay, the seneschal of King Arthur, hated for his insolence. [2,078; *Romaunt* 2,206]

Lachesis: see **Atropos**. [19,739]

Ladre, Saint: St. Lazarus, the brother of Mary and Martha of Bethany, who was raised from the dead by Jesus. [18,439]

Laire a Meün: Meung-sur-Loire, the native town of Jean de Meun. [10,537]

Lavardins: Lavardin, today a village in the *département* of Loir-et-Cher, near Vendôme. [18,699]

Laverne: the goddess of thieves. [9,519]

Lavine: Lavinia, Latinus's daughter, engaged to Turnus, married by Aeneas (*Aeneid* VII). A type of beauty. [20,801]

Lazarus: see **Ladre, Saint**

Lide: Lydia, an ancient country of Asia Minor; Croesus was its last, and most famous, king. [6,461]

Lïenarz, Sainz: St. Leonard, a hermit of the sixth century; the special patron of prisoners, peasants, and the sick. [8,806]

Lifart de Meün, Saint: St. Lifard of Meun was abbot at Meung-sur-Loire, the native town of Jeun de Meun. [13,130]

Loheraigne, Loreyne: Lorraine, now a province of northeastern France. [749; *Romaunt* 766]

Longis: Longinus, or Longius: according to legend, this blind centurion wounded the crucified Christ with his lance. [19,183]

Lucans: Lucan, a Latin poet (39–65) much admired in the Middle Ages, author of the epic *Pharsalia*. [5,630]

Lucina: Roman goddess of childbirth. [10,593]

Lucrece: a type of the woman who prefers death to sexual dishonor. See **Tarquinius**. [8,578]

Maci, Saint: St. Matthew, the evangelist. [11,572]

Macrobes: Macrobius, Roman grammarian who lived c. 400; author of celebrated commentary on Cicero's *Somnium Scipionis*, which provided the Middle Ages with their authoritative text on the significance of dreams. [7]

Maine: province of northwestern France. [7,890]

Mainfrai, Mainfroiz: Manfred (1232–66), king of Sicily, vanquished by **Charles** of Anjou (q.v.). [6,607]

Marcel, Seint: name given to the quarter of Paris where butchers had their shops. [5,023]

Marote, Mariete, Marietta: Robichon and Marote are familiar names of Robin and Marion, traditional shepherd and shepherdess of popular literature. [13,850]

Mars: god of war. Enamored of Venus, he was trapped with her in a net forged by Venus's husband, Vulcan. [13,812]

Marsilliens: rebellious men of Marseille, subdued by **Charles** of Anjou (q.v.). [6,729]

Medee: see **Jason, Eson.** [13,199]

Megera: see **Alletho.** [19,807]

Melan, Milayn: Milan, metropolis of Lombardy in northern Italy, whose inhabitants were reputed to be heretical. [11,695; *Romaunt* 7,023]

Mercurius: Mercury, messenger of the gods and god of eloquence and commerce, who decapitated **Argus** (q.v.). [14,361]

Mermaydens: see **Seraines.** [*Romaunt* 680]

Meün seur Leire: see **Laire a Meün**

Miauz, Meauz: Meaux, town northeast of Paris. [9,358]

Minos: see **Eachus.** [19,824]

Miroër aus Amoreus: "Mirror for Lovers." According to the God of Love, those who hear Jean de Meun reading the *Roman de la Rose* will so name it, provided that they ignore Reason. [10,621]

Mirra: see **Cynaras.** [21,161]

Moÿsi, Moyses: Moses. [11,575; *Romaunt* 6,889]

Myro: Myron, celebrated Greek sculptor (fifth century B.C.). [16,153]

Narcisus: according to the classical legend, Narcissus was a young man, tormented by love, who became enamored of his own reflection and died of this passion. The *Roman* associates him with the *fonteine perilleuse* (see **Fontaine d'Amors**), in the garden of *Deduit*, which has at its bottom the *miroërs perilleus*. In medieval literature, Narcissus is a type of irrational, self-destructive love. [1,436]

Nerons, Nero: the vicious Emperor Nero, an example of those whom Fortune irrationally causes to rise and fall. [6,155]

Normandie: Foul Mouth has soldiers from Normandy, who are (perhaps for that reason) especially formidable and oppressive. [3,872]

Nuiz, Nuit: Night, wife of Acheron, mother of the Furies. [16,896]

Oenone: a nymph, wife or mistress of Paris, whom he betrayed for Helen; an example of deceived women. [13,185]

Of Age, Old Age, On Old Age: see *Viellece, De*. [*Romaunt* 4,884]

Omer: Homer. [6,750]

Omer, Seint: a Merovingian saint, born in Switzerland, died c. 670. [7,093]

Orace: the Roman poet Horace, to whom Reason ascribes good sense and grace. [5,705]

Origenés: Origen, the Alexandrian church father (185–254) who castrated himself. [17,022]

Orpheüs: legendary poet and musician of antiquity, condemned by Genius for sexual perversion. (Cf. Ovid, *Met*. X.78–85.) [19,621]

Ospital: the Hospitallers, or Order of St. John of Jerusalem: a military order founded in 1048, confirmed as a spiritual order in 1113. They greatly distinguished themselves in the crusades. [11,389]

Ostel Dieu: the Hôtel-Dieu, oldest hospital of Paris, formerly situated next to Notre Dame. [4,979]

Ovides: the Roman poet Ovid, who often wrote about love. [7,956]

Pallas: Pallas Athena, Greek divinity sometimes associated with the snake, who advised Cadmus to sow the teeth of a serpent. [19,706]

Pan: Greek nature deity, associated especially with flocks, shepherds, huntsmen, and all rural inhabitants. [17,921]

Paphus: son of Pygmalion and his animated statue, and eponym of the island of Paphos. [21,155]

Paraboles, Parablis: the scriptural book of Proverbs. [11,249; *Romaunt* 6,530]

Paraclit, Paraclete: the monastery founded by Pierre Abelard near Nogent-sur-Seine, of which Heloise (see **Heloÿs**) was prioress. [8,731]

Parasyus, Parrasius: Parrhasius, celebrated Greek painter, born c. 420 B.C. [16,149]

Paris: see *Oenone.* [13,185]

Pavie: Pavia, an important Italian city in Lombardy. [1,618]

Penelope: wife of Ulysses, who remained faithful to him during his long absence at the siege of Troy and subsequent voyages; a model of feminine fidelity and chastity. [8,622]

Pepin, **Pepyn:** king of France (751–68), second of the Carolingian dynasty; father of Charlemagne. [1,426; *Romaunt* 1,458]

Pere, Saint; Pierre: St. Peter the Apostle, head of the church of Christ. [9,291]

Perrette: a woman's name of undetermined significance. [13,854]

Perse: Persia. [6,743]

Phanie: Phania, wise daughter of Croesus (see **Cresus**), who interpreted his dreams. [6,483]

Pharisien, **Pharisen:** the Pharisees. [11,578; *Romaunt* 6,893]

Phebus: the classical deity Phoebus, or Apollo, emblematic of the sun. [6,478]

Philebert, Saint: St. Philibert (died 684) was a Merovingian abbot. [9,291]

Phillis: Phyllis, who hanged herself after being abandoned by her lover Demophoön; an example of deceived women. [13,181]

Phoroneus: a legendary king of Argos, who wished he had never married. [8,715]

Pierres Abailarz: Pierre (Peter) Abelard (1079–1142), famous scholastic theologian and philosopher, lover of Heloise (see **Heloÿs**). [8,729]

Pimalion, Pygmalion: legendary Greek sculptor, who fell in love with a statue which he had made, and who induced Venus to give the statue life. [13,058]

Pirra: Pyrrha, wife of *Deucalion* (q.v.). [17,569]

Pluto: deity of the infernal regions and of the dead. [19,832]

Pol, Saint; Poul: St. Paul the Apostle. [11,353]

Policletus: Polycletus, celebrated Greek sculptor (fifth century B.C.). [16,153]

Policratique: the *Polycraticus*, or Statesman's Book, of John of Salisbury (1110–80), English scholastic philosopher and bishop of Chartres. The work is a discursive, encyclopedic treatise on human behavior and the welfare of the state. [6,664]

Posthumus: a man whose intention of marrying is discussed with incredulity in Juvenal (VI. 21–37). [8,706]

Priant: Priam, king of Troy and husband of **Hecuba** (q.v.). [6,740]

Protheüs: Proteus, a sea deity with the gift of prophecy. In order to avoid questioners, he could change his form at will. [11,151]

Provance: see **Charles**

Ptolemy: see *Tholomee*

Pytagoras, Pictagoras: see *Vers Dorez.* [4,995; *Romaunt* 5,649]

Quartage: see **Cartage**

Radamantus: see **Eachus.** [19,824]

Rasis: Rhases, celebrated Arab physician, born c. 860. [15,931]

Regarz: Observations, influential treatise on optics by Alhazen (see **Alhacem**). [18,006]

Remi, Saint: see **Roumi, Saint**

Renart: Reynard, personification of the fox, from the satirical beast epic *Roman de Renart.* [14,984]

Renouart au Tinel: Renouart de la Pole (Renouart of the Staff), a type of bravery, from the *chansons de geste.* [15,316]

Rethorique: the *Rhetoric (De Inventione)* of Cicero. [16,167]

Roberz, **Robert:** a distinguished name (by contrast with Robin). [11,169; *Romaunt* 6,337]

Roberz d'Artais: Robert II of Anjou (c. 1250–1302), nephew of St. Louis, much admired for his chivalry. [18,671]

Robichon: see **Marote.** [13,851]

Robichonet: Robichonnet, name of a young man. [8,499]

Robin, **Robyn:** a common name, in contrast to the more distinguished name Robert. [11,169; *Romaunt* 6,337]
　　Traditional name for leader of village dance. [12,099]

Rolant, Rolanz: Roland, most famous of Charlemagne's paladins, slain in the ambush at Roncesvalles; immortalized in the *Chanson de Roland.* [7,834]

Romenie: Romagna, province of northeastern Italy. [9,359]

Roncevaus: Roncesvalles, where Roland (see **Rolant**) was slain. [7,835]

Roumi, Saint: St. Remi (437–533), archbishop of Reims, who persuaded Clovis I, the Merovingian king, to convert to Catholicism, and baptised him in 496. [14,639]

Sac, **Sacked Freeres:** the friars of the sack (*Frères de la Pénitence).*

[12,107; *Romaunt* 7,460]

Saier, Frere; Seier: Brother Seier. If the reference is to a particular person, he has not yet been identified. [12,054]

Saint Amor: see **Guillaume de Saint Amor**

Salemon, Salomon: King Solomon. [8,140]

Saluste: Sallust (86–34 B.C.), Roman historian of Catiline's conspiracy and the wars of Jugurtha. [15,148]

Sanson: Samson, the Jewish hero, paragon of strength; betrayed by Dalila. St. Augustine (*City of God* XVIII.19) bracketed him with Hercules. [9,153]

Sardaigne, Cerdagne: the Mediterranean island of Sardinia. [18,128]

Sarradin: Saracen or Moslem: a type of the enemies of Christianity. [6,726]

Scypion, Cipioun: Scipio Aemilianus Africanus the Younger (185–129 B.C.), Roman soldier and statesman, the conqueror of Carthage. According to Cicero in a section of his *Republic* now lost, Scipio had a dream in which his distinguished grandfather by adoption, Scipio Africanus the Elder, appeared to him. See **Macrobes.** [10]

Sebile, Sibyl: the sibyls were legendary prophetesses and oracles of classical antiquity. [8,980]

Secile: the Mediterranean island of Sicily. [6,607]

Seneque: Seneca (2–66), Roman philosopher, instructor of Nero, ultimately put to death by him; a victim of Fortune. [6,155]

Seraines, Sereyns, Sirens: sea nymphs, half woman and half fish or bird, whose seductive songs lured travelers to their destruction. [670; *Romaunt* 684]

Sisicambris: Sisigambis, mother of King Darius Codomannus (see **Daire**), victim of Fortune. [6,742]

Sisyfus: Sisyphus, for his wickedness, was condemned after his death eternally to roll a great stone up a hill, from which it would immediately roll back. [19,269]

Solin: Solinus, a Roman grammarian and encyclopedist, probably of the third century A.D. [5,827]

Suctonius, Sutonius: Suetonius (c. 69–c. 141), Roman historian, author of the anecdotal *Lives of the Twelve Caesars.* [6,428]

Tample, Templers: Templers, or Knights of the Temple: a religious and military order, established by the crusaders at Jerusalem in 1118 to protect pilgrims and the Holy Sepulchre. [11,389; *Romaunt* 6,693]

Tantaluz: Tantalus, mythical king of Lydia, condemned by Jupiter to be ever thirsty and tempted by water, but unable to drink it. [19,252]

Tarquinius: L. Tarquinius Superbus, seventh and last king of Rome, the traditional dates of whose violent and arbitrary reign are 534–510 B.C. His son Sextus Tarquinius raped **Lucrece**. (q.v.). [8,581]

Tarse: Tarsus, city in Asia Minor. St. Paul was born there. [7,350]

Thebes: ancient city in Greece (Boeotia), said to have been founded by **Cadmus** (q.v.). [19,715]

Themis: Olympian goddess, personification of order, law, and justice. Her attributes are a cornucopia and a pair of scales. [17,580]

Theofrastus: see **Aureole**. [8,531]

Thesiphoné: see **Alletho**. [19,805]

Thimee, Timee: *Timaeus*, a very important dialogue of Plato's, in which the doctrine of ideas as well as a philosophy of nature are advanced. [7,074]

Tholomee, Ptolemy: see **Almageste**. [7,008]

Tibauz, Saint; Tibaut: St. Thibaut (Theobald), an eleventh-century hermit saint of France. [9,262]

Tiberz, Dam: Tibert, a personification of the cat, from the *Roman de Renart*. Cf. **Gibbe**. [11,038]

Tibullus: Roman poet of the first century B.C., author of tender and gracious love poetry. [10,478]

Ticius, Tycius: Tityus, a mythological giant, who was punished for his crimes by being placed in hell, where vultures (or, alternatively, a serpent) continually devoured his liver or entrails. [19,276]

Titus Livius: the great Roman historian Livy (59 B.C.–A.D. 19), author of the *Annals*. [5,564]

Tritholemus: Triptolemus, mythological figure, a favorite of Ceres (goddess of harvest), who taught him agriculture, and gave him her chariot, drawn by two dragons, in which to travel over the earth and distribute grain. [10,156]

Triton: a sea deity, son of Neptune, usually represented as blowing a shell. [9,480]

Tulles, Tulius: Tully (i.e., Cicero). [4,400; *Romaunt* 4,882]

Ulixés: Ulysses, legendary Greek hero, who (among many other feats) escaped the enchantments of Circe (see **Cyrcé**). [14,377]

Valerius: Valerius Maximus, a first-century A.D. Latin writer of historical anecdotes, thought in the Middle Ages to be the author of a letter to Rufinus against marriage. The *Epistola Valerii ad Rufinum* is now ascribed to Walter Map. [8,659]

Vers Dorez, Verses Aureate: *Golden Verses*, a poetical composition attributed in the Middle Ages to Pythagoras, the Greek philosopher and mathematician of the sixth century B.C. [4,997]

Viellece, De: *De Senectute* (*On Old Age*), a celebrated treatise of Cicero's. [4,401]

Virgine, Virginia: see **Appius**. [5,562]

Virginius: see **Appius**. [5,563]

Vulcanus: see **Mars**. [13,811]

Welle of Love: see **Fontaine d'Amors**. [*Romaunt* 1,627]

White Monkes: Cistercians, a Benedictine reform movement founded in 1098 by St. Robert of Molesme and several other brethren. [*Romaunt* 6,695]

William Seynt Amour: see **Guillaume de Saint Amor**. [*Romaunt* 6,763]

Wyndesore: see **Guindesores**. [*Romaunt* 1,250]

Xantus: the Xanthus, a river in Asia Minor, which flows into the Mediterranean. [13,195]

Ycarus, Icarus: see **Dedalus**. [5,197]

Yo, Io: a priestess of Juno, loved by Jupiter. According to the usual myth, Jupiter changed Io into a beautiful heifer, which Juno commanded the hundred-eyed Argus to watch. [14,358]

Yolé: Iole, daughter of a Peloponnesian king, was loved by Hercules, to whom her father promised (but later refused) her. [9,169]

Ypocras: Hippocrates (c. 460–c. 357 B.C.), the most famous physician of antiquity, born on the island of Cos, off Asia Minor. [15,929]

Yxion, Ixion: king of the Lapithae, a mythical people inhabiting the mountains of Thessaly. Ixion was condemned to be chained forever to a turning wheel. [19,249]

Zephyrus: Zephyr, personification of the gentle west wind; husband of the nymph Flora (Chloris), goddess of spring and flowers. [5,911]

Zeusys, Zeuzis: Zeuxis (464–398 B.C.), celebrated Greek painter, said to have been born at Heraclea in Sicily. [16,155]

Four

Some Useful Texts

The *Roman de la Rose* is an intensely literary poem. That is to say, its texture is shot through with echoes and quotations from other books. Guillaume and Jean of course share this feature with the other late medieval masters. Their age venerated the great *auctores* of antiquity, borrowed freely from them as well as from more modern authors, and had not yet learned to equate verbal novelty or philosophical eccentricity with originality. But it is unlikely that even Dante or Chaucer is more allusive than the poets of the *Roman*. One has only to skim over the copious notes in, say, Langlois's edition to recognize how thoroughly saturated were their minds and sensibilities with certain writings of Cicero, Ovid, and a significant roster of other authors down to their own time. To adequately appreciate the *Roman*, one must know something of these earlier works which fertilized our poets' imaginations and nourished their minds.

The first four texts below—from Macrobius, Alanus de Insulis, and Andreas Capellanus—are excerpts from books which conspicuously found their way into the *Roman*. The other five are important examples of the criticism which it evoked, from the Quarrel of 1400 to the revival of interest in 1735. All are surveyed in Part One of this book. Most of these texts are still relatively inaccessible to many readers and students, and the last four of them appear here for the first time in English translation.

13

Ambrosius Theodosius Macrobius (c. 400): Commentary on the Dream of Scipio[1]

Book One, Chapter Three

. . . We must first describe the many varieties of dreams recorded by the ancients, who have classified and defined the various types that have appeared to men in their sleep, wherever they might be. Then we shall be able to decide to which type the dream we are discussing belongs.

All dreams may be classified under five main types: there is the enigmatic dream, in Greek *oneiros*, in Latin *somnium*; second, there is the prophetic vision, in Greek *horama*, in Latin *visio*; third, there is the oracular dream, in Greek *chrematismos*, in Latin *oraculum*; fourth, there is the nightmare, in Greek *enypnion*, in Latin *insomnium*; and last, the apparition, in Greek *phantasma*, which Cicero, when he has occasion to use the word, calls *visum*.

The last two, the nightmare and the apparition, are not worth interpreting since they have no prophetic significance. Nightmares may be caused by mental or physical distress, or anxiety about the future: the patient experiences in dreams vexations similar to those that disturb him during the day. As examples of the mental variety, we might mention the lover who dreams of possessing his sweetheart or of losing her, or the man who fears the plots or might of an enemy and is confronted with him in his dream or seems to be fleeing him. The physical variety might be illustrated by one who has overindulged in eating or drinking and dreams that he is either choking with food or unburdening himself, or by one who has been suffering from hunger or thirst and dreams that he is craving and searching for food or drink or has found it. Anxiety about the future would cause a

156

man to dream that he is gaining a prominent position or office as he hoped or that he is being deprived of it as he feared.

Since these dreams and others like them arise from some condition or circumstance that irritates a man during the day and consequently disturbs him when he falls asleep, they flee when he awakes and vanish into thin air. Thus the name *insomnium* was given, not because such dreams occur "in sleep"—in this respect nightmares are like other types—but because they are noteworthy only during their course and afterwards have no importance or meaning.

Virgil, too, considers nightmares deceitful: "False are the dreams *(insomnia)* sent by departed spirits to their sky."[2] He used the word "sky" with reference to our mortal realm because the earth bears the same relation to the regions of the dead as the heavens bear to the earth. Again, in describing the passion of love, whose concerns are always accompanied by nightmares, he says: "Oft to her heart rushes back the chief's valour, oft his glorious stock; his looks and words cling fast within her bosom, and the pang withholds calm rest from her limbs." And a moment later: "Anna, my sister, what dreams *(insomnia)* thrill me with fears?"[3]

The apparition *(phantasma* or *visum)* comes upon one in the moment between wakefulness and slumber, in the so-called "first cloud of sleep." In this drowsy condition he thinks he is still fully awake and imagines he sees specters rushing at him or wandering vaguely about, differing from natural creatures in size and shape, and hosts of diverse things, either delightful or disturbing. To this class belongs the incubus, which, according to popular belief, rushes upon people in sleep and presses them with a weight which they can feel.

The two types just described are of no assistance in foretelling the future; but by means of the other three we are gifted with the powers of divination.

We call a dream oracular in which a parent, or a pious or revered man, or a priest, or even a god clearly reveals what will or will not transpire, and what action to take or to avoid. We call a dream a prophetic vision if it actually comes true. For example, a man dreams of the return of a friend who has been staying in a foreign land, thoughts of whom never enter his mind. He goes out and presently meets his friend and embraces him. Or in his dream he agrees to accept a deposit, and early the next day a man runs anxiously to him, charging him with the safekeeping of his money and committing secrets to his trust. By an enigmatic dream we mean one that conceals with strange shapes and veils with ambiguity the true meaning of the information being offered, and requires an interpretation for its understanding. We need not explain further the nature of this dream since everyone knows from experience what it is. There are five varieties of it: personal, alien, social, public, and universal. It is called personal when one dreams that he himself is doing or experiencing something; alien, when he dreams this about someone else; social, when his dream involves others and himself; public, when he dreams that some misfortune or benefit has befallen the city, forum, theater, public walls, or other public enterprise; universal, when he dreams that some change has taken place in the sun, moon, planets, sky, or regions of the earth.

The dream which Scipio reports that he saw embraces the three reliable types mentioned above, and also has to do with all five varieties of the enigmatic dream. It is oracular since the two men who appeared before him and revealed his future, Aemilius Paulus and Scipio the Elder, were both his father, both were pious and revered men, and both were affiliated with the priesthood.[4] It is a prophetic vision since Scipio saw the regions of his abode after death and his future condition. It is an enigmatic dream because the truths revealed to him were couched in words that hid their profound meaning and could not be comprehended without skillful interpretation.

It also embraces the five varieties of the last type. It is personal since Scipio himself was conducted to the regions above and learned of his future. It is alien since he observed the estates to which the souls of others were destined. It is social since he learned that for men with merits similar to his the same places were being prepared as for himself. It is public since he foresaw the victory of Rome and the destruction of Carthage, his triumph on the Capitoline, and the coming civil strife. And it is universal since by gazing up and down he was initiated into the wonders of the heavens, the great celestial circles, and the harmony of the revolving spheres, things strange and unknown to mortals before this; in addition, he witnessed the movements of the stars and planets and was able to survey the whole earth.

It is incorrect to maintain that Scipio was not the proper person to have a dream that was both public and universal inasmuch as he had not yet attained the highest office but, as he himself admitted, was still ranked "not much higher than a private soldier." The critics say that dreams concerning the welfare of the state are not to be considered significant unless military or civil officers dream them, or unless many plebeians have the same dream. They cite the incident in Homer when, before the assembled Greeks, Agamemnon disclosed a dream that he had had about a forthcoming battle. Nestor, who helped the army quite as much with his prudence as all the youth with their might, by way of instilling confidence in the dream said that in matters of general welfare they had to confide in the dream of a king, whereas they would repudiate the dream of anyone else.[5] However, the point in Scipio's favor was that although he had not yet held the consulship or a military command, he—who himself was destined to lead that campaign—was dreaming about the coming destruction of Carthage, was witnessing the public triumph in his honor, and was even learning of the secrets of nature; for he excelled as much in philosophy as in deeds of courage.

Because, in citing Virgil above as an authority for the unreliability of nightmares, we excerpted a verse from his description of the twin portals of dreams, someone may take the occasion to inquire why false dreams are allotted to the gate of ivory and trustworthy ones to the gate of horn. He should avail himself of the help of Porphyry, who, in his *Commentaries*, makes the following remarks on a passage in Homer presenting the same distinction between gates: "All truth is concealed. Nevertheless, the soul, when it is partially disengaged from bodily functions during sleep, at times gazes and at times peers intently at the truth, but does not apprehend it; and when it gazes it does not see with clear and direct vision, but rather with a dark obstructing veil interposed." Virgil attests that this is natural in the following lines: "Behold—for all the cloud, which now, drawn over thy sight, dulls thy mortal vision and with dank pall enshrouds thee, I will tear away."[6] If, during sleep, this veil permits the vision of the attentive soul to perceive the truth, it is thought to be made of horn, the nature of which is such that, when thinned, it becomes transparent. When the veil dulls the vision and prevents its reaching the truth, it is thought to be made of ivory, the composition of which is so dense that no matter how thin a layer of it may be, it remains opaque.

14

Alanus de Insulis (1114–c. 1203):
Anticlaudianus[7]

Book Seven, 397–480

After the others, Fortune's daughter, Nobility, kinswoman of Chance that is ever at hand, would have willingly and gladly given her gifts, if anything entirely her own, that she could by Nature's law control, had fallen to her lot. But since she has power over nothing except what Fortune supplies, she does nothing without consulting Fortune: in fact the daughter decides to make her way to her mother's abode, sets out on her journey and successfully makes her way over the long road.

There is a rock in mid-ocean on which the sea forever beats, which the conflicting waves charge, which is harassed in various ways and pounded with a never-ending assault. Now it is totally hidden, buried in the waves; now shaking off the sea, it breathes in the air above. It maintains no one aspect; minute after minute transforms it with successive changes. When Zephyrus blows his gentle breath over everything, the rock sprouts choice flowers and rejoices in an abundance of greenery. But soon fierce Boreas ravishes the flowers and ruins the greenery: *finis* is written to the flower's history just as it opens and the flower is mocked by a moment of life. In the same way raging Aquilo plunders everything, mows down the flowers with the sword of cold and wipes out a former joy. Here grows a varying grove and trees that differ. This remains barren, that one bears fruit; one rejoices in renewed foliage, another leafless laments; one flourishes, quite a few wither; one blooms, others are bloomless; some rise on high, the rest hug the ground; one sprouts, the others decay. Thus various accidents alter them and they all alternate in successive changes. The fall of the dice brings here many things that run counter to the normal. The cedar, brought low, and sinking to a pygmy's height, ceases to be a giant and the dwarf myrrh assumes giant stature: thus one takes the form of the other. The laurel pines, the myrtle bears fruit; the olive withers, the willow becomes fruitful, the pear tree is barren, the apple tree is bereft of fruit, while in produce the elm contends with the vine. Here the thorn-hedge, armed with its darts, threatens careless hands with wounds and the prickly yew hurts them. Here Philomena rarely sings, the lark seldom thrills: more often the horned owl, the harbinger of misfortune and herald of grief, foretells sad chance. Here two streams flow down, differentiated by unlike rising-places, different appearance, diverse shades of color, dissimilar taste and separate source-springs. One has very sweet water, gives honey-sweet draughts, leads many astray by its sweetness. A draught of its waters causes a greater thirst for them; it intoxicates those who drink from it, nay while the water is slaking thirst, it is producing it; a drink from the stream gives a thirst for the stream and it causes dropsy in countless drinkers. It bickers along with faint murmur, murmurs in a sweet whisper and flows over the rock in a quiet stream. At the head of this river many keep their place and there is no opening for them to go further. They scarcely touch and barely taste the sweet waters of the river. They long to feast further on this great delicacy, they long to be more fully immersed in the stream, to have all their limbs drenched in its waters. Others go further: these an ampler stream holds immersed in a deep eddy and deeper water carries them along. However, when they have been touched with the great sweetness of the stream, a gentle wave carries them back and sets them on the bank again.

The other river tumbles down in fast-flowing fall, black with sulphurous waters. The water by its bitterness causes wormwood to grow and its raging heat resembles a furnace. Its color clashes with the eyes, its flavor with the taste, its crash with the ears. Zephyrus does not ripple these waters but Boreas, making the waters heave from their depths, raises them to mountain height, proclaiming a war between the waves and involving kinsfolk in battle. On the river's bank floods of tears are overwhelming many who are afraid of being sunk in the deep torrent of the raging river and of having to bear the violence of its flood. Many people go down into this stream, are buried in the deep waters and are carried along by the swollen river.

The flowing water now sucks men in, now spews them out. Those it plunges into the waters, these it allows a short respite, but the abyss so sucks in most that they cannot retrace their steps and escape to the world above and no tracks are left to mark the way back. This river, running with various windings, enters the flood of very sweet water, forces that stream to degenerate and makes it share its corruption. The cloudy darkens the clear, the bitter sours the sweet, the warm spoils the cool, the fetid ruins the fragrant.

Book Eight, 1–63

The house of Fortune, clinging on high to a sheer rock and threatening to tumble down, sinks into a steep slope. It is subject to every raging wind and bears the brunt of every tempest of heaven. Rarely does the gentle breeze of Zephyrus make that house calm and clear and rather seldom does its soft, kind breath wipe out the storms of Notus and the cold of Boreas. One part of the house sits atop the mountain rock, the other crouches on the rock's base and as though on the verge of sliding off, shows signs of falling. One part of the house glitters with silver, shines with gems, is alight with gold; the other part lies debased with worthless material. The former part prides itself on its lofty roof; the latter stands uncovered in a gaping cleft. Here is Fortune's abode, if indeed the unstable ever abides, the wandering takes up residence, the moving becomes fixed. For Fortune complete rest is flight, permanence is change, to stand still is to revolve, to be in a fixed position is to run to and fro, a fall is an ascent. For her reasoned procedure is to be without reason, reliability is to be reliably unreliable, devotion is to be devotedly undevoted. She is fickle, unreliable, changeable, uncertain, random, unstable, unsettled. When one thinks that she has taken a stand, she falls and with a counterfeit smile she feigns joy. She is rough in her gentleness, overcast in her light, rich and poor, tame and savage, sweet and bitter. She weeps as she smiles, roams around as she stands, is blind as she sees. She is constant in fickleness, steadfast in faltering, true to falsehood, false to truth, unchangeable in changeability. She keeps this constant rule—that she is not constant; she faithfully maintains this one principle—that she knows not how to be faithful; she remains true to this one tenet—that she always proves false; she is settled on this one thing—that she ever goes her unsettled way. Her appearance with its twofold aspect misleads the viewer. The front of her head is covered with a rich growth of hair, the back bemoans its baldness. One eye dances mischievously, the other overflows with tears; the latter is dull and heavy, the former sparkles. Part of her face is alive, aflame with natural color; part is dying in the grip of pallor; as the charm of the countenance fades, the face grows dull and its beauty melts away. One hand gives a gift, the other takes it away; one increases the gift, the other diminishes it; one offers it, the other withdraws it; one hand grips tightly, the other loosens its grip. Her steps are unequal, retrograde, reeling, wandering: as she advances she goes backwards; at once fast and slow on her feet, she falls far back as she goes forward. Now she shines forth in finer toga, now slumming, she wallows in the clothes of the poor; now left without a dress to her name, she offers herself to the public and is seen bemoaning her honors of old. She keeps her wheel in fast motion and no rest brings an end to the toil of movement, no leisure-time stops the motion. For when that labor, as it often does, tires her right hand, her left hand takes its place, comes to the aid of its weary sister and plies the wheel in faster motion. Its whirl is ravenous, its swoop is fast, its attack on two fronts. It envelops mankind, exempts no one from its downward spin but forces all to put up with the antics of fate and drives men down into all kinds of misfortune. It increases the pressure on some, lightens the burden for others; hurls some down, raises others up. While Croesus is at the top of the wheel, Codrus is at the bottom. Julius is on his way up, Magnus on his way down, and Sulla is at the bottom. Marius is coming up but, with a turn of the wheel, Sulla is on his way back and Marius is being forced down. Thus the wheel sweeps everything up in turn and spiralling Fortune changes our fates.

15

Alanus de Insulis (1114–c. 1203):
The Complaint of Nature[8]

Metre One

I change from laughter to tears, joy to sorrow, merriment to lament, mirth to grief, when I behold the decrees of Nature ignored; when society is ruined and destroyed by the monster of sensual love; when Venus, fighting against Venus, makes men women; when, with her magic art, she unmans men. . . . Alas! Where has the loveliness of Nature, the beauty of character, the standard of chastity, the love of virtue departed? Nature weeps, character passes away, chastity is wholly banished from its former high station, and becomes an orphan. The sex of active nature trembles shamefully at the way in which it declines into passive nature. Man is made woman, he blackens the honor of his sex, the craft of magic Venus makes him of double gender. . . .

[*In Prose One, the melancholy narrator has a vision of Nature as an exquisite, regally adorned virgin.*]

Prose Three

. . . "Alas!" said she, "what blindness of ignorance, what delirium of mind, what failing of the senses, what infirmity of the reason has placed a cloud on your understanding, has forced your spirit into exile, has dulled the power of your feeling, has made your mind to sicken, so that not only is your intellect cheated out of its quick recognition of your Nourisher, but also your power of discerning, as if it were smitten by a strange and monstrous sight, suffers a collapse at my very appearance? Why has recognition of my face strayed from your memory? You, in whom my gifts announce me, who have blessed you with such abundant favor and kindness; who, from your early age, as vice-regent of God the Creator, have ordered by sure management your life's proper course; who in time past brought the fluctuating material of your body out from the impure essence of primordial matter into true being; who pitied your misshapen countenance, which, so to speak, cried often to me, and marked it with the stamp of human appearance, and ennobled it, destitute before of beauty and grace of lineament, with the more excellent vesture of features. And here, arranging the different duties of the members for the protection of the body, I ordered the senses, as guards of the corporeal realm, to keep watch, that like spies on foreign enemies they might defend the body from external assault. So would the material part of the whole body, being adorned with the higher glories of nature, be united the more agreeably when it came to marriage with its spouse, the spirit; and so would the spouse, in disgust at the baseness of its mate, not oppose the marriage. Your spirit, also, I have stamped with vital powers, that it might not, poorer than the body, envy its successes. And in it I have established a power of native strength, which is a hunter of subtle matters in the pursuit of knowledge, and establishes them, rendered intelligible, in the understanding. On it, also, I have impressed the seal of reason, to set aside by the winnowing fan of its discrimination the emptiness of falsehood from the serious matters of truth. Through me, also, the power of memory serves you, hoarding in the treasure-chest of its recollection the glorious wealth of knowledge. With these gifts, then, I have blessed both, that neither might groan over its own poverty, or complain at the other's affluence.

"And just as this marriage is brought to pass by my consent, so is the same marital bond dissolved according to my decision. Not in you particularly, but also in all things generally, shines out the abundance of my power. I am she who has fashioned the form and eminence of man into the likeness of the structure of the universe, so that in him, as in a mirror of the world itself, Nature's lineaments might appear. For just as, of the four elements, the concordant discord, the single plurality, the dissonant consonance, the dissenting agreement, produce the structure of the palace of earth, so, of four ingredients, the similar unsimilarity, the unequal equality, the unformed conformity, the separate identity, firmly erect the house of the human body. And those qualities which come together as mediators among the elements—they establish a firm peace among the four humors. And just as the army of the planets opposes with contrary motion the fixed rolling of the firmament, so in man is found a continual hostility between lust and reason. For the activity of reason, taking its rise from a celestial source, passes through the low levels of earth, and, watchful of heavenly things, turns again to heaven. The activities of lust, on the other hand, wandering waywardly and contrary to the firmament of reason, turn and slip down into the decline of things on earth. Now the latter, lust, leads the human mind into the ruin of vices, so that it perishes; the former, reason, bids it, as it rises, to ascend to the serenity of virtue. The one dishonors man, and changes him to a beast; the other mightily transfigures him into a god. Reason illuminates the darkness of the brain by the light of contemplation; lust extinguishes the radiance of the mind by the night of desire. Reason makes man to talk with angels; lust forces him to wanton with brutes. Reason teaches man to find in exile a home; lust forces him in his home to be an exile. And, in this, man's nature cannot reproach me for my ordering and management. For, out of the council of wisdom, I have set such a war of opposition between these antagonists that if, in this strife, reason bend down lust to defeat, the victory will not be without its following reward. For prizes won by victories shine more fairly than other presents. Gifts acquired by labor are brighter and more delightful than all those that are free. And he deserves the commendation of greater praise who toils and receives little, than he who receives much at ease. The earlier labor, pouring a certain sweetness into the following recompense, rewards the worker with greater favor. . . .

"But lest I should seem, in this my prerogative and power, to be detracting arrogantly from God, I profess most emphatically that I am the lowly disciple of the Supreme Ruler. For I, as I work, am not able to press my step in the footprints of God as He works, but I contemplate Him in His activity from a long way off, as if with longing. His operation is simple, mine is multiform; His work is faultless, mine is defective; His is marvelous, mine is transient; He is incapable of being born, I was born; He is the maker, I am the made; He is the

Creator of my work, I am the work of the Creator; He works from nothing, I beg work from another; He works by His own divine will, I work under His name. . . ."

Prose Four

. . . Then said she: "Since all things are by the law of their being held subject to my laws, and ought to pay me a rightful and established tribute, almost all, with just dues and with seemly presentation, regularly obey my commands; but from this general rule man alone is excluded by an abnormal exception. He, stripped of the cloak of decency, exposes himself in unchastity for a professional male prostitute, and not only dares to stir tumult and strife against the majesty of his queen, but also to inflame the madness of intestine war against his mother. Other creations, on which I have bestowed the lesser gifts of my favor, throughout the rank of their activities are bound in willing subjection to the inviolability of my commands. But man, who exhausted the treasury of almost all my riches, tries to overthrow the natural impulses of nature, and arms against me the violence of wicked lust. . . ."

While, in the progess of this narrative, mention was being made of Cupid, I slipped a question of the following tenor into an interruption, with which I had broken in, saying: "Stay! Stay! Did I not fear to incur disfavor from your kindness by rude interruption of your speech, and by the burden of my questions, I would desire to know, from your discernment and by your delineation, the nature of Cupid, on whom your speech has touched before with some slight mention. For though various authors have pictured his nature under the covering wrap of allegory, they have yet left us no marks of certainty. And his authority over the human race is seen from experience to be so powerful that no one, whether marked with the seal of nobility, or clothed in the beauty of exceptional wisdom, or fortified with the armor of courage, or robed in the garment of loveliness, or honored with distinctions of other graces, can except himself from the comprehensiveness of the power of love."

Then she, slowly shaking her head, said in words foretelling rebuke: "I believe that you are serving as a paid soldier in the camp of

Cupid, and are connected with him by some relationship and close intimacy. For you eagerly try to explore his tangled maze, though you ought rather to be applying your mind's attention the more closely to my discourse, rich in treasures of thought. But nevertheless, before it advances into the course of my further speech, since I sympathize with the weakness of your humanity, I am obliged to dispel, as far as in my small ability lies, the shadows of your ignorance, Besides, I am bound to the solving of your problems by solemn obligation and promise. So, either through describing with faithful description, or defining with correct definition, a matter that is non-demonstrable I shall demonstrate, one that is inextricable I shall untangle, although this, which is not bound in obedience by connections with any substance, and does not desire the scrutiny of the intellect, cannot be stamped with mark or any description. Then let there be given this representation of the subject, as I have determined it; let this issue as the explanation of a nature inexplicable; let this be the conception of a subject unknown, this theory be given of a matter not ascertainable—and yet, withal, in chastened and lofty style:

Metre Five

"Love is peace joined with hatred, faith with fraud, hope with fear, and fury mixed with reason; pleasant shipwreck, light heaviness, welcome Charybdis, healthy sickness, satisfied hunger, famished satiety, drunken thirst, deceptive delight, glad sorrow, joy full of pains, sweet evil, evil sweetness; pleasure bitter to itself, whose scent is savory, whose savor is tasteless; grateful tempest, clear night, shadowy day, living death, dying life, agreeable misfortune, sinful forgiveness, pardonable sin, laughable punishment, holy iniquity, nay, even delightful crime, unstable play, fixed delusion, weak vigor, changeable firmness, mover of things established, undiscerning reason, mad prudence, sad prosperity, tearful laughter, sick repose, soothing hell, sorrowful paradise, pleasant prison, vernal winter, wintry spring, calamity; bold worm of the mind, which the purple of the king feels, and which does not pass by the toga of a beggar. Does not Cupid, working many miracles by changing things into their opposites, transform the whole race of men? When the monk and the adulterer have both been foreign to a man, he yet compels these two to possess and dwell in him at the same time. While his madness rages, Scylla lays aside her fury, the good Aeneas begins to be a Nero, Paris lightens with his sword, Tydeus is gentle in love, Nestor becomes young and Melicerta old, Thersites begs Paris for his beauty, Davus begs the beauty of Adonis and into Davus goes all of Adonis, rich Crassus is in want and Codrus has abundance in poverty, Bavius produces poetry, the muse of Virgil is dull, Ennius is eloquent, Marcus is silent, Ulysses becomes foolish, Ajax in his folly is wise. . . .

"But why should I tell more? Under the spear of Cupid must each lover go, and pay him his dues. He wages war against all; his rule excepts hardly a one; he smites all things with the anger of his lightning, and against him neither probity nor prudence will be of effect, nor beauty of form, nor abundance of riches, nor the height of nobility. Thefts, lies, fear, anger, fury, deceit, violence, error, sadness possess his strange dominions. Here it is reason to be without reason, moderation to be unrestrained, faith to have no faith. Displaying the sweet, he adds the bitter, instills poison, and finishes best things with an evil end. Attracting he seduces, laughing he jeers, with smarting ointment he anoints, laying hold he corrupts, loving he hates. Yet you can yourself bridle that madness, if you flee—no stronger medicine is given. If you would escape Love, shun his places, his times; both place and time give him nourishment. If you follow him, he waits; by fleeing, he is put to flight; if you retreat, he retires; if you flee, he flies.

Prose Five

"Now the theory of the art of love has appeared clearly to you from my skillful presentation, and through the book of experience you will be able to acquire for yourself its practice. And it is not strange if in this portrayal of Cupid I intersperse slight signs of blame, although he is allied to me by the connection of blood-relationship. Disparaging malice, with its deep rust, did not drive me to these upbraiding and reproving censures, nor did the intensity of burning hate breaking forth from within, nor the tyrant of jealousy raging furiously without—but the fear lest I should seem to strangle clear and eloquent truth by silence. I do not deny the essential nature of love honorableness if it is checked by the bridle of moderation, if it is restrained by the reins of sobriety, if it does not transgress the determined boundaries of its natural character, or its heat boil to too great a degree. But if its spark shoots into a flame, or its little spring rises to a torrent, the rankness of the growth demands the pruning-knife, and the swelling and excess require an assuaging medicine; for all excess disturbs the progress of well-regulated temperance, and the pride of unhealthy extravagance fattens, so to speak, into ulcers of vices.

"The former poetical discourse, then, which strayed into playful jest, is set before you as a treat for your childishness. Now let the style, which had slightly wandered toward the boyish and light verses of your youth, return to the ordered theme of the narration previously planned. As I showed in touching on the subject before, I appointed Venus to build up a progeny from the living creatures of earth, that in her work of producing things she might shape the various rough materials, and lay them before me. But I, in the manifold formation of their natures, was to add the final and polishing hand. And in order that faithful tools might exclude the confusion of poor work, I have assigned to her two lawful hammers, by which she may bring the stratagems of the Fates to naught, and present to view the multiform subjects of existence. I also appointed for her work anvils, noble instruments, with a command that she should apply these same hammers to them, and faithfully give herself up to the forming of things, not permitting the hammers to leave their proper work, and become strangers to the anvils. For the office of writing I provided her with an especially potent reed-pen, in order that, on suitable leaves desiring the writing of this pen (in the benefit of my gift of which leaves she had been made a sharer), she might, according to the rules of my orthography, trace the natures of things, and might not suffer the pen to stray in the least measure possible from the path of proper description into the by-track of false writing. . . ."

[*Nature describes how Venus, having become self-indulgent and corrupt, ignores her great task, betrays her lawful husband Hymen, and as a result of her adultery with Antigenius, gives birth to an illegitimate son, Mirth.*]

Prose Eight

[*Nature has now been joined by Hymen, Chastity, Temperance, Generosity, and Humility. Nature is speaking.*]

". . . I perceive, with a mature and deep-rooted understanding, what is the reason for your coming together, what the occasion for your arrival, what the cause of your lamentation, what the source of your grief. For men, who are fashioned only in the beauty of humanity, and who yet are sunk into bestial ugliness, and whom I grieve to have invested with the robe of manhood, are endeavoring to disinherit you from your patrimony of an earthly habitation, and are seizing all power on earth, and forcing you to repair to your celestial home. Since, then, my welfare is affected, when the partition-wall between is flaming with fire, I feel compassion for your suffering, sympathize in your grief, read my groans in your groans, and find my loss in your adversity. Therefore, passing over nothing of what has happened, I will attain my own goal myself, and I will smite these men with vengeance answering to their sin, so far as I am able to extend the arm of my might. But since I cannot exceed the limit of my power, and it is not in my control to root out the poison of this pestilence completely, I will follow the measure of my ability, and brand the men who are caught in these crooked vices with the mark of anathema.

"But it is fitting to ask Genius, who assists me in the priestly office, to cast out, with the aiding presence of my judiciary power, with your assent and favoring help, and with the pastoral rod of excommunication, those men from the catalogue of the things of nature, from the bounds of my jurisdiction. Hymen, the highly proved, will be the executor of this mission. In him shine the stars of glittering eloquence, and in his possession is placed the armory of the examining council."

Then they rose, and, resting from their tears and lament, bowed their heads in deep humility, and freely gave to Nature abundant signs of their gratitude. And Hymen, who humbled himself on bended knee in the immediate sight of Nature, declared himself obedient to the appointed mission. Then she marked and inscribed with a reed-pen a papyrus sheet with an epistolary composition of this sort:

"Nature, by the grace of God delegated protectress of the worldly realm, to Genius, her other self, greeting, and a wish that in everything he be befriended by the favors of fair fortune! Since similarities rejoice in a scorn of things unlike them, and in the friendly appearance of things like them, I, who find in thee, as in the mirror of Nature, myself again in marked resemblance, am bound to thee by the knot of most ardent love, so that I am with thee in all things, advance in thy progress, or, in like measure, droop in thy failure. Therefore ought our love to be reciprocal, so that thou wouldest answer with equal affection, and make our fortunes one. The evidence of evil committed tells thee fully, in the form of a loud wail, of the shipwreck of the human race. For thou seest how men debase the original dignity of their natures with bestial pleasures, and transgress humanity's privileged state, changing in their degenerate practices to beasts, and how, in following their own desires in the pursuit of lust, going to shipwreck in the whirlpools of intemperance, seething in the heat of avarice, flying upon the false wings of pride, giving way to the bites of envy, gilding others with the hypocrisy of flattery, they fall far from their natural and noble state. No one is ready with medicinal remedies for these vicious diseases. No one restrains the torrent of these crimes with a dyke of defence. No harbor checks unchangeably the flood-tides of these evil deeds. Therefore the virtues, being wholly unable to bear the assault of such a hostile conflict, have fled to us, as to a refuge of defence and a succor to their life. Since our common interests are thrown into confusion by the fierce attack, I entreat thee with prayers, enjoin thee by the virtue of obedience, both warn as I command and command as I warn, that thou banish all deception and excuse, and hasten thy approach to us; and that, with the aiding presence of myself and my women, thou sever the children of abomination from the holy communion of our congregation, and, in the due solemnity of thine office, smite them with the hard rod of excommunication."

Thereupon she gave the letter, which had been sealed and marked with a signet, on which an artist's skill had engraved the name and image of Nature, to her legate to deliver. Then Hymen, ending his acts of thanks with a graver countenance of joy, received his appointed embassy, and, rousing his companions from dull idleness, bade them take up their instruments of music, and, stirring them from dumb silence, summon them to the measures of harmonious melody. Then, caressing their instruments in a few preludes, they struck out a sound of many notes in one, of quality unlike yet consonant, of manifold tone.

Prose Nine

. . . After the mutual rejoicing had been consummated in an end of satisfaction, Genius, with hand raised in request, enjoined silence, and, following this, coined the material of his voice into this form of speech:

"O Nature, I do not believe that without the divine breath of inspiration has that imperial edict gone out from thine even judgment, to the effect that all who try by abuse and neglect to reduce our laws to ruin should not rejoice in the high day of our festival, but should be smitten with the sword of anathema. And since this law and legitimate decree does not oppose the rule of justness, and since the scales of thy careful judgment sit quiet on the balance-tongue of my consideration, I hasten more quickly to strengthen the ruling of thine edict. For though my mind, which has been tormented by the odious vices of men, and which has traveled into the depth of sorrow, is unacquainted with the paradise of gladness, yet the beginning of delight and joy smells sweetly in this, that I see thee striving with me toward the attainment of vengeance due. And it is not strange if in the harmonious union of our wills I find the music of concord, since one original thought and idea conforms us with each other, and has brought us into the same mind, since the official rank of one administration makes us alike, and since hypocritical love does not join our minds with the band of shallow affection, but the virtue of pure love dwells in the inner secret places of our souls."

While Genius was limiting the course of his speech to these few words, Nature drew aside a little the shadows of sorrow with what was like the rising dawn of an exclamation, and, though with the honor of her position preserved, showed to Genius her proper gratitude. Then Genius, after laying aside his common garment, and being adorned more honorably with the higher ornaments of the sacerdotal vestment, called out from the secret places of his mind the order of excommunication referred to, under this form of words, and proceeding in this way of speech:

"By the authority of the Absolute Being and of His eternal thought, and with the approbation of the celestial soldiery, and the agreement of Nature and the assisting ministry of the attendant virtues beside, let him be separated from the kiss of heavenly love, as the desert of ingratitude demands; let him be degraded from the favor of Nature; let him be isolated from the harmonious assembly of the things of Nature, whoever turns awry the lawful course of love, or is often shipwrecked in gluttony, or swallows greedily the delirium of drunkenness, or thirsts in the fire of avarice, or ascends the shadowy pinnacle of insolent pride, or suffers the deep-seated destruction of envy, or keeps company with the false love of flattery. Let him who makes an irregular exception to the rule of love be deprived of the sign of love. Let him who is deep in the abyss of gluttony be chastised by shamefaced beggary. Let him who sleeps in the Lethean stream of drunkenness be tormented with the fires of perpetual thirst. Let him in whom burns the passion to possess incur the continual needs of poverty. Let him who, exalted on the precipice of pride, throws out a spirit of arrogance, fall ingloriously into the valley of dejected humility. Let him who envies and gnaws like the moth of detraction at the riches of another's happiness first find himself an enemy to himself. Let him who hunts gifts from the rich by the hypocrisy of flattery be cheated by a reward of deceptive worth."

After Genius, in the utterance of this anathema, had made an end to his speech, the assembly of the women approved of the curse with quick word of ratification, and confirmed his edict. Then the lights of the tapers in their hands became drowsy, sank to the earth with a scorn of extinction, and seemed to be fallen asleep. With the mirror of this visionary sight taken away, the previous view of the mystic apparition left me, and I awoke from my ecstatic dream.

16

Andreas Capellanus (c. 1185): *The Art of Courtly Love*⁹

Book One

CHAPTER 1. WHAT LOVE IS

Love is a certain inborn suffering derived from the sight of and excessive meditation upon the beauty of the opposite sex, which causes each one to wish above all things the embraces of the other and by common desire to carry out all of love's precepts in the other's embrace.

That love is suffering is easy to see, for before the love becomes equally balanced on both sides there is no torment greater, since the lover is always in fear that his love may not gain its desire and that he is wasting his efforts. He fears, too, that rumors of it may get abroad, and he fears everything that might harm it in any way, for before things are perfected a slight disturbance often spoils them. If he is a poor man, he also fears that the woman may scorn his poverty; if he is ugly, he fears that she may despise his lack of beauty or may give her love to a more handsome man; if he is rich, he fears that his parsimony in the past may stand in his way. To tell the truth, no one can number the fears of one single lover. This kind of love, then, is a suffering which is felt by only one of the persons and may be called "single love." But even after both are in love, the fears that arise are just as great, for each of the lovers fears that what he has acquired with so much effort may be lost through the effort of someone else, which is certainly much worse for a man than if, having no hope, he sees that his efforts are accomplishing nothing, for it is worse to lose the things you are seeking than to be deprived of a gain you merely hope for. The lover fears, too, that he may offend his loved one in some way; indeed he fears so many things that it would be difficult to tell them.

That this suffering is inborn I shall show you clearly, because if you will look at the truth and distinguish carefully you will see that it does not arise out of any action; only from the reflection of the mind upon what it sees does this suffering come. For when a man sees some woman fit for love and shaped according to his taste, he begins at once to lust after her in his heart; then the more he thinks about her the more he burns with love, until he comes to a fuller meditation. Presently he begins to think about the fashioning of the woman and to differentiate her limbs, to think about what she does, and to pry into the secrets of her body, and he desires to put each part of it to the fullest use. Then after he has come to this complete meditation, love cannot hold the reins, but he proceeds at once to action; straightway he strives to get a helper and to find an intermediary. He begins to plan how he may find favor with her, and he begins to seek a place and a time opportune for talking; he looks upon a brief hour as a very long year, because he cannot do anything fast enough to suit his eager mind. It is well known that many things happen to him in this manner. This inborn suffering comes, therefore, from seeing and meditating. Not every kind of meditation can be the cause of love; an excessive one is required, for a restrained thought does not, as a rule, return to the mind, and so love cannot arise from it.

Chapter 2. Between What Persons Love May Exist

Now, in love you should note first of all that love cannot exist except between persons of opposite sexes. Between two men or two women love can find no place, for we see that two persons of the same sex are not at all fitted for giving each other the exchanges of love or for practicing the acts natural to it. Whatever nature forbids, love is ashamed to accept.

Every attempt of a lover tends toward the enjoyment of the embraces of her whom he loves; he thinks about it continually, for he hopes that with her he may fulfill all the mandates of love—that is, those things which we find in treatises on the subject. Therefore in the sight of a lover nothing can be compared to the act of love, and a true lover would rather be deprived of all his money and of everything that the human mind can imagine as indispensable to life rather than be without love, either hoped for or attained. For what under heaven can a man possess or own for which he would undergo so many perils as we continually see lovers submit to of their own free will? We see them despise death and fear no threats, scatter their wealth abroad and come to great poverty. Yet a wise lover does not throw away wealth as a prodigal spender usually does, but he plans his expenditures from the beginning in accordance with the size of his patrimony; for when a man comes to poverty and want he begins to go along with his face downcast and to be tortured by many thoughts, and all joyousness leaves him. And when that goes, melancholy comes straightway to take its place, and wrath claims a place in him; so he begins to act in a changed manner toward his beloved and to appear frightful to her, and the things that cause love to increase begin to fail. Therefore love begins to grow less, for love is always either decreasing or increasing. I know from my own experience that when poverty comes in, the things that nourished love begin to leave, because "poverty has nothing with which to feed its love."

But I do not tell you this, my friend, with the idea of indicating by what I say that you should follow avarice, which, as all agree, cannot remain in the same dwelling with love, but to show you that you should by all means avoid prodigality and should embrace generosity with both arms. Note, too, that nothing which a lover gets from his beloved is pleasing unless she gives it of her own free will.

Chapter 3. Where Love Gets Its Name

Love gets its name (*amor*) from the word for hook (*amus*), which means "to capture" or "to be captured," for he who is in love is captured in the chains of desire and wishes to capture someone else with his hook. Just as a skillful fisherman tries to attract fishes by his bait and to capture them on his crooked hook, so the man who is a captive of love tries to attract another person by his allurements and exerts all his efforts to unite two different hearts with an intangible bond, or if they are already united he tries to keep them so forever.

177

CHAPTER 4. WHAT THE EFFECT OF LOVE IS

Now it is the effect of love that a true lover cannot be degraded with any avarice. Love causes a rough and uncouth man to be distinguished for his handsomeness; it can endow a man even of the humblest birth with nobility of character; it blesses the proud with humility; and the man in love becomes accustomed to performing many services gracefully for everyone. O what a wonderful thing is love, which makes a man shine with so many virtues and teaches everyone, no matter who he is, so many good traits of character! There is another thing about love that we should not praise in few words: it adorns a man, so to speak, with the virtue of chastity, because he who shines with the light of one love can hardly think of embracing another woman, even a beautiful one. For when he thinks deeply of his beloved the sight of any other woman seems to his mind rough and rude.

I wish you therefore to keep always in mind, Walter my friend, that if love were so fair as always to bring his sailors into the quiet port after they had been soaked by many tempests, I would bind myself to serve him forever. But because he is in the habit of carrying an unjust weight in his hand, I do not have full confidence in him any more than I do in a judge whom men suspect. And so for the present I refuse to submit to his judgment, because "he often leaves his sailors in the mighty waves." But why love, at times, does not use fair weights I shall show you more fully elsewhere in this treatise.

CHAPTER 5. WHAT PERSONS ARE FIT FOR LOVE

We must now see what persons are fit to bear the arms of love. You should know that everyone of sound mind who is capable of doing the work of Venus may be wounded by one of Love's arrows unless prevented by age, or blindness, or excess of passion. Age is a bar, because after the sixtieth year in a man and the fiftieth in a woman, although one may have intercourse his passion cannot develop into love; because at that age the natural heat begins to lose its force, and the natural moisture is greatly increased, which leads a man into various difficulties and troubles him with various ailments, and there are no consolations in the world for him except food and drink. Similarly, a girl under the age of twelve and a boy before the fourteenth year do not serve in love's army. However, I say and insist that before his eighteenth year a man cannot be a true lover, because up to that age he is overcome with embarrassment over any little thing, which not only interferes with the perfecting of love, but even destroys it if it is well perfected. But we find another even more powerful reason, which is that before this age a man has no constancy, but is changeable in every way, for such a tender age cannot think about the mysteries of love's realm. Why love should kindle in a woman at an earlier age than in a man I shall perhaps show you elsewhere.

Blindness is a bar to love, because a blind man cannot see anything upon which his mind can reflect immoderately, and so love cannot arise in him, as I have already fully shown. But I admit that this is true only of the acquiring of love, for I do not deny that a love which a man acquires before his blindness may last after he becomes blind.

An excess of passion is a bar to love, because there are men who are slaves to such passionate desire that they cannot be held in the bonds of love—men who, after they have thought long about some woman or even enjoyed her, when they see another woman straightway desire her embraces, and they forget about the services they have received from their first love and they feel no gratitude for them. Men of this kind lust after every woman they see; their love is like that of a shameless dog. They should rather, I believe, be compared to asses, for they are moved only by that low nature which shows that men are on the level of the other animals rather than by that true nature which sets us apart from all the other animals by the difference of reason. Of such lovers I shall speak elsewhere.

Chapter 6. In What Manner Love May Be Acquired, and In How Many Ways

From the Fifth Dialogue: "A nobleman speaks with a noblewoman"

. . ."To my request [the King of Love] answered, 'You have been permitted to see our mighty works that through you our glory may be revealed to those who know it not, and that this sight which you now

179

see may be a means of salvation for many ladies. We therefore command and firmly enjoin upon you that wherever you find a lady of any worth departing from our pathway by refusing to submit herself to love's engagements, you shall take care to relate to her what you have seen here and shall cause her to leave her erroneous ideas so that she may escape such very heavy torments and find a place here in glory. Know, then, that the chief rules in love are these twelve that follow:

    I. Thou shalt avoid avarice like the deadly pestilence and shalt embrace its opposite.

    II. Thou shalt keep thyself chaste for the sake of her whom thou lovest.

    III. Thou shalt not knowingly strive to break up a correct love affair that someone else is engaged in.

    IV. Thou shalt not choose for thy love anyone whom a natural sense of shame forbids thee to marry.

    V. Be mindful completely to avoid falsehood.

    VI. Thou shalt not have many who know of thy love affair.

    VII. Being obedient in all things to the commands of ladies, thou shalt ever strive to ally thyself to the service of Love.

    VIII. In giving and receiving love's solaces let modesty be ever present.

    IX. Thou shalt speak no evil.

    X. Thou shalt not be a revealer of love affairs.

    XI. Thou shalt be in all things polite and courteous.

    XII. In practicing the solaces of love thou shalt not exceed the desires of thy lover."

Book Two

CHAPTER 8. THE RULES OF LOVE (*excerpt*)

    I. Marriage is no real excuse for not loving.

    II. He who is not jealous cannot love.

    III. No one can be bound by a double love.

IV. It is well known that love is always increasing or decreasing.

V. That which a lover takes against the will of his beloved has no relish.

VI. Boys do not love until they arrive at the age of maturity.

VII. When one lover dies, a widowhood of two years is required · of the survivor.

VIII. No one should be deprived of love without the very best of reasons.

IX. No one can love unless he is impelled by the persuasion of love.

X. Love is always a stranger in the home of avarice.

XI. It is not proper to love any woman whom one would be ashamed to seek to marry.

XII. A true lover does not desire to embrace in love anyone except his beloved.

XIII. When made public love rarely endures.

XIV. The easy attainment of love makes it of little value; difficulty of attainment makes it prized.

XV. Every lover regularly turns pale in the presence of his beloved.

XVI. When a lover suddenly catches sight of his beloved his heart palpitates.

XVII. A new love puts to flight an old one.

XVIII. Good character alone makes any man worthy of love.

XIX. If love diminishes, it quickly fails and rarely revives.

XX. A man in love is always apprehensive.

XXI. Real jealousy always increases the feeling of love.

XXII. Jealousy, and therefore love, are increased when one suspects his beloved.

XXIII. He whom the thought of love vexes eats and sleeps very little.

XXIV. Every act of a lover ends in the thought of his beloved.

XXV. A true lover considers nothing good except what he thinks will please his beloved.

XXVI. Love can deny nothing to love.

XXVII. A lover can never have enough of the solaces of his beloved.

XXVIII. A slight presumption causes a lover to suspect his beloved.

XXIX. A man who is vexed by too much passion usually does not love.

XXX. A true lover is constantly and without intermission possessed by the thought of his beloved.

XXXI. Nothing forbids one woman being loved by two men or one man by two women.

17

Documents of the Quarrel[10]

Pierre Col to Christine de Pisan (mid-1402)

After I had heard people speak of your high understanding, your clear intellect, and of your melodious eloquence, I desired very greatly to see your letters and other small things of like kind. Thus after great care in seeking them, there has come into my hand a certain letter of yours, addressed, as I note, to my seigneur and especial master, Monsieur le Provost of Lisle, which began: "Reverence, honor," etc.[11] In this letter you make an effort to reproach the very devout Catholic and very excellent theologian, the most divine orator and poet and most perfect philosopher, Master Jean de Meun, in some particular parts of his book of the *Rose*. Yet I myself scarcely dare to open my mouth in praise of this book, lest I should set my foot into an abyss. For as we read of Herod, he did more good to the Innocents through hatred by having them killed than he could possibly have done through love. Perhaps it will be the same for you and others who strive with you to impugn this most noble writer Master Jean de Meun. You will perhaps praise him more in thinking to condemn him than I would be able to praise him if all my members were changed into tongues and employed at the task. For I am unequal to the task not only on account of the dullness of my intellect, the heaviness of my understanding, my weak memory, and my poorly ordered language, but more especially on account of the vast abundance of good things which are in that work impossible to express. . . .

First of all, you begin, without reason, with the chapter in which Reason appears, and you say that she names the secret members of man by their proper names. And I respond to such an argument that God made the things; hence, they are good, and indeed can be called by their proper names. You do say, in fact: "I confess that God created all things pure and clean coming from Himself, so that in the State of Innocence there would have been no wickedness in naming them; but man became impure by the pollution of sin." Further, you use as an example Lucifer, who was first beautiful and whose name was beautiful, but who subsequently was reduced to a horrible ugliness by sin, whereby the name, although it is beautiful of itself, horrifies those who hear it. Besides, you say that the name does not make the thing dishonorable; but the thing, the name. Here you resemble the pelican: you kill yourself with your beak.[12] If you believe that the thing makes the name dishonorable, what name can you give to the thing which would not be dishonorable, if the thing is not changed when the name is? Then I come to the place where you say that in the State of Innocence it was permitted to name the secret members, and that God formed them in such a state. I ask you whether you would speak of the secret members of a two- or three-year-old child—for you would not deny that God creates us all. Would you dare name them by their proper name? If you say no, nevertheless he is in the state of innocence without pollution in word or deed. And it is useless for you to reply that you spoke of original sin, for it came about through disobedience. And if the pollution of our first parents made the secret members so shameful that one is not permitted to name them, I say that by a stronger reason one ought not to call our first parents by name. For they are the ones who sinned; not their members. If you say yes, it is permissible for one to name the secret members of a child, I ask you to tell us to what age it is permitted to name them, and also whether one can name by their name the secret members of an aged man who has been chaste and virginal all his life. Similarly, would you dare to name the secret members of dumb beasts, for they do not sin at all? Thus, can you teach Reason and the disciples of the aforesaid Meun how they should speak! In fact, in this chapter of Reason, the Lover himself offers a broader and more forceful argument against naming the secret members than you do. And Reason responds to his argument, and yet you do not address yourself to this response at all, as you should have done before you criticized her. Thus there is no more need to answer you with regard to this matter. . . .

First, then, Lady Theological Eloquence says that Master Jean de Meun carries on his forehead the inscribed title of his condemnation by this word *Foolish Lover*, and she continues: "Who brought great Troy to ruin in former days by fire and flame? A foolish lover. Who caused more than a hundred thousand noble men to be destroyed: Hector, Achilles, and others? A foolish lover. Who exiled King Tarquin from Rome? A foolish lover,"—and other such examples. I ask Lady Eloquence if this argument seeks to blame a man for being a foolish lover or to blame the book of the *Rose* because it was made by a foolish lover? If it blames a foolish lover, I will not answer at all. For I admit that being a foolish lover is foolish and irrational, but there is no need for anyone to try to blame a foolish lover more than the book of the *Rose* does. . . . And when Master Jean de Meun calls the secret members of women "sanctuaries" and "relics," he does so in order to show the great folly that is in the Foolish Lover. For a foolish lover thinks only of this little rosebud, and it is his god and he honors it as his god. Also at this point he feigns poetically, and to poets and painters there has always been such license, as Horace says.[13] He, in fact, chooses his words very well when he calls a woman's secret members "sanctuaries," for the gates and walls of a city are by law called holy because if one uses force or trespasses without leave against them, he must suffer the consequences. Thus is it with the secret members of a woman; he who uses force there or who without force unduly trespasses upon them must pay for it. Moreover, the Bible says that it was customary to sanctify the secret members of the woman.

But if the argument seeks to blame the book of the *Rose* because he who made it was a foolish lover, I marvel why Lady Eloquence does not first draw such conclusions against Solomon, David, and other foolish lovers, who were long before Meun, whose books are made a part of holy Scripture and their words a part of the holy mystery of the Mass. Who caused Uriah the good knight to be killed by treachery in order to commit adultery with his wife? A foolish lover. Who caused the temples with the idols to be built for the love of strange women? A foolish lover—and so many others that I pass over.

Against these Lady Eloquence ought to speak first, if she wishes to press her argument. But she does not do so. Do we not read that St. Peter and St. Paul were firmer in the faith after they had sinned, and many others similarly? I say that Master Jean de Meun, because he had been a foolish lover, was very firm in reason; for the better he knew the folly which is in foolish love by experience, the better was he able to scorn it and to praise reason. And when he made this book of the *Rose*, he was no longer a foolish lover (and had repented of being one), as is clear from his speaking so well of Reason. . . .

But let us come to your point. Lady Eloquence, addressing her words to those who support this Foolish Lover, says thus: "Is this not madness to say that one ought to speak bluntly and crudely and without shame, however dishonorable the words in the judgment of all people?" etc. Ha! Lady Eloquence, you are constrained here to present your original premise badly, on which you found all your subsequent argument. But do not hold a grudge against the man who causes you to do so, for I really believe that he does not do this knowingly. Certainly, he found little to please him in this most noble book of the *Rose*, because he scarcely read it, or, as I prefer to believe, he was displeased precisely because he had read it little. . . . I admit that it would be an evil to seek out opportunities to speak of the work of nature and to be cunningly ingenious at speaking of it for mere pleasure—therein lies the impurity that some men abominate so greatly. This is the point made by Cicero in *De Officiis*, and other philosophers who spoke similarly of such matters.[14] But when one speaks on many different subjects, and, without any special predilection, mentions the secret members, it is quite proper for him to do so. This is what Jean de Meun does in the chapter of Reason. And, by God, it is fitting to speak of them at least once, if one does not overstress their importance; and their importance is not overstressed since he speaks of them by name once and never again. And so it is permissible to speak in the way that Reason speaks of them. Thus Holy Scripture names them by their proper name and quite rightly. So do law books in many places. And besides, the secret members are necessary and useful, and profitable, and beautiful, and good. Further, the Bible forbids a man who has had them cut off to enter a church.[15] And they are named there very properly, and I do not believe that Jesus Christ himself had a member that one could not honorably name. . . . [And] women certainly call their own private parts by their proper names. They choose not to name a man's. But I do not see that their parts are more honorable than man's.

See further what Lady Eloquence says: "He observes badly the rules of rhetoric, for he ought to have noted to whom Reason spoke. If she had spoken to a layman, a clerk, or a theologian, it would have been one thing. But she spoke to a Foolish Lover, who by such words can be incited to carnality, as a great clerk or theologian would not be." And it seems by her words that being a clerk, a philosopher, or a theologian is not compatible with being a foolish lover, that they are irreconcilable. Alas, it is, it has been, and it will forever be far otherwise. Look at the examples of David, Solomon, and others. Some teachers even say that Solomon made the Canticles on account of his love of Pharaoh's daughter; yet he was held the wisest man of his time or before. In short, one could bring forth more than a thousand examples of people who were clerks and at the same time foolish lovers. . . . Also, for God's sake, naming the secret members twice or thrice does not move a man to foolish loving, when it is necessary to name them. When Reason names them, she exhorts the Foolish Lover to desist from foolish love. And in speaking of numerous things, she comes properly to speak of the secret members. Truly, if he had always been thus occupied, Lady Idleness would never have opened the gate of the garden to him. Yet although he already was a Foolish Lover, Reason moved him somewhat toward desisting from it, for which the God of Love reproached him. It is clear that in the chapter of Reason, Master Jean de Meun did not stoop to speak of the secret members merely on account of his fondness for speaking bluntly and bawdily, but because it suited his purpose in showing the foolishness of those who claim that it is never permissible to name them by their proper names under any circumstances. . . .

But let us go further. You and Lady Eloquence have exclaimed over the dishonorableness to be found in this chapter of the Old Woman, where, you both say, one finds nothing but filth, and similarly in the chapter of Jealousy; and you say that you would really like to find someone capable of justifying it to you. "What end is served by the many dishonorable words which this book contains?" "But," you say, "I do not condemn the author in all places in the aforementioned book," as if you wish to say that you condemn him in this particular place, and therefore set yourself up as a judge although you have spoken out of prejudice and outrageous presumption. Oh excessively foolish pride! Oh opinion uttered too quickly and thoughtlessly by the mouth of a woman! A woman who condemns a man of high understanding and dedicated study, a man who, by great labor and deliberation, has made the very noble book of the *Rose*, which surpasses all others that were ever written in French. When you have read this book a hundred times, provided you have understood the greater part of it, you will discover that you could never have put your time and intellect to better use. Indeed, he who wrote the Complaint of Lady Eloquence was more deliberate and gracious than you. For he says at the end of the Complaint that he did not hear the sentence given. However, as Terence says, "Truth engenders hatred; flattery, friends"; and I suspect it is because Meun spoke the truth that you wish to bite him.[16] But I advise you to keep your teeth to yourself. I answer Lady Eloquence and you by the same means, and I say that Master Jean de Meun in his book introduced characters, and made each character speak according to his nature, that is, the Jealous Man as a jealous man, the Old Woman as an old woman, and similarly with the others. And it is wrong-headed to say that the author believes women to be as evil as the Jealous Man, in accordance with his character, declares. This is clearly not true of the author. He merely recites what any jealous man says of women invariably, and Meun does this in order to demonstrate and correct the enormous irrationality and disordered passion of jealous men. . . .

Moreover, if Holy Scripture recites the abominable sins of Sodom and Gomorrah, does it exhort one to commit such sins? When you go to a sermon, do you not hear the preachers castigate the vices that men and women commit every day, so that they might lead them into the right way? In good faith, damoiselle, it is true. One ought to call to mind the foot on which one limps in order to walk better. . . .

And in order the better to blame vice, he speaks as if vice lay outside man, just as, in the chapter of the Jealous Man, he says that all the vices made poverty leap out of hell and come to earth. And of Shame he says that she restrains and controls. Yet he speaks more against men than against women. Does he not condemn, in the chapter on Nature, twenty-six vices with which men are corrupted? And in innumerable other places which I pass over. In the chapter on Nature he says that clerks abandoned to vice ought to be punished more than lay men and ordinary people, and that gentility resides in virtue. Among these virtues, he includes honoring ladies and damoiselles. In God's name, this is no attack on the whole feminine sex. I say this in response to your accusation in the closing words of your letter. St. Ambrose, in one of his sermons, blames the feminine sex more, for he says that it is a sex accustomed to deceiving. In truth, you do also—you blame them more than Meun when you say that if one reads the book of the *Rose* before queens, princesses, and other great ladies, they would have to blush with shame. Why should they blush? It appears that they would feel themselves guilty of the vices that the Jealous Man recites of women.

Neither does he condemn religion, as Lady Eloquence says. It is very true that he says that hypocrisy "betrays many a region by semblance of religion" (10,443–10,444). He does not say by religion, but by the *semblance* of religion. . . . And when Lady Eloquence reports that he says that young men are not at all stable in their faith, I say that when a young man enters a religious order because of youth rather than devotion, he is not firm in it. And this is what Master Jean de Meun says in the chapter of the Old Woman; and here are his own words:

> So I say to you that
> When a man enters a religious order
> And later regrets it, he is almost
> Ready to hang himself in his dismay.
>
> [13,937–13,940]

And thus it is clear that he speaks there of a man who repents of having entered into a religious order, as they often have. . . . It is certainly not in accord with man's natural appetite to vow to abstain from meat and to be chaste and poor all his life, or even to promise to be faithful to one woman, or, on the other hand, a woman, to one man. As Lady Eloquence herself suggests, our frailty is inclined to vice. Does she mean to praise the vices by this? Not at all. So, if Master Jean de Meun says that natural appetite is not inclined to religion but to the contrary, he does not wish by this to blame religion and praise its contrary. But you will say to me that I recite the good words and not the evil, which incite to lubricity and teach Jealousy how to take the castle. And Lady Eloquence says that he wishes to drive all women out of chastity. I answer and say to you that in all manners of war it is a greater advantage to be the defender than the assailant, if one is warned ahead of time. For example, suppose Jealousy has had a strong castle constructed and has placed in it good sentries to guard it, but the castle is nevertheless captured by a certain kind of assault. If Jean de Meun has described the way in which it was captured, has he not given a great advantage to the castle guards by showing them how it was captured, so that they may in the future block the gap or place better guards there and thus lessen the chances of the assailants? . . . When Ovid wrote the *Art of Love*, he wrote in Latin, which women did not understand. Therefore, he gave it only to the assailants to teach them how to capture the castle. This was the aim of his book, without speaking through characters. But he, as Ovid, gave all his teaching. On account of this he was exiled, because of the very great jealousy of the Roman husbands. . . .

There is no point in saying that Jean de Meun, in composing his book, drew on Ovid's *Art of Love* and books by many others, for the more varied the forms of attack that he describes the better he teaches the defenders to guard the castle: and it was for this purpose that he wrote it. In fact, an acquaintance of mine, in his efforts to free himself from foolish love, borrowed the *Roman de la Rose* from me, and I have heard him swear by his faith that it was this book which helped him most to disentangle himself. . . .

If his book contains very bawdy words which degrade the feminine sex, it is simply because he quotes other authors who use them, for, as he says, he does nothing more than quote. Thus, it seems to me that one ought to blame the authors rather than those who quote them, as I said before. But you will say to me: "Why does he quote them?" I say that he did it in order to teach more effectively how gatekeepers should guard the castle. Besides, these words are appropriate there. For his purpose was to continue the subject initiated by Guillaume de Lorris, and in so doing to speak of all matters according to their hierarchical rank for the good of the human creature, in both body and soul. Thus he speaks of Paradise and of the virtues to be pursued and the vices to be shunned. And because he places vice beside virtue and hell beside heaven, he is the better able to reveal the beauty of the one and the ugliness of the other. Moreover, he simply follows the work begun by Guillaume de Lorris when he mentions the act of love in the chapter of Jealousy, of the Old Woman, and in various other places. Genius does not grant Paradise to foolish lovers, as Lady Eloquence suggests, but rather to those who perform the works of nature virtuously. There is a vast difference between performing the works of nature virtuously and being a foolish lover. Neither Nature nor Genius exhorts a man to be a foolish lover; rather, they preach that one ought to follow the works of nature. To propagate the human species and to abhor the sin against nature—these are the legitimate aims which they propose. And although I do not dare, and do not wish, to say that it is not sinful, outside the state of marriage, to perform the work of nature for the two above-mentioned reasons, nevertheless I dare say that it *is* permitted within marriage; and this is Master Jean de Meun's point in the chapter of the Old Woman. . . .

As for myself, in good truth, I had rather be among the blamed and scorned for prizing and loving the book of the *Rose* than to be among its blamers and reproachers. And may all those who reproach him know well, that seven thousand remain who will never bow the knee before Baal, and who are full ready to defend him. If he were contemporary with you who blame him, I would say that you have particular hatred for him personally; but you have never so much as seen him. Thus I cannot imagine whence this comes, save that the very loftiness of the book invites the winds of Envy. Your ignorance is not at all the cause of this criticism; this did not come certainly from your sketchy reading of the book of the *Rose*. Perhaps you merely pretend to blame the said book in order to exalt it. . . . At all events, I pray all men and women who wish to criticize or blame him in any part to read him thoroughly first, four times at least, that they may the better understand him. And I will accept such a thorough reading for their absolution. If they decline to do this, let them at least consider the purpose for which he wrote his book, and let them read his justification without prejudice, and I am sure that they will excuse him. . . . For generally he says that he has never said anything which was not for instruction, that is, for each one to have knowledge of himself and others. And finally, "that if he has said any word which Holy Church considers foolish" (15,269–15,270), he is completely ready to amend it. . . . And may the Trinity grant us all a fleece so white that we may, with the said de Meun, crop the grass which grows in the park of the little gamboling lamb. Amen.

Christine de Pisan to Pierre Col (2 October 1402)

To M. Pierre Col, Secretary of the King our Lord.

. . . Despite your beautiful rhetoric, you do not move my heart at all or make me wish to change what I have previously written. On this matter which your recent letter dealt with, namely the debate begun some time ago over the *Roman de la Rose*, I have received and been encouraged by writings addressed to me by other important people. And although I am otherwise engaged and did not intend to write more on the subject, I will nevertheless answer you, bluntly and directly, according to my custom, and speak the truth without any glossing over. And since I did not know how to emulate your good style, may you take into consideration my lack of skill. . . .

First of all, you declare that I condemn without grounds the fact that Reason . . . names the secret members of man by their proper names. Then you repeat my previous objection to this, namely, that God truly created all things good, but by the pollution of our first parents' sin, man became impure; and that Lucifer was first given a beautiful name, but later was transformed into a horrible person; and, finally, that the name does not make the thing dishonorable, but the thing, the name. By saying this, I resemble, you say, the pelican, which kills itself with its beak. This was your conclusion. Then you go on to say that if the thing, therefore, makes the name dishonorable, what name can one give to the thing which would not be dishonorable? Without more ado, I will answer this bluntly, for I am no logician. . . . Indeed, I do admit to you that, because of corrupted will, I could in no way speak of a dishonorable thing, whether the secret members or some other ignoble matter, whatever name I should give them, without the name becoming dishonorable. Nevertheless, if in the case of sickness or some other need, it were necessary to refer specifically to the secret members or whatever else, and if, in such a situation, I were able to make myself clearly understood by using some other name, then I would not at all be speaking dishonorably. The reason is that the purpose for which I spoke in that case would not be dishonorable. Yet, even in such a case, if I were to name them by their proper names, I would indeed be speaking dishonorably, for the primary associations of the thing have already made the name dishonorable. . . .

I am far from alone in the true, just, and reasonable opinion which I hold against the work of the *Rose* on account of its most reprehensible lessons, although there may well be some good in it. Among the other good people who agree with me, a courageous teacher and master of theology—competent, worthy, admirable, estimable, elect among the elect—came forward, after I had written the letter which you say you have seen.[17] Having decided to increase virtue and destroy vice (with which the work of the *Rose* has poisoned many human hearts) by opposing that book, he composed a short work, clearly inspired by pure theology. Concerning this matter, you wrote me that you have seen a work "made in the manner of a Complaint in the Holy Court of Christianity, in which Canonical Justice was established as a judge, and the virtues around her as her council, the chief and chancellor of which was Wise Understanding, accompanied by Lady Reason, Prudence, Knowledge, and others as secretaries. Theological Eloquence was advocate of the Court. The promoter of the suits was Conscience, who brought up and presented a request by Chastity, as follows: 'To Justice the law giver, who holds the place of God on earth, and to the universal Court of his devout and most Christian religion, Chastity, your faithful subject, humbly supplicates and requests that you provide a remedy and a brief warning against the intolerable deeds which a certain Foolish Lover has been doing and continues to do to me,' and he places thereafter eight or nine articles."

You begin the aforementioned letter by addressing me alone, since you consider it easy to repudiate my reasoning on account of my ignorance, because, apparently, you are confident of your own good sense and subtlety. Then, inexplicably, you begin voicing your personal criticism of the words of the above-mentioned notable person in his well-written work, since his opinion is contrary to your own erroneous one. Now consider well, consider well whether I might not reasonably apply to you the insulting words which you addressed to me in some places, saying, "Oh outrageous presumption! Oh excessively foolish pride!" etc. It is not at all my intention, however, to take upon myself the defence of all the questions posed by Lady Eloquence, for these are not related to the purpose of my first letter, save in a few places which raise the subject you would re-argue with me. For I will defer to the man who wrote the said Complaint, since he would be better able to defend it in a few words than I could in an entire lifetime. But I can say this much about the matter: you wish, unreasonably, to accuse him of ignorance—you who think you understand the work better than he, for all his wisdom and deep learning. You say indeed (to speak more courteously about such a notable person) that if he had studied the said book well, just as his understanding towers over all others, so too would his praise and appreciation of it. Praised be God! How good it must be to presume to believe, as you do, that such a man (who, you admit, is a worthy person) would have publicly condemned a work before he had even completely understood it! . . .

In making your response to Lady Eloquence you quote from the *Roman de la Rose* Reason's words, which say essentially that she can indeed name things by their proper names, whether they are good or not. And you say that Jean de Meun does not argue there that one has to name them but that one *may* do so. On behalf of Lady Eloquence, I will reply to you somewhat bluntly. I know perfectly well that duty is constraint and power is will, but nonetheless one's choice of words in such a case can make an offense of speaking openly and fully, as has already been proved and will be again. Yet you maintain, along with Reason, that one can speak of them by their proper names without sin, and you even allege that the Bible and holy writings name them by their proper names, where it is appropriate. I answer you, good friend, that if the Bible or holy writings name them, the manner of speaking and the purpose are wholly different from his work; rather, their aim is far removed from carnal enticement. The Bible certainly is not the work of a female character who called herself the daughter of God, and it never speaks to a Foolish Lover in order to fan the fires of lust. . . . You say that there is no case for claiming that good custom forbids speaking thus plainly, a subject which you do not discuss further. Yet I do not see why you will not speak to the matter whether the custom is good or evil, if you know something good about it. But you report Lady Eloquence as saying that if one thinks the custom is evil, he assumes foolishly that women have never accustomed themselves to it. Yet she is right. And it would be a pity if it were otherwise and if such a reproach could be brought by other countries against the women of this kingdom. For as it is said in the common proverb, "By the tongue, the inclination is known." For even Reason, whom you hold as so great an authority, says that this has never been customary in France. And indeed, it has not been the custom. . . .

You say that you are amazed at the custom of women's naming their own secret members by their proper names, while refusing to name a man's. I answer you that (saving your grace) certainly honorable women do not say the name publicly; and if some women name the things which are private to them more than those which are not, you ought not to be astonished. But you who assert by so many arguments that Master Jean de Meun's Reason is right in saying that they should be called openly by name, I ask you sincerely, you who are his very especial disciple as you say, why you do not name them openly in your own writing without beating around the bush? It seems to me that you are not a good pupil, for you do not follow well at all the doctrine of your master, who teaches you to name them. If you say that this is not customary, are you then afraid of being criticized, so that you take heed to this custom? Do you wish to live by the opinion of other people? Rather, follow good doctrine, in order to show them what they ought to do, for all things must begin somewhere. And if someone blames you at first, you will be praised for it later, when people see that the custom is good and right. Ha! my God! you do not do so. You cannot deny that shame keeps you from it. And where is Master Jean de Meun's Reason? She has little power when shame defeats her. Blessed be such shame that defeats such Reason. If I hated you, I would say, would to God that you had gone against custom in this matter. But I love you for your good sense and the good that people say of you. Although I scarcely know you, I do not wish you the dishonor of speaking frankly. For honorable and virtuous speech is the mark of a praiseworthy person.

It seems to me that you condemn Lady Eloquence's argument that de Meun observed the rules of rhetoric badly, in that he failed to consider to whom Reason was speaking. For, she maintains, Reason spoke to a Foolish Lover, who would simply be more inflamed by her words. And this would not be true of a learned man, since a philosopher or a theologian could not be a lover, a fact which you deny, citing the examples of David, Solomon, and others. Yet I am amazed that you wish to correct in others that very fault into which you yourself have fallen. And you uphold at one point what you wish to refute at another. It is good to know that when the gallant gentleman spoke of the Foolish Lover, he assumed that this man was completely ignorant; in the case of foolish love, he presumed that there was great knowledge in it; and when he said "a great theological clerk," he assumed that the passion of foolish love was not in him. For it is fitting that his fine intellect, which makes no mistakes, should conceive it in this way or even more subtly! But you say that a man will not be influenced by such words to love foolishly, and the reply is that he is already influenced, since he is a foolish lover. But his passion can indeed be increased. . . .

Then you speak of the deep dismay which Lady Eloquence and I express about the great dishonorableness in the chapter of the Old Woman, when we say that one can find nothing there but total filth and vile teaching, and similarly in the chapter of Jealousy. And we say much more that you do not reply to. Then you completely misread my words at the end of my aforementioned letter, remembering this part badly (begging your pardon). For you claim I said that I do not condemn the author or authors in all places in the said book, as if, you say, I meant that I condemned him for those parts which I criticized, charging that I set myself up as judge on the basis of mere opinion. My answer is that, in reality, you have ill chosen the flowers of my writing and have made a clumsily arranged bouquet (saving your grace). It was not by opinion but by certain knowledge that I declared that he spoke in a gross and most dishonorable manner in several places, and generally gave an evil exhortation. This judgment is easy to make, for it is proved by the work itself. Thus you or I or anyone else who understands French can condemn him on this point. Yet because he does not speak so dishonorably throughout, I say that I do not condemn him throughout. Further, you report correctly my wishing I could find someone to explain to me how so many dishonorable things could be good. And, nevertheless, you do not provide this explanation, but rather pass over it without fulfilling the wish. And since you are angry with me without reason, you attack me harshly with "Oh outrageous presumption! Oh excessively foolish pride! Oh opinion uttered too quickly and thoughtlessly by the mouth of a woman! A woman who condemns a man of high understanding and dedicated study, a man who, by great labor and mature deliberation, has made the very noble book of the *Rose*, which surpasses all others that ever were written in French. When you have read this book a hundred times, provided you have understood the greater part of it, you will discover that you could never have put your time and intellect to better use!" My answer: Oh man deceived by willful opinion! I could assuredly answer but I prefer not to do it with insult, although, groundlessly, you yourself slander me with ugly accusations. Oh darkened understanding! Oh perverted knowledge blinded by self will, which judges grievous poison to be restoration from death; perverse doctrine to be healthful example; bile to be sweet honey; horrible filthiness to be satisfying beauty. A simple little housewife sustained by the doctrine of Holy Church could criticize your error! Flee and eschew the perverse doctrine which could lead you to damnation. When God has once enlightened you with true knowledge, you will be horrified by it, when you turn around and look back down the dangerous path you travelled.

You say in order to reprove me that truth engenders hatred and flattery friends, as Terence says. And on account of this, you suspect that I wish to bite him, and counsel me to watch my teeth. Know this for a certainty, that you lack somewhat in your thinking there (saving your reverence), for because there are so many deceiving lies and such lack of truth in the book, I wish not only to bite, but to pull up by the roots the very great fallacious lies which it contains. You respond to Lady Eloquence and me that Master Jean de Meun introduced characters in his book, and made each one speak fittingly, according to what pertained to him. I readily admit that the proper equipment is necessary for any particular game, but the will of the player manipulates such equipment to his own purpose. And it is clearly true (may it not displease you) that he was at fault in attributing to some of his characters functions which do not properly belong to them: as with his priest he calls Genius, who insistently commands men to bed the ladies and to continue the work of nature without leaving off. And yet he then has Genius say that one ought to flee women above all things, accusing them of as much evil and villainy as possible. I do not understand how it pertains to his office or even to the function of many other characters who say the same. You say that it is the role of the Jealous Man to speak in such a way; my reply is that never, in all his characters, can Meun resist the temptation to slander women viciously. They are, thanks to God, none the worse for this. But, anyway, in my other letter, I spoke of this matter fully, to which remarks you scarcely responded, a fact which leaves me hardly anything to say.

Since this book of the *Rose* is so necessary and so important for teaching the good moral life, tell me, pray, what benefit to the common good can come from a collection of such immoral lessons as those espoused by the character called the Old Woman. For if you say that Meun's purpose is to teach men to guard themselves from these evils, I reply that most people, I believe, have never had anything to do with the kind of devilment that she describes and do not even know that such things exist. Therefore, from innocence like this, no harm can befall the general good, when most people are unaware of such evil in the first place. . . .

Moreover, you reply to Lady Eloquence and me by asking whether a man's citing of the crime reported by another can lead a person to commit the same crime. . . . Is, therefore, Holy Scripture, which recounts the abominable sins of Sodom and Gomorrah, guilty of exhorting men to commit such sins? You speak very well and to the point, you believe, but I ask you whether these authors, or Holy Scripture itself, in recounting such things, makes use of invented characters or soft, alluring words which support and sustain treachery, heresy, and other evils. You know very well that it is not so, for wherever such evils are recounted in books, they are condemned in such a way that they sound unpleasant to all who hear. And you used the example of the preacher's calling to mind in his sermon the foot on which one limps, because I had said previously that one need not remind nature of this, in order to make her walk straighter. But how does he call it to mind? How? Does he say, "My children, play! Rejoice! Take your ease—do so; this is the way to paradise"? By God, my lord, he does not; rather, he calls to mind this foot in such a way that it horrifies the hearers. One could say, "God grant you good day," in such a way that it sounds evil and bitter. . . .

You have said before that he does not blame women, but rather speaks well of them. But I am waiting for the proof. And you say that Saint Ambrose blamed the feminine sex more than he did, for he says that it is a sex accustomed to deceive. I will answer you in this: you know well that the writings of the theologians, and even the sermons of Jesus Christ himself, made use of a double meaning. Thus it is good to know that Saint Ambrose never made such a statement in condemnation of women: I am convinced that the good man blamed only vice. For he knew very well that there were many holy women, but he wished to say that it is the feminine sex through which man frequently deceived his own soul, just as Solomon said that the misdeed of a man is worth more than the good deed of a woman.[18] We know well that this is not to be taken according to the letter. . . .

You answer Lady Eloquence's criticism of Meun's attacks and slanders on religion by saying that he has not attacked religion at all. My reply is this, that as a public defamer (saving your grace) he defames religion excessively and without any exception. The good and devout Catholic, who is capable of criticizing wrongdoing, understands this, and I rely upon his opposition, for it is not pertinent to what I said in my first letter. And as you yourself rightly say, I could tell you that you quote the good words and select from them whatever suits your purpose, while ignoring the bad ones. To Lady Eloquence's complaint that, in teaching one to capture Jealousy's castle, he desired to drive chastity out of all women, you answer, incredibly, that he wished rather to teach the guards how to block the places through which it could be captured, or to place better guards there. And then you say that in all manner of wars the assailants have the advantage only when they are well informed. Now let us speak for a moment between us two about wars. I say to you that there are some kinds of wars in which the assailants have the advantage. Do you know when this is? When the captain or general is very malicious and wise in the ways of war and is dealing with an innocent party not accustomed to war. Then there is another point which often injures the defenders, even when they are strong: the treachery or false flattery by those very people on whom they rely. In such a way, the strong castle of Ilion was captured long ago. Moreover, when a castle is under attack, you cannot advise someone how to block the holes from treachery, since that treachery is so well concealed. Master Jean de Meun teaches how the castle of Jealousy will be attacked and captured. He does nothing at all to help the defenders in closing up the gaps, for he does not speak to them at all and is not on their side. Rather, he aids and abets the assailants in every form of assault. Thus, if I were to advise you how to conquer your enemy, this would clearly not be in order for him to guard himself against you.. And if you suggest that Meun does not teach it but simply relates how it was captured, I say to you that a man who describes an evil way of making counterfeit money or how someone had done so, he teaches it rightly enough. Hence, I say with certainty that he did it for no other purpose than to admit the assailants.

Afterward, you introduce Ovid's *Art of Love* for your purpose—and you are caught here in your own trap, if you would but consider it. And you give further proof of it, for which I am grateful, when you say that he was wrongly exiled for writing it. You say that Ovid wrote the work in Latin, which women did not understand, and that he gave it to the attackers only, in order to teach them how to attack the castle. This was the purpose of his book, and for this very reason he was exiled—without cause, you say—by the very great jealousy of the Roman men. Certainly, it seems to me that if you had been well advised, you would never have brought into the discussion at this point Ovid's *Art of Love* as an excuse for your master. The only way you could have introduced it to good effect would have been to say that it is the basic foundation and principle of this book of the *Rose*, which is the mirror and exemplar of the good and chaste life, which ideas he took from Ovid, who spoke of nothing save chastity. Ha! God! How obvious it is that sheer will has blinded your good sense, when you say that he was exiled without cause. The Romans, who governed all their deeds with excellent judgment, at that time exiled him, wrongfully you say, on account of jealousy. And since you say afterward that Meun put in his book not only Ovid's *Art of Love* but also the work of many other authors, then even by your own reasoning it is proved that Meun speaks to the attackers, just like Ovid from whom he borrowed. But you say that the more diverse the methods of attack he recounts, the better he teaches the castle guards the art of defence. Indeed, he is like a man who attacks and tries to kill you (may God preserve you); he merely teaches you how to defend yourself! Such teaching would be priceless, and you ought to thank him for it! At least you cannot deny that he does not teach how to harm the assailants, whatever the strength of the defenders. . . .

Ha! *Art of Love*! A book badly named! For of love there is nothing. It could well be called the art of falsely and maliciously deceiving women. This is a beautiful doctrine! Is then everything gained by deceiving women well? Who are women? Who are they? Are they serpents, wolves, lions, dragons, monsters, or ravishing, devouring beasts and enemies to human nature that it is necessary to make an art of deceiving and capturing them? Read then the *Art*. Learn then how to make traps, capture the forts, deceive them, con-demn them, attack this castle, take care that no woman escape from you men, and let everything be given over to shame! And, by God, these are your mothers, your sisters, your daughters, your wives, and your sweethearts: they are you yourselves and you yourselves are they. Now deceive them fully, for it is "much better, dear master, to deceive," etc.

I laugh at your saying that you lent your book of the *Rose* to a foolish lover so that he could free himself from foolish loving. This book helped him so much that you have heard him swear by his faith that it was this that helped him the most in freeing himself. You claim you mention this because of the words at the end of my letter, "How many have become hermits because of it?" My answer: if you had lent to your friend a book of Saint Bernard's devotions or some other holy legend which demonstrates that there is but one good love in which one ought to set his heart and affections, as Lady Philosophy shows Boethius, or some similar work, then I promise you that you would have done him far more good. But beware lest you have given him the means of withdrawing from the warmth of the sun and throwing himself into a blazing furnace. . . .

You say that it is because [Jean de Meun] placed vice beside virtue and hell beside paradise that he is able to show the blessedness of the one and the ugliness of the other. My answer: he does not show the blessedness of paradise at all when he says that evil doers will go there. Rather, he brings paradise into the filthy things that he describes in order to give greater authority to his book. But if you wish to hear paradise and hell described more subtly and, theologically, portrayed more advantageously, poetically, and efficaciously, read the book of Dante, or have it explained to you, because it is written splendidly in the Florentine language. Without wishing to displease you, I say that you will find there sounder principles, and you will be better able to profit from it than from that *Roman de la Rose* of yours. It is one hundred times better written; there is, be not offended, no comparison. . . .

And you say: "There is a vast difference between performing the work of nature virtuously and being a foolish lover." My answer: not once does he speak of performing this task virtuously. But I say to you that it is worse to be lecherous in many places, as he wishes to teach, than to be deeply in love in a single place. You say that Nature and Genius do not encourage people to be foolish lovers, but that they do encourage the performance of these same works, which are permissible to courtly lovers. My answer: do you then mean to say, since Nature does not preach it, that it is against nature to be deeply in love? This simply is not true (saving your grace). But since he says that the works of nature are permissible to courtly lovers, it would be worth knowing how they should carry out this purpose. You say that the work of nature is intended for the continuance of the human species and the abandonment of the vice that one ought not to name. My answer: it is pointless to debate this, because, thank God, nature does not lack in anything, and it is a foolish waste of time to tell water to follow its natural course. And the other sin which he mentions is not widespread, God be praised, in France. It is scarcely necessary to put such words in anybody's mouth. You say that, "although I do not dare, and do not wish, to say that it is not sinful, outside the state of marriage, to perform the said work." I give you these answers, without more ado: God knows you thought it, and another disciple like you dared to say it. But it is necessary to keep quiet about it, and for good reason. Nevertheless, you say this: "Is it permitted in marriage?" My answer: God be praised for it, we know this well. Nevertheless, the book of the *Rose*, unlike you, does not make this point about marriage in any place. . . . The question of marriage is far removed from the purpose of Genius. . . for he never gave marriage a thought, the good man. Nor do you believe that he ever did, whatever you say, God help me. In your efforts to excuse Meun, you choose to read the passage as implying that one may licitly perform the said work, at least within marriage. Yet it seems inappropriate that in that state one should have to perform the work so fully and diligently. Then, at the same time, he condemned the marriage state so excessively, when he said that there is so much strife in it that no one knowingly would enter into it, however eager to marry. How, then, according to him, can the work of nature be continued? He ought rather to have praised the state of marriage, in which the work can licitly be performed, in order to whet man's appetite for marriage. . . .

I do not know why we are debating these questions so fully, for I do not believe that we will be able to change each other's opinions. You say that he is good; I say that he is evil. Now show me which of the two is right. And when you and your accomplice, in your subtle ways, have been able to change evil into good, then will I believe that the *Roman de la Rose* is good. But I know well that this book is suitable for those who desire to live in wickedness and are more concerned with selfishly protecting themselves than others. For those, however, who desire to live in virtuous simplicity, and not embroiled in worldly desires, deceiving none, nor being deceived, this book has little to offer. . . .

18

Jean Molinet (1433–1507):
Prologue to
Roman de la Rose Moralisie[19]

Saint Augustine says that love is a kind of life which joins or
desires to unite or couple two things together: that is, the lover and
the beloved.[1] Rabanus says that in true love, nothing is too hard,
nothing too bitter, nothing too grievous, nothing too mortal. He says
further that love is so strong that one may ask what weapon or
wound, what pain or death can conquer it. Saint Denis says in the
book of holy names that love joins superiors with inferiors, inferiors
with superiors, and equals with equals. . . . Those who love always
die and yet are never dead. According to the various definitions of
love cited here, with their diverse characteristics, we can discern
three branches: divine love, natural love, and foolish love [*amour
fatuelle*]. Divine love is blazing fire, brilliant light, sweet honey, rich
wine, radiant sunshine; the unspeakable treasure which surrounds
the cherubim, brought to mankind by the Son of God, which topples
the gates of iron, redeems mankind, and admits the heavenly glory;
which will reward the righteous when everything else perishes,
withers, disappears, dies, except the inextinguishable, unfading, in-
comprehensible love of God. Natural love, lawful and proper, maintains the human species, sustains the generations of children,
nourishes the young of the animals, unites princes in peace, joins
cities in concord, draws together diverse spirits, so that without love
nothing is agreeable, useful, or enduring. Foolish love is vain
pleasure, frequent cogitation, a blazing and inextinguishable fire, insatiable ambition, incredible deception, diabolical illusion, of rage
the bitter portion, of true repose the destruction, of carnal music the
invention, of gifts habituation, of words multiplication, of foolishness

accumulation, of honor retrogradation, of sense annihilation, of famine the expansion, of health retardation, of good manners corruption, of vices the generation, of praise the suppression, of poverty repletion, of purse evacuation, of fraudulent images the profusion, of natural color the mutation, of light privation, of strength diminution, of spirit perturbation, of bodily members desiccation, of life abbreviation, of human body perdition, and of the soul damnation. . . .

If we should try to moralize the opening episode, the person who is said to be in bed, sleeping and dreaming, represents a young child in that initial state which philosophers call "embryo," resting in its maternal bed: that is, in its mother's belly, where it reposes and dreams of the fortune which it will experience in the world. It arises in the gracious month of May, the time of love, full of grace, when little birds sing—who signify the preachers and doctors of Holy Church, who urge us toward love of our Lord. And when the child is up, clothed, shod, and surrounded by the miseries of this world which generate cold, heat, hunger, thirst, he seeks to elude the world, evade the wind of vainglory, and avoid being soiled by the world's vile actions. He washes his hands and stitches his great sleeves, according to the usage of those times, and, joyously advancing to the song of birds, advances to a clear fountain, which is the holy fountain of baptism that descends abruptly from the high celestial mountain: this is the gentle and healthful water, wide and spacious, which extends from one end of the earth to the other. . . .

19

Clément Marot (1496–1544):
Preface to *Roman de la Rose*
(Moral Exposition)[20]

. . .I should say, first of all, that the Rose which the Lover so much desires represents the condition of wisdom, which is most appropriate to the Rose by virtue of that flower's merits, sweetnesses, and odors. . . . And, thus, the Rose is prefigured by the Papal Rose, which is composed of three things: that is, of gold, musk, and balm; for true wisdom is golden, signifying the honor and reverence which we owe to God our Creator; it is akin to musk, because of the fidelity and justice which we owe to our neighbors; and it partakes of balm with respect to ourselves, as we must hold our souls dear and precious as pure balsam, above all worldly things.

Secondly, we may interpret the Rose as the condition of grace, which is apparently difficult to obtain—not on the part of the one who gives it, for God is omnipotent, but on the part of the sinner, who is always separated from Him who gives it. This type of spiritual Rose, cool and fragrant, we may see in those Roses which enabled great Apuleius to recover his original form, as he writes in his book of the *Golden Ass*, in which he found a chaplet of roses hanging from the sistrum of Ceres, goddess of grain.[21] For even as Apuleius, who had been transformed into an ass, regained thereby his original human form and rationality, so a human sinner, converted into a brute beast by comparable irrationality, regains his first state of innocence through the grace of God, which he receives when he finds the chaplet or crown of Roses, which is to say the condition of penitence, hanging from the gentle sistrum of Ceres, which is the sweetness of divine mercy.

Thirdly, we may see in the Rose the glorious Virgin Mary,

through her gifts, joys, and perfections of grace, which I shall not pursue at present. Know that heretics cannot easily find this virginal Rose, and not only because *Male Bouche* keeps them away from its goodness, for they have spoken ill of it, wishing to stain and disparage its natural honor by claiming that we need not come before it and call it Mother of pity and mercy: for it is the white Rose which we shall find in Jericho, planted, as Solomon tells us, "like the planting of a Rose in Jericho."[22]

Fourthly, we may understand by the Rose the sovereign, infinite goodness and glory of eternal beatitude, which, as true lovers of its perpetual joy and delight, we can obtain by avoiding the vices which encumber us, and availing ourselves of the aid of the virtues, which will lead us to the garden of infinite joy, up to the Rosebush of all good and glory which is the beatific vision of God's essence. . . .

The natural Rose, then, can signify the infinite good and true celestial glory, which is not false and deceptive, like worldly glory, which deceives us to the extent that we believe it is true though it is not. Therefore, I say to whoever wishes to interpret the *Roman de la Rose* in this way, that he will find there much good, profit, and utility hidden beneath the surface of the text, which should not be disdained. For there is a double gain to be found in it: recreation of spirit and delightful pleasure with respect to the literal sense, and usefulness with respect to the moral meaning. Fables are made and contrived in order for their mystical sense to be revealed; and one should not, therefore, condemn them. . . .

20

The Collins Gloss (c. 1500–1520)[23]

3 (580)

The start of all carnal voluptuousness arises from Idleness, and because of this, Ovid says, in his book on the art of loving, "Ocia si tollas periere cupidinis Artes."[24]

4 (603)

The consequence of worldly *Deduit* is to dwell with Villainy, Hate, Poverty, and the other images painted on the wall of *Deduit*.

5 (629–42)

Note that Idleness runs after all vices, and flees all virtues, and in this way the young person enters into carnal love.

6 (722)

When the man is sated by Idleness with voluptuousness, he exults, as if stupefied in spirit, to see young girls and young men dancing, and he deems all these vanities a great glory.

7 (868–79)

By the God of Love and his garments, we should understand the voluptuous young man who wears clothes of various fashions.

8 (925)

By the five arrows of the God of Love, we should understand five temptations of the flesh, through which the young man falls into voluptuousness.

10 (1,299–1,320)

When the young man is in the worldly garden and is handsome, rich, generous, open, and devoted to the company of Lady Idleness, who governs him, he soon abandons himself to voluptuousness. As Ezechiel witnesses in his sixteenth chapter: "Hec sint iniquitas Sodonne; saturitas panis et ocium."[25]

11 (1,580)

By Narcissus, who admires himself in the mirror, should be understood the foolish, proud, voluptuous young men who admire themselves in their false vanities, which intoxicate them, and plunge into the sorrowful, deceiving darkness of the false fountain, in which they are given to taking their voluptuousnesses, which flee them and lead them on to death. And afterward, they are washed in a water called Styx, as was Narcissus. This Styx is one of the bogs of hell, and represents suffering or sorrow.

17 (1,953)

When the voluptuous young man has fallen for Base Love, he renders him homage. That is, he forsakes all virtues, even the service of God, and, having become traitor, idolator, a man of blinded understanding, he becomes a slave of created things and of vices.

18 (2,035)

After the voluptuous young man undertakes to serve Carnal Concupiscence, he is not satisfied to abase himself with his chattel and physical strength, but he also gives him his heart and declares him to be his god.

30 (3,068)

When the young man is drunk with indecent love, he repudiates all reason and all correction, for his ardent sensual concupiscence expels all law, both divine and pragmatic. Thus Boethius witnesses in

Latin, in the third book of his *Consolation*, where he speaks of Orpheus and Eurydice: "Quis legem det amantibus maior lex amor est sibi."[26]

31 (3,129)

By Friend, we may understand carnal delight, which incites and compels the man who has fallen into demented love [*amour fole*] and lost all his reason to strive toward his pleasurable but indecent end. After the man has been so incited, he hopes to find a way of approaching the one he loves, in order to have what he desires; but danger of losing her good name makes her at first hesitate. . . .

33 (3,287)

When the young girl finds herself pursued by anyone who looks respectable—her weak, feminine nature not contemplating the end result, and any preceding signs of love—she is conquered by youth, which now rules her. And because everyone is attracted to his like, she attracts the one whom she loves, and, without scruple for parents or reputation, she expels and totally rejects *Dangier*.

34 (3,386)

When access is certain, and *Dangier* has been expelled from Fair Welcome—that is, from the girl who is loved—this girl gives herself to the one she loves; and were it not for the fear of losing her chastity, she would allow him to kiss her and to pluck the rosebud—that is, she would permit him to have her virginity.

35 (3,422)

After *Dangier* is expelled from Fair Welcome—that is, from the amorous maiden, and the young man is allowed to see the rose—that is, she enjoys the company of the young man who is in love with her, by reason of her consent to lewd and lustful words, she is entirely burned by the flaming torch of Venus—that is, carnal love for him.

40 (3,778)

How Jealousy—that is, the suspicious friends of Fair Welcome, who is the young girl—puts Fair Welcome in the tower—that is, he is guarded so closely that his mother, aunt, or sister do not allow him to talk to man or woman, and keep him away from dances, social affairs, and all gatherings of young men.

48 (4,305–15)

Voluptuous desire subdues all estates: that is, it attracts all who are inclined toward disordered will, and draws them away from the true love of God.

56 (4,617)

The Lover's repudiation of the words of Reason, and his indifference to them, signifies that the voluptuous young man acknowledges no law or reason which are to him stronger than his desire to accomplish his vile scheme.

61 (5,346)

Here the voluptuous Lover replies to Reason that it is exceedingly difficult for him to leave disordered Love in order to cleave to True Love, which is true charity.

70 (5,896–5,975)

The house of Fortune is seated on a hard rock (pride and ambition), in the midst of the sea (the human heart). Two waves, ever changing, surround it (good and bad fortune). When Zephyrus, the gentle wind (worldly prosperity), makes the stars flare out (apparent riches), Bise (adversity) cuts and mows the flowers (banishes all worldly joys and wealth). From Fortune come diverse trees (rational creatures with various fortunes). One is barren (unhappy in worldly goods), the other bears fruit (has good fortune) and flourishes, but is not able to pursue its good fortune. The one tree, always without leaves, is orphaned (is deprived of fortune); the other retains its verdure (is on good terms with fortune, but never attains fortune's great goods). The one rises (that is, toward worldly goods); the other bows toward the ground (that is, is deprived of these goods). And there are several which become faded (that is, unhappy). When buds come to one, several become faded (that is, when one begins to prosper, by contrast several become wretched). There the laurel and the olive wither (every virtue and all virtuous men are unhappy). The nightingale rarely sings there (that is, there is never joy or solace), but the screech owl sings (that is, there is much fear, dread, and bad luck). From there come two rivers, good fortune and bad.

84 (6,878)

The refusal of Reason by the Lover signifies that the voluptuous young man has no care for reason or instruction, but only for the pursuit of his voluptuous desire, as he is estranged from all virtue.

86 (7,242)

When Reason leaves the Lover, Friend returns and comforts him by suggesting ways to consummate his voluptuous love. By "Friend," as was stated earlier, we should understand carnal delight. After Reason has been banished from the voluptuous Lover's understanding, his delight and disordered carnal appetite tempt and blind him very much, compelling him to come to his sin by way of various other kinds of sins.

88 (7,358)

Friend—that is, carnal delight—warns the voluptuous Lover to appease Foul Mouth (that is, those whose speech exposes foolish love) if he wishes to satisfy his disordered appetite, so that he may be better able to approach the rose (his loved one).

93 (7,712)

Other advice of Friend to the Lover: that he model himself on his loved one. This signifies that voluptuous pleasure subjects a man utterly to feminine will, in order to consummate his lust.

94 (7,866)

Friend advises the Lover to capture the castle in which is Fair Welcome, against the will of Foul Mouth and the other gatekeepers, by means of Foolish Generosity. This signifies that voluptuous desire compels a man to waste his goods, extravagantly and foolishly, in order to attain consummation of his foolish love. Through this Foolish Generosity, young girls lose their shame and fear of sin.

105 (10,332)

After Wealth has refused to allow the voluptuous Lover on the road of Give-Too-Much, the God of Love returns to him; and because he has remembered well the god's commandments, Love promises him help and sends him certain people, who come to him. This signifies that when the voluptuous Lover is unable to give presents, or to send such things to his beloved in order to attract her to voluptuousness, the God of Love (that is, ardent lust) comes again to him with these persons: which means that he must become idle, open, generous, happy, humble, handsome, a singer, a dancer; and take up all other fashionable youthful follies, in order to please her whom he loves.

106 (10,440)

By False Seeming and Constrained Abstinence, we may understand those who seem to be devout men or religious men by their appearance, but in their hearts are more sinful than worldly men. They come to Cupid to serve him: that is, they are the cause of lechery.

108 (10,689)

The way to seize the castle in which is Fair Welcome (the beautiful girl), to whom the gatekeepers deny access—that is, on account of the evil gossip which they fear, and by reason of *Dangier*, Fear and Shame, which originally are part of young persons. And for this reason the barons of the host of Love (that is, all the vices by which one falls into voluptuous love, such as Idleness, Joy, Openness, Foolish Generosity, *Deduit*, Beauty, Youth, Foolish Boldness) join together—that is, set in motion the voluptuous Lover to seize the castle holding Fair Welcome, which signifies finding a way to appease those who prevent him from fulfilling his foolish love. And the voluptuous Lover sends to Foul Mouth, the first gatekeeper (that is, those who talk about him), False Seeming and Constrained Abstinence, two personages whose garments and behavior have the appearance of piety, in order to keep him from talking further. After Foul Mouth is appeased, Courtesy and Generosity attack the Old Woman who guards Fair Welcome. This signifies that when the Lover has appeased Foul Mouth, he behaves courteously to the Old Woman who guards the beautiful girl, and corrupts her with gifts. And when the Lover has won over the Old Woman, Delight and Skillful Concealment assail Shame—that is, the Lover seduces the beautiful girl into foolish love, and promises and swears to her that he will protect her honor above all. It also signifies that the girl, who delights in seeing and hearing him, becomes emboldened and loses shame. Once Shame is conquered, there remain Fear and *Dangier*, to whom are sent Openness and Pity. This may be understood as follows: when the young girl has lost Shame, she receives the requests and gifts of the voluptuous Lover, through which she shows her pity for him—which means that she consents to his wishes.

120 (12,158)

The approach of False Seeming and Constrained Abstinence to Foul Mouth, sent by the God of Love to attack him, who, as first gatekeeper, guards Fair Welcome: this can signify that the voluptuous Lover, prevented from having access to his beloved (and devising delights and novel tricks of folly and vain love in order to fulfill his voluptuousness) by Foul Mouth, for fear of the neighbors' gossip and evil chatter, and that of the parents, sends Constrained Abstinence and False Seeming. This means that he sends some man of religion to whom he has told his story (with dissimulation and the false appearance of charity, as well as the pretence of humble dress and behavior, pretending while he is with them to be living like St. John the Baptist) to chastise their sinful tongues and preach to them feigned words and parables, in order to suppress the gossip so that the Lover may achieve his ends.

121 (12,375)

After Constrained Abstinence and False Seeming have preached to Foul Mouth, False Seeming confesses him, and in so doing he cuts off his tongue with a knife. By this we may understand that after the "religious" man, who has been sent to neighbors or parents by the voluptuous Lover, has admonished them about their tongues, he obliges them to confess, and while they confess he cuts their tongues—that is, he gives them as penance the prohibition against ever talking about the Lover, no matter what they see, as if everything were for the best.

122 (12,451)

When False Seeming has cut Foul Mouth's tongue, he enters through the gate, accompanied by Courtesy and Generosity. They approach the Old Woman who guards Fair Welcome, and False Seeming gives her a chaplet for Fair Welcome. This signifies that when the feigned and hypocritical religious has appeased the evil tongues, as we have said, with regard to the approach of the volup-tuous Lover to the beautiful girl, then he comes with gifts to the woman who guards this girl, and persuades her that love is good; and, giving her hope of profit, tells her that she will be committing a great sin in preventing their access, and that she need have no suspi-cions for he has already suppressed all bad talk and defamatory tongues. . . .

126 (12,794)

When the young girl has taken the Lover's chaplet from the Old Woman, and this woman has conveyed to her the Lover's love, as do many such women, who, having been lewd in their youth, are glad to make others like themselves—this Old Woman, well instructed in the theory of lewdness, and also following her own nature (for as Ovid says, at the beginning of his book on the art of love, women know the art of love by nature),[27] shows her all the tricks and dodges which clever, amorous girls play on their deluded lovers.

134 (14,771)

After Fair Welcome has received the Lover, through the media-tion of the Old Woman, and Fair Welcome (that is, the beautiful girl) gives herself honorably to him, which is the pretext of amorous young-girls, the Lover wishing to take the rose (the girl), for the sweet offer which she had made to him, and to have his pleasure with her—there appear *Dangier*, Fear, and Shame, who prohibit the Lover from touching her. That is to say, the amorous young girl—at first for fear of her friends, and shame of being defamed by losing her virginity—becomes angry and pretends to be troubled, repudiating the Lover with various words and allegations of resistance. . . .

135 (15,077)

At the time of the repudiation of the Lover of Fair Welcome by *Dangier*, Shame, and Fear, the God of Love comes with all his host to help the Lover. That is, when the amorous young girl, on account of the resistance and fear of her friends, and because of the shame and bad name with which she fears to be besmirched, rejects her beloved, the God of Love comes with all his host (that is, the carnal love which she has for her beloved)—Youth, Foolish Pity, Fleshly Delectation, Idleness, remembrance of the Lover's great Generosity—and urges her to forget and ignore Fear and Shame.

141 (15,762)

The coming of Venus to the siege, through the appeal of her son, Love. Once again they besiege the castle in which is Fair Welcome. That is, when the Lover has pursued his beloved to the point where, if not for fear of her friends, he would be ready to have his pleasure with her, she, moved by foolish love, falls into carnal delight by an affection of her will; and when her Lover assaults her—that is, implores her—Fear defends her with little wands taken from the garden of *Dangier* (that is, expressions of the fear of her parents).

158 (19,437)

The arrival of Genius among the host of Love: this can be taken to mean that in disordered love, Genius, who represents joy in engendering, is responsible for the consummation of libidinous love.

162 (19,941)

In this chapter Genius urges that one should do one's best to enter the park of the Lamb and be among the ewes whose shepherd has the white fleece, and wishes these ewes to be clothed like himself. This means that we must purge ourselves through confession in order to have the robe of innocence, as does the blessed Son of God; the ewes are the elect, the park of the Lamb is paradise, where there is no night, no past and no future.

166 (20,249)

The difference between the heavenly park—that is, paradise—and the garden of *Deduit*, where Idleness is gatekeeper—that is, the garden of worldly vanities.

167 (20,317)

Note that the things in the garden of *Deduit* are all fraudulent, mortal, and corruptible.

175 (20,638)

Genius's candle and flame represent carnal pleasure, to which all men and women, according to their nature, are drawn, and to which they are subject.

178 (20,766)

Venus throws a burning torch at Shame and Fear: that is, lechery and the carnal pleasure of amorous women banish shame and the fear of God, of friends, and of the world, so that sin may be accomplished. The natural lechery of women (*luxuria mulieris in umbilico*).

180 (21,237)

When the fiery torches are thrown into the castle by Venus, *Dangier*, Shame, and Fear flee the burning castle. That is, when the girl or woman is burned with carnal love, she cares nothing of the fear of God, nor of her friends, nor of shame before God or the world, if only she may satisfy her disordered will; and she has no concern for the evils or great dangers which may come. The poor sinner is burned by voluptuousness, and is deprived of all reason and virtue.

181 (21,288)

After Fear and Shame have left the [burning] tower, Courtesy, Openness, and Pity come to Fair Welcome, and beg him not to allow himself to be burned up, but to give the Lover what he asks. That is, after the amorous young girl has been burned by voluptuousness, having lost both fear and shame, she abandons herself voluntarily to foolish and dishonorable love.

21

Lenglet du Fresnoy:
Preface to *Roman de la Rose* (1735)[28]

Our ancestors had such a high estimation of the *Roman de la Rose* that we would be lacking in respect, or guilty of gross ingratitude, if we did not do the same. The number of manuscripts, which is greater even than that of the printed editions, reveals clearly that this was the book of our fathers; and if its language were not so different from our own—less refined, even somewhat affected—this might also be the book of our children. I can say, however, that it has never been entirely neglected. Knowledgeable persons have long recognized that one cannot wholly understand our language unless one puts this work at the head of one's reading list. I will say, further, that I regard the *Roman* not only as our Ennius, as Clément Marot asserted, but also as our Homer. . . .

Guillaume de Lorris, who started the poem, was from the little town in Gâtinais whose name he bears. . . . His work . . . displays the accomplishment of his talent. We find there not only a fluent ver-sification, but also (taking into account the age) a charming and learnedly diverse imagination, expressing feelings, manners, and ideas. We must not, however, suppose that we shall find there that elevation, enthusiasm, or refinement which the sixteenth century sought to recapture for French poetry by imitating the ancients, and which reached their perfection only in the seventeenth. We will find, rather, a kind of expression which is simpler and more of a piece: there is, indeed, in the *Roman* a uniformity which comes very near to monotony. But we must excuse this, in view of the character of its age, whose simplicity is well depicted in the works of our ancestors.

Jean de Meung, surnamed *Clopinel* because of a defect in one of his legs, came after, and brought the *Roman* to its end—I should say even to its perfection. He had more vivacity than Guillaume de Lorris; he was as good a poet, but knew less of manners and feelings than his predecessor. He had the opportunity to continue a beautiful poem which had fallen into his hands, and he did this with such success that this book, the oracle of our fathers, is still today enjoyed by persons of discrimination who have the time to read it and the ability to understand it. . . .

The Lover's object of enjoying the Rose, which is his chief aim, leads him to hear and follow all the advice of the God of Love, all the consolation which his Friend gives him, and the methods which an experienced Old Woman suggests to him. He seeks to overcome the obstacles and perils which Love, in order to test lovers' constancy, puts in his way. Neither the wise counsels of Reason, nor the murmurs of Jealousy, nor the impediments which are put before him by all the enemies whom fate opposes to his desires, prevent him from following his plan. The greater his difficulties, the greater his ardor. . . . If this were a refined love, leading to a meeting of spirits, a union of hearts, we would have to admire such praiseworthy efforts. (I might myself feel this way, though with some reserve.) But it is nothing like that: scarcely has he consummated his desires but he abandons this mistress for whom he has done so much, and who has done so much for him. He has a lively recollection of the pleasures which he has enjoyed with her, and even evokes their memory with some satisfaction; but he knows nothing of what has happened to her since he left her to what I dare say was an unpleasant fate. We see this only too abundantly wherever he speaks of these physical pleasures, which nearly always cause the shipwreck of impetuous love affairs.

Nevertheless, that is not to say that we do not find in the *Roman* the laws of love that is tender and delicate, the passion of beautiful souls who know no true good save loving. He has even given us their maxims in more than one place. But as he has depicted too violent a lover to be controlled by such noble ideas, he is obliged to fall back often on that physical love toward which nature only too often inclines. . . .

Satire is not less conspicuous in this *Roman* than love; it is perhaps even more judiciously treated than that passion. The poem quickly turns to the defects of the sex, which it exaggerates a bit too strongly, and in terms which have properly been cause for reproach; sometimes it addresses the difference between lovers' conduct before and after marriage; sometimes it attacks the licentiousness of the cloister, where chastity itself is not secure; and I may say that (under royal sovereignty) it dares paint a rather bold picture of how peoples acquire kings. After having taken up the simple, natural life of primitive men, it shows us the dissensions and evils brought by property and the division of goods. . . .

Our fathers always wished to season their happiest works with a dash of morality. They did not take the trouble to give us those delicate nuances of morals which the ancients have taught us to insert gently into our writings; they preferred sermons rendered tiresome by tedious length and trivial maxims. We always know what they are going to say before they have even said it. There is a specimen of this at the very beginning of the *Roman*; but, happily, it is not sustained to the point of disgusting us. The author allows us to glimpse what he might do, but he has the discretion not to condemn us entirely to the taste of his century.

There are two kinds of morality in the *Roman*. The first, the more ingenious, is concealed in the structure of his work, and cannot be perceived until we have finished reading it. I have already pointed out that he depicts a young man seduced by purely external graces, and who gives himself to the most irrational kind of love. He is uneasy, agitated, unquiet; he seeks ways to satisfy himself; he is frustrated; but he is only the more trapped by Love. He gives himself to this divinity; he listens to his laws and observes them; he hopes for solace and receives only disappointment. Reason appears, hoping to dissuade him from loving. Wise as she is, she cannot make herself heard by youth predisposed to *fol amour*. . . . His insurmountable difficulties lead him to beg help of the forces of the God of Love, who assembles them all on his behalf. What an effort is needed! But finally he arrives at his goal. . . . All these troubles, pains, questions asked, counsels heard, disappointments experienced, unhappiness endured—all lead to a single instant of pleasure. One wakens immediately from this lethargy; hardly has one reflected upon one's moment of joy when memories of the long, exhausting pains come crowding back. This is the basis of the morality contained in this *Roman*, and which is revealed in the last two verses only, to those who know to look for them. . . .

There is another morality in this work, sown in the form of maxims. Some of these, simply expressed but delicately conceived, would still do honor today to those who might express them with a fittingly sage and noble elegance. Is there anything in the old simplicity of our language more ingeniously, wisely conceived than what is said of the justice rendered by Wealth to misers, of the vengeance which she extracts from them, on account of the captivity which they have imposed upon her (by nature a sociable and friendly lady)? . . .

Finally . . . apart from morality, we find in this *Roman* a delicacy of manners which does honor to our nation, inasmuch as we achieved it more than four centuries before our neighbors were able to do so. There are likewise strokes of politics, characterization, portraits, maxims, rules of conduct, philosophical truths, feelings; and all this makes us recognize how right they were to regard this book, in its own time, as an essential work for the practise of civilized life, for there are few books of that time in which we find such a great variety of necessary, useful, and agreeable things. . . .

This is, then, a romance [*roman*], but it is not written with the design prescribed by the rules of art. It is, indeed, also a poem, though it has nothing of what we call "heroic." We have, however, given it the name of poem because it is composed in measured and rhyming verses, and poetry as such requires no more. It is a romance because it presents a contrived and imagined story, as much for the sake of turning us away from love as giving us its rules. But the work has nothing of the sort that one seeks today in such productions: that is to say, a foundation of verisimilitude which would lead us sometimes to believe, or at least wish, that everything in it were true. What is marvellous here is absurd; but the absurdity does not cease to be instructive. Yet we must excuse our fathers; they could not do better. There is, nevertheless, a certain order in this romance. Things always happen by degrees, and with a kind of proportion. Thus, the real conclusion does not appear in the beginning of the work, as in such things as *Amadis*; there is a more natural, better delineated order, for the more progress the Lover makes, the more entangled he becomes as he heads toward the real conclusion, which comes only at the end of the work.

The *Roman* is filled with incidents, some of which are quite ingeniously related to the subject, but others of which are thrown in for heaven knows what reason. The stories, above all, are disposed so curiously that any other place than the one which they occupy would seem to be equally suitable.

221

FIVE

Select Research Bibliography

We have not tried to embrace in this bibliography everything that has been published on the *Roman*: that would be both impossible and pointless. We have tried, however, to include—together with many lesser items—everything of primary value, as well as bibliographical tools which can lead readers to the rest. Materials of exceptional importance are identified by asterisks.

The entries are gathered into eleven sections: bibliographies and concordances; scholarship on manuscripts of the *Roman de la Rose*; French printed editions (arranged chronologically), eighteenth century to the present; French modernizations; translations; scholarship and criticism before the twentieth century; scholarship and criticism of the twentieth century; materials and scholarship relating to the Quarrel; ancillary materials for study of the *Roman*; *Romaunt of the Rose*; Chaucer's relation to the *Roman de la Rose*.

22

Bibliographies and Concordances

[Roman de la Rose]

Batany, Jean. *Approches du Roman de la Rose*. Paris, 1974. Contains useful annotated bibliography, though there are misprints, and the reader should use with care.

* Bossuat, Robert. *Manuel Bibliographique de la Littérature Française du Moyen Age*. Melun, 1951.

* ———. *Supplément (1949–1953)*. Paris, 1955.

* ———. *Second Supplément (1954–1960)*. Paris, 1961.

* Dahlberg, Charles, trans. *The Romance of the Rose*. Princeton, 1971. Contains extensive bibliography, especially rich in related cultural materials.

Dahlberg, Charles, and Gunn, Alan M. F. "*Rose* Scholarship, 1970–73." *Encomia* 1, no. 2 (1976): 8A–8J.

Danos, Joseph R. *A Concordance to the Roman de la Rose of Guillaume de Lorris*. Chapel Hill, 1975. Professor Danos has completed a concordance to Jean de Meun's part of the poem, which is to be published in the near future.

Encomia. Publishes each spring an international bibliography of scholarship in courtly literature, starting spring 1976 for 1974.

* Gunn, Alan M. F. *The Mirror of Love*. Lubbock, Texas, 1952. Contains very extensive bibliography, which seeks "proximate completeness." Sections on "Studies in the Rhetoric of *Amplificatio*" (pp. 529–31) and "Literary, Philosophical, and Cultural Context" (pp. 531–44) are especially valuable.

* Holmes, Urban T., Jr., ed. *A Critical Bibliography of French Literature: Vol. I: The Mediaeval Period*. 2d ed. Syracuse, 1952.

226

* Jung, Marc-René. "Der *Rosenroman* in der Kritik seit dem 18. Jahrhundert." *Romanische Forschungen* 78 (1966): 203–52.

Klapp, Otto. *Bibliographie der Französischen Literaturwissenschaft.* Frankfurt-am-Main, 1960– . An annual bibliography, starting with 1956.

Knudson, Charles, and Misrahi, Jean. "French Medieval Literature." In *The Medieval Literature of Western Europe: A Review of Research, Mainly 1930–1960,* edited by John Fisher. New York, 1966.

* *MLA International Bibliography of Books and Articles on the Modern Languages and Literatures.* An annual bibliography, 1956–.

* Ott, Karl A., ed. and trans. *Der Rosenroman.* 3 vols. Munich, 1976–79. There is an excellent bibliography, 3:1158–74.

Poirion, Daniel. *Le Roman de la Rose.* Paris, 1973. Contains a partially annotated bibliography (pp. 208–14).

[*Romaunt of the Rose* and Chaucer's Relation to the *Roman*]

Baird, L. Y. *A Bibliography of Chaucer, 1964–1973.* Boston, 1977.

Crawford, William R. *Bibliography of Chaucer 1954–1963.* Seattle, 1967.

Griffith, D. D. *Bibliography of Chaucer 1908–1953.* Seattle, 1955.

Hammond, E. P. *Chaucer: A Bibliographical Manual.* New York, 1908.

* *MLA International Bibliography of Books and Articles on the Modern Languages and Literatures.* An annual bibliography, 1956–.

Studies in the Age of Chaucer: Yearbook of the New Chaucer Society. Annotated Chaucer bibliography, starting with 1975 in Vol. 1 (1979).

Tatlock, J. S. P., and Kennedy, A. G., *A Concordance to the Complete Works of Geoffrey Chaucer and to the Romaunt of the Rose.* Washington, D.C., 1927.

23

Scholarship on Manuscripts of the
Roman de la Rose

Dean, R. J. "Un Manuscrit du *Roman de la Rose* à Jersey." *Romania* 65 (1939): 233–37.

Dorgan, C. W. "Notes on Rare Books and Manuscripts: *Le Roman de la Rose.*" *Boston Public Library Quarterly* 6 (1954): 58–61.

Ewert, A. "Two Fragments of the *Roman de la Rose.*" MLR 26 (1931): 182–87.

Fawtier, R. "Deux Manuscrits du *Roman de la Rose.*" *Romania* 58 (1932): 265–73.

Fourez, Lucien. "Le *Roman de la Rose* de la Bibliothèque de la Ville de Tournai." *Scriptorium* 1 (1946–47): 213–39.

Ham, E. B. "The Cheltenham Manuscripts of the *Roman de la Rose.*" MLR 26 (1931): 427–35.

Hawkins, R. L. "The Manuscripts of the *Roman de la Rose* in the Libraries of Harvard and Yale Universities." *Romanic Review* 19 (1928): 1–24.

Jung, Marc-René. "Ein Fragment des *Rosenromans* in der Stiftsbibliothek Engelberg." *Vox Romanica* 24 (1965): 234–37.

* Kuhn, Alfred. "Die Illustration des *Rosenromans.*" *Jahrbuch der Kunsthistorischen Sammlungen der Allerhöchsten Kaiserhauses* 31 (1913–14): 1–66.

* Langlois, Ernest. *Les Manuscrits du Roman de la Rose: Description et Classement.* 1910. Reprint. Geneva, 1974. This standard monograph should be supplemented by Langlois's remarks in his edition of the *Roman*, 1:48–55.

* Lecoy, Félix, ed. *Le Roman de la Rose.* 3 vols. Paris, 1965–70. Lecoy discusses the MSS in 1:xxxv–xliii.

* Luria, Maxwell. "A Sixteenth-Century Gloss on the *Roman de la*

Rose." Mediaeval Studies 44 (1982). An annotated text of the Collins gloss in the Philadelphia Museum of Art (see pp. 72–73, 207–17 above).

Monnier, P. "*Le Roman de la Rose* (Manuscript Fragment 178)." *Librarium* 2 (1968): 125–36.

Pickford, Cedric E. "The *Roman de la Rose* and a Treatise Attributed to Richard de Fournival: Two Manuscripts in the John Rylands Library." *Bulletin of the John Rylands Library* 34 (1952): 333–65.

Roques, M. "Fragments de Manuscrits du *Roman de la Rose*." *Romania* 55 (1929): 263–65.

Ruggieri, J. "Uno Sconosciuto Frammento del *Roman de la Rose*." *Archivum Romanicum* 9 (1930): 417–36.

Samaran, C. "Fragments de Manuscrits." *Romania* 76 (1955): 241–43.

Vitale-Brovarone, A. "Un Nuovo Frammento del *Roman de la Rose*." *Studi Francesi* 60 (1976): 497–98.

See also "Scholarship and Criticism of the Twentieth Century": Dahlberg 1971, Fleming 1969, Robertson 1962, and Tuve.

24

French Printed Editions (Arranged Chronologically), Eighteenth Century to the Present†

Lenglet du Fresnoy, l'Abbé N., ed. *Le Roman de la Rose, par Guillaume de Lorris et Jean de Meun dit Clopinel. Revu sur plusieurs éditions et sur quelques anciens manuscrits. Accompagné de plusieurs autres ouvrages, d'une préface historique, de notes et d'un glossaire.* 3 vols. Paris, 1735. The edition was also published at Amsterdam in the same year.

———. *Le Roman de la Rose par Guillaume de Lorris et Jean de Meung dit Clopinel, édition faite sur celle de Lenglet Dufresnoy, corrigée avec soin et enrichie de la dissertation sur les auteurs de l'ouvrage, de l'analyse, des variantes et du glossaire publiés en 1737 par J. B. Lantin de Damerey.* 5 vols. Paris, 1798.

* Méon, M., ed. *Le Roman de la Rose par Guillaume de Lorris et Jehan de Meung: Nouvelle Edition, Revue et Corrigée sur les Meilleurs et Plus Anciens Manuscrits, par M. Méon.* 4 vols. Paris, 1814. Reprint (with introduction by D. Poirion). Paris, 1973.

Michel, Francisque, ed. *Le Roman de la Rose, par Guillaume de Lorris et Jean de Meung. Nouvelle édition revue et corrigée.* 2 vols. Paris, 1864.

Croissandeau, J. [Pierre Marteau], ed. *Le Roman de la Rose. Edition accompagnée d'une traduction en vers, précédée d'une introduction, notices historiques et critiques, suivie de notes et d'un glossaire.* 4 vols. Orleans, 1878–79. 5 vols. Paris, 1878–80.

* Langlois, Ernest, ed. *Le Roman de la Rose, par Guillaume de Lorris et Jean de Meun, Publié d'Après les Manuscrits.* 5 vols. Paris,

---

†For listing and description of earlier French editions, see chapter two, "Manuscripts, Editions, and Translations."

1914–24. One of the two standard texts (together with Lecoy).

Cohen, Gustave, ed. *Le Roman de la Rose.* Paris, 1929. Reprint. Paris, 1973. A text with commentary and bibliographical references.

Thuasne, Louis, ed. *Le Roman de La Rose.* Paris, 1929.

Linker, R. W., ed. *Li Romanz de la Rose.* Chapel Hill, 1937. Guillaume's section only.

* Lecoy, Félix, ed. *Le Roman de la Rose par Guillaume de Lorris et Jean de Meun.* 3 vols. Paris, 1965–70. One of the two standard texts (together with Langlois).

Poirion, Daniel, ed. *Le Roman de la Rose; Chronologie et établissement du texte par Daniel Poirion.* Paris, 1974. Text based on MS B.N. fr. 25523. See review article by Eric Hicks, "De l'Histoire Littéraire comme Cosmogonie." *Critique* 32 (1976): 510–19.

25

French Modernizations

Baridon, Silvio, ed. *Le Roman de la Rose par Guillaume de Lorris et Jean de Meung. Dans la version attribuée à Clément Marot.* 2 vols. Milan, 1954–57. An early sixteenth-century verse modernization by a distinguished poet. For a discussion of this and other early redactions in French, see pp. 60, 69–72 above.

Croissandeau, J. [Pierre Marteau], ed. *Le Roman de la Rose. Edition accompagnée d'une traduction en vers, précédée d'une introduction, notices historiques et critiques, suivie de notes et d'un glossaire.* 4 vols. Orleans, 1878–79. 5 vols. Paris, 1878–80. Croissandeau's verse translation was reprinted, Paris, 1965.

Gorce, M. M., ed. *Le Roman de la Rose. Texte essentiel de la scolastique courtoise préfacé et commenté.* Paris, 1933. Extracts slightly modernized, with a valuable commentary.

Goublet, Juliette, trans. *Roman de la Rose d'après Guillaume de Lorris.* Paris, 1963.

Huard, Etienne, trans. *Le Roman de la Rose, traduction libre et en vers.* Paris, 1835.

* Lanly, André, trans. *Le Roman de la Rose, traduction en français moderne.* 3 vols. Paris, 1971–76. The most reliable French modernization.

Mary, André, trans. *Le Roman de la Rose mis en français moderne.* 1928. Reprint. Paris, 1960. A prose translation with many passages omitted or summarized, intended for wide readership.

Vertut, Georges, ed. *Le Roman de la Rose, par Guillaume de Lorris et Jean de Meung. Renouvelé par Georges Vertut.* Paris, 1956. A modernized text, accompanied by illustrations from an early printed edition.

26

Translations

Battaglia, Salvatore, ed. *Le Roman de la Rose. Testo, versione, introduzione e glossario.* Naples, 1947. Contains the original text together with a good Italian translation.

Cipriani, Lisi, trans. *Selections from the Romance of the Rose.* Urbana, Ill., 1906.

* Dahlberg, Charles, trans. *The Romance of the Rose by Guillaume de Lorris and Jean de Meun.* Princeton, 1971. An excellent prose translation, accurate and readable. See review by M. A. Grellner in *Medium Aevum* 42 (1973): 69–73.

Ellis, Frederick Startridge, trans. *The Romance of the Rose by W. Lorris and J. Clopinel.* 3 vols. 1900. Reprint. New York, 1975. The first nearly complete English version (Ellis refused to translate the scabrous ending), now of historical interest only; the tetrameter couplets provide a very free and inexact rendering of the original.

Fährmann, Heinrich, trans. *Das Gedicht von der Rose.* Berlin, 1839. The first German translation.

Gregor, J., trans. *Der Roman von der Rose.* Vienna, 1921. Contains commentary of Emil Winkler and illustrations from MS Vienna, National Library of Austria, Cod. 2592.

Ineichen, G., trans. *Der Rosenroman.* Berlin, 1967.

Ott, Karl A., ed. and trans. *Der Rosenroman.* 3 vols. Munich, 1976–79. Contains French text and German translation on facing pages. Vol. 1 has a long introduction which surveys critical issues.

Robbins, Harry W., trans. *Le Roman de la Rose.* New York, 1962. In serviceable but freely rendered blank verse. Better than Ellis, inferior to Dahlberg (especially for readers who require scholarly exactness.).

Sutherland, Ronald, ed. *The Romaunt of the Rose and the Roman de la Rose: A Parallel-Text Edition*. Oxford, 1967. See chapter thirty-one for other editions of the *Romaunt*.

Teza, E., trans. *Dal Romanzo della Rosa, di Guglielmo de Lorris*. Padua, 1896.

Vervijs, Eelco, ed. *Die Rose van Einric van Aken, met de Fragmenten der twede Vertaling*. The Hague, 1868. An edition of the two Dutch translations of the late thirteenth or early fourteenth century.

27

Scholarship and Criticism Before the Twentieth Century

Ampère, J. J. "Poésie du Moyen-Age: *Le Roman de la Rose.*" *Revue des Deux Mondes* 3 (1843): 441–73, 574–81.

Bouhours, Père Dominique, S. J. *Les Entretiens d'Ariste et d'Eugène.* Paris, 1671.

Cénac-Moncaut, J. E. M. *Les Jardins du Roman de la Rose Comparés avec ceux des Romains et ceux du Moyen Age.* Paris, 1869.

Goujet, Abbé Claude-Pierre. *Bibliothèque Françoise ou Histoire de la Littérature Françoise.* Paris, 1745. See 9: 26–71.

Guillon, Félix. *Etude Historique et Biographique sur Guillaume de Lorris, Auteur du Roman de la Rose, d'après Documents Inédits et Revision Critique des Textes des Auteurs.* Orleans, 1881.

Hanscom, Elizabeth D. "The Allegory of De Lorris's *Roman de la Rose.*" *MLN* 8 (1893): 151–53.

Heinrich, Fritz. *Über den Stil von Guillaume de Lorris und Jean de Meung.* Ausgaben und Abhandlungen aus dem Gebiete der Romanischen Philologie, vol. 29. Marburg, 1885.

Huot, Paul. *Etude sur le Roman de la Rose.* Orleans, 1853.

Joret, Charles. *La Rose dans l'Antiquité et au Moyen Age.* Paris, 1892.

* Langlois, Ernest. *Origines et Sources du Roman de la Rose.* Paris, 1891. Should be supplemented by the introduction and notes in Langlois's edition of the *Roman.*

———. "Le Roman de la Rose." In *Histoire de la Langue et la Littérature Française*, edited by L. Petit de Julleville, 2:105–61. Paris, 1896.

Lanson, Gustave. "Un Naturaliste du XIIIe Siècle: Jean de

Lanson, Gustave. "Un Naturaliste du XIIIe Siècle: Jean de Meung." *Revue Bleue Politique et Littéraire* 2 (1894): 34–41.

* Lantin de Damerey, J. B. *Supplément au Glossaire du Roman de la Rose, Contenant des Notes Critiques, une Dissertation sur les Auteurs, l'Analyse de ce Poème, un Discours sur l'Utilité des Glossaires, les Variantes Restituées sur un MS. de M. le Président Bouhier de Savigny, et une Table des Auteurs Cités dans cet Ouvrage.* Dijon, 1737. Important eighteenth-century commentary.

Lenient, C. *La Satire en France au Moyen Age.* Paris, 1859. 4th ed. Paris, 1893.

Massieu, Abbé Guillaume. *Histoire de la Poésie Françoise.* Paris, 1739. See pp. 165–70, 179–206.

Nisard, D. *Histoire de la Littérature Française.* Paris, 1867. See 1: 160–91.

* Paris, Gaston. "*Roman de la Rose.*" *La Littérature Française au Moyen Age (XIe–XIVe Siècle). Paris,* 1888.

* Paris, Paulin. "*Roman de la Rose.*" *Histoire Littéraire de la France.* Paris, 1856. 23: 1–61.

Paulmy, Antoine René, Marquis de. "De la Lecture des Livres François Considérée comme Amusement." *Mélanges Tirés d'une Grande Bibliothèque.* Paris, 1780. 4: 9–18, 51–55.

Püschel, R. *Li Romanz de la Rose, Première Partie par Guillaume de Lorris.* Berlin, 1872.

Saint-Evremond, Charles de. "Sur le *Roman de la Rose.*" In *Oeuvres de M. de Saint-Evremond,* edited by Des Maizeaux. New edition. London, 1711.

Sorel, Charles. *La Bibliothèque Françoise.* Paris, 1664. See pp. 222–23.

See also "Materials and Scholarship Relating to the Quarrel": Piaget.

28

Scholarship and Criticism of the Twentieth Century†

Adler, A. "The Topos *Quinque Lineae Sunt Amoris* Used by Ronsard in *Amours* (1552), CXXXVI." *Bibliothèque d'Humanisme et Renaissance* 15, no. 2 (1953): 220–25.

Badel, Pierre-Yves. *Introduction à la Vie Littéraire au Moyen Age.* Paris, 1969.

———. "Pierre d'Ailly, Auteur du *Jardin Amoureux.*" *Romania* 97 (1976): 369–81.

———. "Raison, 'fille de Dieu,' et le Rationalisme de Jean de Meun." *Mélanges de Langue et de Littérature du Moyen Age et de la Renaisssance, Offerts à Jean Frappier.* Geneva, 1970. See pp. 40–52.

Baker, David Jeffrey. "Allegory and Exegesis in Jean de Meun's *Roman de la Rose.*" Ph.D. dissertation, Yale University, 1978.

Baker, Denise N. "The Priesthood of Genius: A Study of the Medieval Tradition." *Speculum* 51 (1976): 277–91.

Bargreen, Melinda L. "The Author in his Work: The Priest/Pupil Narrative Topos." Ph.D. dissertation, University of California, Irvine, 1972. Treats Ovid, Andreas, Guillaume, Jean, Gower, and Chaucer.

* Barney, Stephen A. *Allegories of History, Allegories of Love.* Hamden, Conn., 1979. Chapter 6 treats the *Roman.* See also chapter 1 (on allegory) and chapter 2 (on Prudentius), and the valuable bibliographical notes.

Batany, Jean. *Approches du Roman de la Rose.* Paris, 1974. A student's guide, which surveys *Roman*'s place in the history of love

†Publications concerned with the Quarrel are listed in chapter twenty-nine.

poetry, allegory, and marriage satire.

———. "Paradigmes Lexicaux et Structures Littéraires au Moyen Age." *Revue d'Histoire Littéraire de la France* 70 (1970): 819-35.

Battaglia, Salvatore. "Il *Roman de la Rose* di Guillaume de Lorris." *La Cosciènza Letteraria del Medioevo*. Naples, 1965. See pp. 417-34.

Baumgartner, E. "De Lucrèce à Héloïse; Remarques sur Deux Exemples du *Roman de la Rose* de Jean de Meun." *Romania* 95 (1974): 433-42.

Beltran, L. "La Vielle's Past." *Romanische Forschungen* 84 (1972): 77-96.

* Benedetto, Luigi Foscolo. *Il Roman de la Rose e la Letteratura Italiana*. Halle, 1910.

———. "Per la Cronologia del *Roman de la Rose*." *Atti della R. Accademia delle Scienze di Torino* 44 (1909): 471-87.

Bossuat, Robert. *Histoire de la Littérature Française*. edited by J. Calvet. Vol. 1, *Le Moyen Age*. Rev. ed. Paris, 1955. See pp. 195-202.

Bouché, Thomas. "Ovide et Jean de Meun." *Le Moyen Age* 83 (1977): 71-87.

* Bourdillon, F. W. *The Early Editions of the Roman de la Rose*. London, 1906. The standard monograph on this subject. (Appended to this work is a "supplementary note": *A Verard Fragment of the Roman de la Rose*. London, 1913.)

Bourneuf, A. *"Le Testament* of Jean de Meun." Ph.D. dissertation, Fordham University, 1956.

Brumble, Herbert D. "Genius and Other Related Allegorical Figures in the *De Planctu Naturae*, the *Roman de la Rose*, the *Confessio Amantis*, and the *Faerie Queene*." Ph.D. dissertation, University of Nebraska, 1970.

Brüning, Detlef. *Clement Marots Bearbeitung des Rosenromans (1526): Studien zur Rezeption des Rosenromans im frühen sechzehnten Jahrhundert*. Berlin, 1972.

Burchardt, A. *Beiträge zur Kenntnis der französischen Gesellschaft in der zweiten Halfe des XIII. Jahrhunderts auf Grund der Werke Rutebeufs, des Roman de la Rose, des Renart le Nouvel, und des Couronnement Renart*. Coburg, 1910.

Butturff, Diane, and Butturff, Douglas. *"Le Roman de la Rose* and the Sophistry of Love." *The French Review*, special no. 3 (fall

1971): 52–58.

Chamard, Henri. *Les Origines de la Poésie Française de la Renaissance.* 1920. Reprint. Geneva, 1973.

Cherniss, Michael D. "Irony and Authority: The Ending of the *Roman de la Rose.*" MLQ 36 (1975): 227–38.

———. "Jean de Meun's *Reson* and Boethius." *Romance Notes* 16 (1975): 678–85.

Cocito, L. "La 'Fontanne de Benimor' et la 'Fontaine d'Amour.'" *Convivium* 35 (1967): 227–30.

* Cohen, Gustave. *"Le Roman de la Rose." Tableau de la Littérature Française* 1 (1962): 89–101.

Cohn, Norman. *The World-View of a Thirteenth-Century Parisian Intellectual: Jean de Meun and the Roman de la Rose.* Durham, N.C., 1961.

Contini, Gianfranco. "Un Nodo della Cultura Medievale: la Serie *Roman de la Rose, Fiore, Divina Commedia.*" *Lettere Italiane* 25 (1973): 162–89.

Coville, Alfred. *Recherches sur Quelques Ecrivains du XIVᵉ et du XVᵉ Siècle.* Paris, 1935. See pp. 129–74.

Curtius, Ernst Robert. *European Literature and the Latin Middle Ages.* Translated by Willard R. Trask. New York, 1953. See especially chapter 6.

———. "Natura Mater Generationis." *Zeitschrift für Romanische Philologie* 58 (1938): 180–97.

Dahlberg, Charles. "First Person and Personification in the *Roman de la Rose:* Amant and Dangier." *Mediaevalia* 3 (1977): 37–58.

* ———. "Love and the *Roman de la Rose.*" *Speculum* 44 (1969): 568–84.

* ———. "Macrobius and the Unity of the *Roman de la Rose.*" SP 58 (1961): 573–82.

* ———, trans. *The Romance of the Rose by Guillaume de Lorris and Jean de Meun.* Princeton, 1971. Contains valuable introduction and notes, as well as copious illustrations from MSS.

Defourney, Michel. "Observations sur la Première Partie du *Roman de la Rose.*" In *Mélanges Offerts à Rita Lejeune.* 2:1163–69, Gembloux, 1969.

* ———. "Le *Roman de la Rose* à travers l'Histoire et la Philosophie." *Marche Romane* 17 (1967): 53–60.

Demats, P. "D'Amoenitas à Deduit: André le Chapelain et Guillaume de Lorris." In *Mélanges de Langue et de Littérature du Moyen Age et de la Renaissance, Offerts à Jean Frappier*, 2 vols., pp. 217–33. Geneva, 1970.

Denkinger, T. "Die Bettelorden in der französischen didaktischen Literatur des 13. Jahrhunderts, besonders bei Rutebeuf und im *Roman de la Rose.*" *Franziskanische Studien* 2 (1915): 286–313.

Di Stefano, Giuseppe. "Situation de la *Rose.*" In *Mélanges Littéraires Publiés à l'Occasion du 150ᵉ Anniversaire, Université McGill de Montréal*, edited by J. Ethier-Blais et al. Montreal, 1971.

Dragonetti, R. "Pygmalion ou les Pièges de la Fiction dans le *Roman de la Rose.*" In *Orbis Mediaevalis: Mélanges de Langue et de Littérature Médiévales Offerts à Reto Raduolf Bezzola*, edited by G. Güntert et al., pp. 89–111. Berne, 1978.

———. "Le 'Singe de Nature' dans le *Roman de la Rose.*" *Travaux de Linguistique et de Littérature* 16 (1978): 149–60.

Eberle, Patricia J. "The Lovers' Glass: Nature's Discourse on Optics and the Optical Design of the *Romance of the Rose.*" *University of Toronto Quarterly* 46 (1976–77): 241–62.

Economou, George D. "The Character Genius in Alan de Lille, Jean de Meun, and John Gower." *Chaucer Review* 4 (1970): 203–10.

* ———. *The Goddess Natura in Medieval Literature*. Cambridge, Mass., 1972.

———. "The Two Venuses and Courtly Love." In *In Pursuit of Perfection: Courtly Love in Medieval Literature*, edited by Joan M. Ferrante and George D. Economou, pp. 17–50. Port Washington, N.Y., 1975.

Edelman, Nathan. *Attitudes of Seventeenth-Century France Toward the Middle Ages.* New York, 1946. See pp. 383–93 and passim.

Egbert, V. W. "Pygmalion as Sculptor." *Princeton University Library Chronicle* 28 (1966): 20–23.

Ettmayer, K. R. *Der Rosenroman (Erster Teil), Stilistiche, Grammatische, und Literarhistorische Erlaüterungen zum Studium und zur Privatlektüre des Textes.* Heidelberg, 1919.

Eusebi, M. "Saggio sulla Edizioni Cinquecentesche del *Roman de la Rose* Attribuite a Clément Marot." *Rendiconti* 92 (1958): 527–57.

Faral, Edmond. "La Littérature Allégorique et le *Roman de la Rose.*" In *Histoire de la Littérature Française*, edited by J. Bédier and Paul Hazard. Paris, 1923.

———. "Le *Roman de la Rose* et la Pensée Française au XIIIe Siècle." *Revue des Deux Mondes*, 7th Ser. 35 (September 1926): 430–57.

Fenley, G. W. "Faus-Semblant, Fauvel, and Renart le Contrefait: A Study in Kinship." *Romanic Review* 23 (1932): 323–31.

Fenzi, Enrico. "Boezio e Jean de Meun: Filosofia e Razione nelle Rime Allegorische di Dante." In *Studi di Filologia e Letterature Dedicati a Vincenzo Pernicone*. Genoa, 1975.

Fialova, M. "Les Expressions de la Laideur dans le *Roman de la Rose*." *Etudes Romanes de Brno* 5 (1971): 63–68.

* Fleming, John V. "The Moral Reputation of the *Roman de la Rose* Before 1400." *Romance Philology* 18 (1965): 430–35.

* ———. *The Roman de la Rose: A Study in Allegory and Iconography*. Princeton, 1969. A very important (though controversial) study, based on examination of the MS illustrations, and containing valuable material on cultural backgrounds. See reviews by A. Gunn in *MP* 69 (1971): 57–59; A. David in *ELN* 9 (1971): 134–39; W. Calin in *Speculum* 47 (1972): 311–13; F. L. Utley in *Medievalia et Humanistica* 3 (1972): 308–14; M. A. Grellner in *Medium Aevum* 42 (1973): 69–73; and L. J. Friedman in *Romance Philology* 28 (1975): 743–48.

Fox, John. *A Literary History of France*. Edited by P. E. Charvet. Vol. 1, *The Middle Ages*. New York, 1974. See pp. 216–24.

Francon, M. "Jean de Meun et les Origines du Naturalisme de la Renaissance." *PMLA* 59 (1944): 624–45.

———. "The *Roman de la Rose* and Vauquelin de la Fresnaie." *MLN* 68 (1953): 410–11.

Frappier, Jean. "Variations sur le Thème du Miroir, de Bernard de Ventadour à Maurice Scève." *Cahiers de l'Association Internationale des Etudes Françaises* 11 (1959): 134–58.

Freeman, M. A. "Problems in Romance Composition: Ovid, Chrétien de Troyes, and the *Romance of the Rose*." *Romance Philology* 30 (1976): 158–68.

Friedman, A. B. "Jean de Meun an Englishman?" *MLN* 65 (1950): 319–25.

* Friedman, Lionel J. "Gradus Amoris." *Romance Philology* 19 (1965): 167–77.

* ———. "Jean de Meun and Ethelred of Rievaulx." *L'Esprit Créateur* 2 (1962), 135–41.

* ———. "'Jean de Meung,' Antifeminism, and 'Bourgeois Realism.'" *MP* 57 (1959–60): 13–23.

Galpin, S. L. "Dangiers li vilains." *Romanic Review* 2 (1911): 320–22.

———. "Fortune's Wheel in the *Roman de la Rose.*" *PMLA* 24 (1909): 332–42.

———. "Geber and the *Roman de la Rose.*" *MLN* 23 (1908): 159.

———. "Influence of the Mediaeval Christian Visions on Jean de Meun's Notions of Hell." *Romanic Review* 2 (1911): 54–60.

Garvey, Sister Calixta. "The Syntax of the Declinable Words in the *Roman de la Rose.*" Washington, D.C., 1936.

George, F. W. A. "Jean de Meung and the Myth of the Golden Age." In *The Classical Tradition in French Literature: Essays Presented to R. C. Knight*, edited by H. T. Barnwell et al., pp. 31–39. Edinburgh, 1977.

Gill, R. "A Study in Traditional Elements in Middle High German Literature, with Special Reference to the *Tristan* of Gottfried von Strassburg and its Similarities with the *Roman de la Rose* of Guillaume de Lorris." Ph.D. dissertation, University of London, 1959.

Glunz, H. H. *Die Literarästhetik des Europäischen Mittelalters: Wolfram—Rosenroman—Chaucer—Dante.* 1937. Reprint. Frankfurt, 1963.

Gröber, G. "Grundriss der Roman." *Philologie* 2 (1902): 734–41.

Gros, Gaston. *L'Amour dans le Roman de la Rose.* Paris, 1925.

Guillon, F. *Jean Clopinel dit de Meung: Le Roman de la Rose Considéré comme Document Historique du Règne de Philippe le Bel.* Paris, 1903.

* Gunn, Alan M. F. *The Mirror of Love: A Reinterpretation of the Romance of the Rose.* Lubbock, Tex., 1952. An indispensable study, widely acknowledged to be one of the best works on the *Roman.* Particularly valuable for its treatment of rhetorical elements, and its appendix, "Figures of Amplification" (pp. 509–22).

———. "Teacher and Student in the *Roman de la Rose*: A Study in Archetypal Figures and Patterns." *L'Esprit Créateur* 2 (1962): 126–34.

Hall, Ellen W. "A Study of Rabelais' Thought in the Context of Jean de Meung's *Roman de la Rose.*" Ph.D. dissertation, Bryn

Mawr College, 1973.

Ham, E. B. "Régionalismes dans le *Roman de la Rose.*" *Mélanges de Linguistique Française Offerts à M. Charles Bruneau*, pp. 235–39. Geneva, 1954.

Hanson-Smith, E.A. "Be Fruitful and Multiply: the Medieval Allegory of Nature." Ph.D. dissertation, Stanford University, 1972.

* Hatzfeld, Helmut. "La Mystique Naturiste de Jean de Meun." *Wissenschaftliche Zeitschrift der Friedrich-Schiller-Universität Jena* 5 (1955–56): 259–69.

Heisig, K. "Arabische Astrologie und Christliche Apologetik im *Rosenroman.*" *Romanische Forschungen* 71 (1959): 414–19.

Hicks, Eric. "Le Visage de l'Antiquité dans le *Roman de la Rose.* Jean de Meung, Savant et Pédagogue." Ph.D dissertation, Yale University, 1965.

Hilder, Gisela. "Abu Ma'shars *Introductorium in Astronomiam* und der Altfranzösischen *Roman de la Rose.*" *Zeitschrift für Romanische Philologie* 88 (1972): 13–33.

———. *Der Scholastische Wortschatz bei Jean de Meun.* Tübingen, 1972.

Hill, Thomas. "La Vieille's Digression on Free Love: A Note on Rhetorical Structure in the *Romance of the Rose.*" *Romance Notes* 8 (1966): 113–15.

———. "Narcissus, Pygmalion, and the Castration of Saturn: Two Mythographical Themes in the *Roman de la Rose.*" *SP* 71 (1974): 404–26.

Hipolito, Terrence. "*Roman de la Rose*: Nature's Grace." *Comitatus* 1 (1970): 47–79.

* Huizinga, Johan. *The Waning of the Middle Ages.* Translated by F. Hopman. London, 1924. See chapters 8, 9, 12, and passim.

Hult, David F. "In Quest of the *Rose*: Guillaume de Lorris and Jean de Meun." Ph.D. dissertation, Cornell University, 1977.

Irribarria-Huettig, Maria S. "Système Métaphorique du *Roman de la Rose.*" Ph.D. dissertation, University of Kansas, 1975.

Jauss, Hans R. "Form und Auffassung der Allegorie in der Tradition der Psychomachia (von Prudentius zum ersten *Romanz de la Rose).*" In *Medium Aevum Vivum: Festschrift Walter Bulst*, edited by H. R. Jauss and Dieter Schaller, pp. 179–206. Heidelberg, 1960.

————. *Genèse de la Poésie Allégorique Française au Moyen Age (de 1180 à 1240)*. Heidelberg, 1962.

————. "La Transformation de la Forme Allégorique entre 1180 et 1240: d'Alain de Lille à Guillaume de Lorris." In *L'Humanisme Médiéval dans les Littératures Romanes du XIIe au XIVe Siècles*, edited by A. Fourrier, pp. 107–45. Paris, 1964.

Jeanroy, Alfred. *Histoire de la Nation Française*, edited by G. Hanotaux. Vol. 12, *Histoire des Lettres*. Paris, 1921. See pp. 404–18.

Jung, Marc-René. *Etudes sur le Poème Allégorique en France au Moyen Age*. Berne, 1971. See pp. 292–310 and passim.

————. "Gui de Mori et Guillaume de Lorris." *Vox Romanica* 28 (1968): 106–37.

————. "Jean de Meun et l'Allégorie." *Cahiers de l'Association Internationale des Etudes Françaises* 28 (1976): 21–36.

Kaminska, Alexandra B. "Literary Confessions from 1215 through 1550: Development in Theme and Form of French, German, and English Confessions from the Fourth Lateran Council through the Reformation." Ph.D. dissertation, University of Maryland, 1972.

Kanduth, E. "Der *Rosenroman*: Ein Bildungsbuch?" *Zeitschrift für Romanische Philologie* 86 (1970): 509–24.

Kelly, Douglas. "'Li chastiaus . . . Qu'Amors prist puis par ses esforz': The Conclusion of Guillaume de Lorris' *Rose*." In *A Medieval French Miscellany*, edited by N. J. Lacy, pp. 61–78. Lawrence, Kans., 1972.

————. *Medieval Imagination: Rhetoric and the Poetry of Courtly Love*. Madison, Wis., 1978.

King, Peter. "Flos Veneris." In *Texts and Manuscripts: Essays Presented to G. I. Lieftinck*, edited by J. P. Gumbert and M. J. M. de Haan, 2: 61–72. Amsterdam, 1972. Treats rose as female pudendum.

Köhler, E. "Lea, Matelda und Oiseuse." *Zeitschrift für Romanische Philologie* 78 (1962): 464–69.

* ————. "Narcisse, la Fontaine d'Amour et Guillaume de Lorris." *Journal des Savants* (1963): 86–103. Also in *L'Humanisme Médiéval dans les Littératures Romanes du XIIe au XIVe Siècles*, edited by A. Fourrier, pp. 147–66. Paris, 1964.

Kolb, H. "Oiseuse, die Dame mit dem Spiegel." *Germanisch-*

romanische Monatsschrift 15 (1965): 139–49.

* Kuhn, Alfred. "Die Illustration des *Rosenromans.*" *Jahrbuch der Kunsthistorischen Sammlungen der allerhöchsten Kaiserhauses* 31 (Vienna, 1913–14): 1–66. An earlier version was published at Freiburg in 1911. A pioneering study (though flawed by errors) of the MS illustrations, containing fifteen plates and forty-five text figures.

Kunitzsch, Paul. "Das Abu Ma'sar-Zitat im *Rosenroman.*" *Romanische Forschungen* 82 (1970): 102–11.

Kupka, Paul. *Zur Chronologie und Genesis des Roman de la Rose.* Gardelegen, 1901.

* Langlois, Ernest. "Gui de Mori et le *Roman de la Rose.*" *Bibliothèque de l'Ecole des Chartes* 68 (1907): 249–71. Langlois was one of the greatest editors and critics of the *Roman.* A bibliography of his writings was published by Noël Dupire, Paris, 1929.

Lanly, A. "La Hardiesse de Pensée de Jean de Meun." In *Linguistique et Philologie (Applications aux Textes Médiévaux): Actes du Colloque des 29 et 30 Avril 1977, publ. par les soins de Danielle Buschinger.* Paris, 1977. See pp. 345–58.

Larmat, J. *Le Moyen Age dans le Gargantua de Rabelais.* Nice, 1973.

Larsen, Judith C. "Proverbial Material in the *Roman de la Rose.*" Ph.D. dissertation, University of Georgia, 1978.

Lecoy, Félix. "Une Mention du *Roman de la Rose* au XVIᵉ Siècle." *Romania* 87 (1966): 119–20. Lecoy is editor of one of the two standard editions of the *Roman.*

———. "Sur la Date du *Roman de la Rose.*" *Romania* 89 (1968): 554–55.

———. "Sur un Passage Délicat du *Roman de la Rose.*" *Romania* 85 (1964): 372–76.

Le Gentil, P. *La Littérature Française du Moyen Age.* Paris, 1963. See pp. 130–40.

Lejeune, Rita. "A propos de la Structure du *Roman de la Rose* de Guillaume de Lorris." In *Etudes de Langue et de Littérature du Moyen Age Offertes à Félix Lecoy,* pp. 315–48. Paris, 1973.

———. "Propos sur l'Identification de Guillaume de Lorris, Auteur du *Roman de la Rose.*" *Marche Romane* 26 (1976): 5–17.

Lepage, Yvan G. "Le *Roman de la Rose* et la Tradition Romanesque au Moyen Age." *Etudes Littéraires* 4 (1971): 91–106.

Levine, Don E. "The Style of Morality." Ph.D. dissertation,

Princeton University, 1972. A study of Guillaume's part of the *Roman* and of Chaucer's *Knight's Tale.*

Levy, R. "Le Rôle de la Charaierresse dans le *Roman de la Rose.*" *Neophilologus* 36 (1952): 75–79.

* Lewis, C. S. *The Allegory of Love.* London, 1936. See especially chapter 3. One of the most influential of studies on the *Roman.* Lewis's views with regard to "courtly love," the radical dif ference between Guillaume's and Jean's parts of the *Roman,* and the putative inferiority of Jean as a literary artist, were widely accepted, though they have been rejected in recent years by such scholars as Robertson, Dahlberg, and Fleming.

Lord, Carla. "Tintoretto and the *Roman de la Rose.*" *Journal of the Warburg and Courtauld Institutes* 33 (1970): 315–17.

* Louis, René. *Le Roman de la Rose: Essai d'Interprétation de l'Allégorisme Erotique.* Paris, 1974.

Luquiens, F. B. "The *Roman de la Rose* and Medieval Castillan Literature." *Romanische Forschungen* 20 (1905): 284–320.

* Luria, Maxwell. "A Sixteenth-Century Gloss on the *Roman de la Rose.*" *Mediaeval Studies* 44 (1982).

Lyons, F. "Some Notes on the *Roman de la Rose*: The Golden Chain and Other Topics in Jean de Meun." In *Studies in Medieval Literature and Languages in Memory of Frederick White-head,* edited by W. Rothwell, pp. 201–08. Manchester, 1974.

McKean, Sister M. Faith. "The Role of Faux-Semblant and Astenance Contrainte in the *Roman de la Rose.*" In *Romance Studies in Memory of Edward Billings Ham,* edited by U. T. Holmes, pp. 103–08. Hayward, Calif., 1967.

Maler, B. "La Prophétie d'Albumasar dans le *Roman de la Rose.*" *Studia Neophilologica* 18 (1945–46): 47–48.

Milan, Paul B. "The Golden Age and the Political Theory of Jean de Meun: A Myth in *Rose* Scholarship." *Symposium* 23 (1969): 137–49.

Morawski, J. "Parodie d'un Passage du *Roman de la Rose* dans un *Sermon Joyeux.*" *Romania* 52 (1926): 159–60.

Müller, F. W. *Der Rosenroman und der Lateinische Averroïsmus des 13. Jahrhunderts.* Frankfurt-am-Main, 1947.

* Muscatine, Charles. *Chaucer and the French Tradition.* Berkeley, 1957. An important study of "bourgeois" and "courtly" styles in medieval French poetry. Considers Chaucer's relation to the

Roman and to other French works.

* ———. "The Emergence of Psychological Allegory in Old French Romance." *PMLA* 68 (1953): 1160–83.

Nichols, Stephen G., Jr. "Marot, Villon, and the *Roman de la Rose*: A Study in the Language of Creation and Re-Creation." *SP* 63 (1966): 135–43, and 64 (1967): 25–43.

———. "The Rhetoric of Sincerity in the *Roman de la Rose*." In *Romance Studies in Memory of Edward Billings Ham*, edited by U. T. Holmes, pp. 115–29. Hayward, Calif., 1967.

Novati, F. *Freschi e Minii del Dugento: Conferenze e Letture*. Milan, 1908. Rev. ed. Milan, 1925. See pp. 207–40, rev. ed.

Oster, Daniel. "Grandeur et Décadence de l'Hypocrisie." *Nouvelles Littéraires*, no. 2452 (September 1974): 11.

Ott, Karl A. "*Armat* und *Reichtum* bei Guillaume de Lorris." In *Beiträge zum Romanischen Mittelalter*, edited by K. Baldinger, pp. 282–305. Tübingen, 1977.

* Paré, Gérard M. *Les Idées et les Lettres au XIIIᵉ Siècle: Le Roman de la Rose*. Montreal, 1947. This work appeared in an earlier edition as *Le Roman de la Rose et la Scolastique Courtoise*, Paris and Ottawa, 1941. Important study of Jean de Meun's thought and his role in the intellectual life of his age.

Payen, Jean-Charles. "Attention au *Roman de la Rose*." *Nouvelles Littéraires*, no. 2561 (December 1976): 8.

———. "Le Comique de l'Enormité: Goliardisme et Provocation dans le *Roman de la Rose*." *L'Esprit Créateur* 16 (1976): 46–60.

———. "Le *Roman de la Rose* et la Notion de Carrefour Idéologique." *Romanistische Zeitschrift für Literaturgeschichte* 1 (1977): 193–203.

* *La Rose et l'Utopie: Révolution Sexuelle et Communisme Nostalgique chez Jean de Meun*. Paris, 1976.

———. "A Semiological Study of Guillaume de Lorris." *Yale French Studies* 51 (1975): 170–84.

Pézard, A. "Lune et Fortune chez Jean de Meun et chez Dante." In *Studi in Onore di Italo Siciliano*, 2 vols., pp. 985–95. Florence, 1966.

Pickens, R. T. "*Somnium* and Interpretation in Guillaume de Lorris." *Symposium* 28 (1974): 175–86.

Picone, Michelangelo. "Dante e il Mito di Narciso: Dal *Roman de la Rose* alla *Commedia*." *Romanische Forschungen* 89 (1977): 382–97.

Piehler, P. *The Visionary Landscape: A Study in Medieval Allegory.* Montreal, 1971.

Planche, A. "Les Robes du Ciel: Autour d'une Image de Jean de Meun." *Romania* 98 (1977): 349–66.

Poirion, Daniel. "Les Mots et les Choses selon Jean de Meun." *L'Information Littéraire* 26 (1974): 7–11.

———. "Narcisse et Pygmalion dans le *Roman de la Rose.*" In *Essays in Honor of Louis Francis Solano,* edited by R. Cormier and U. T. Holmes, pp. 153–65. Chapel Hill, 1970.

* ———. *Le Roman de la Rose.* Paris, 1973. A critical survey of the poem.

Polak, L. "Plato, Nature, and Jean de Meun." *Renaissance and Modern Studies* 3 (1977): 80–103.

Pucci, Robert G. "The Metaphorical Rose: Mythology, Language, and Poetics in the *Roman de la Rose.*" Ph.D. dissertation, Brown University, 1974.

Quilligan, Maureen. "Words and Sex: The Language of Allegory in the *De Planctu Naturae,* the *Roman de la Rose,* and Book III of the *Faerie Queene.*" *Allegorica* 1 (1977): 195–216.

* Rand, E. K. "The Metamorphosis of Ovid in *Le Roman de la Rose.*" In *Studies in the History of Culture: The Discipline of the Humanities,* pp. 103–21. Menasha, Wis., 1942.

Raynaud de Lage, G. "Nature et Génius chez Jean de Meung et chez Jean Le Maire des Belges." *Le Moyen Age* 58 (1952): 125–43.

Ribard, Jacques. "Introduction à une Etude Polysémique du *Roman de la Rose* de Guillaume de Lorris." In *Etudes de Langue et de Littérature du Moyen Age Offertes à Félix Lecoy,* pp. 519–28. Paris, 1973.

* Robertson, D. W., Jr. "The Doctrine of Charity in Medieval Literary Gardens: A Topical Approach through Symbolism and Allegory." *Speculum* 26 (1951): 24–49. Reprinted in Robertson, *Essays in Medieval Culture,* Princeton, 1980. An important discussion of the gardens in the *Roman.*

* ———. *A Preface to Chaucer: Studies in Medieval Perspectives.* Princeton, 1962. See especially pp. 91–104, 196–207, 361–65, and passim. A work of capital importance with respect to the *Roman,* Chaucer, other medieval texts, and late medieval literary aesthetics generally. Controversial and indispensable.

Rossi, Luciano. "Notula sul Re dei Ribaldi." *Cultura Neolatina* 33

(1973): 217–21.

Rossman, Vladimir R. "The Art of Contradiction in the *Romance of the Rose.*" *Beiträge zur Deutschen Philologie* 21 (1977): 270–81.

———. *Perspectives of Irony in Medieval French Literature.* The Hague, 1975. See pp. 122–57.

Rychner, Jean. "Le Mythe de la Fontaine de Narcisse dans le *Roman de la Rose* de Guillaume de Lorris." In *Le Lieu et la Formule: Hommage à Marc Eigeldinger*, edited by Y. Bonnefoy et al. Neuchâtel, 1978.

Ryding, William W. "Faus-Semblant: Hero or Hypocrite?" *Romanic Review* 60 (1969): 163–67.

Sasaki, Shigemi. "Sur le Personnage d'Oiseuse." *Etudes de Langue et Littérature* 32 (March 1978): 1–24.

Sichi, Edward, Jr. "'These Two Imparadis't': A Comparative Study of the Gardens in *Paradise Lost* and the *Roman de la Rose.*" Ph.D. dissertation, Duquesne University, 1977.

Siciliano, I. *François Villon et les Thèmes Poétiques du Moyen Age.* Paris, 1934. Treats the *Roman*'s great influence on Villon.

* Sneyders de Vogel, K. "'Le cercle dont le centre est partout, la circonférence nulle part' et le *Roman de la Rose.*" *Neophilologus* 16 (1931): 246–50.

* ———. "Encore une Fois 'le cercle dont le centre est partout, la circonférence nulle part.'" *Neophilologus* 17 (1932): 211–12.

———. "Marot et le *Roman de la Rose.*" *Neophilologus* 17 (1932): 269–71.

———. *De Rozeroman, een Beeld Uit Het Middel-Eeuwsche Cultuurleven.* The Hague, 1942. A critical study.

———. "L'Unité du *Roman de la Rose.*" *Neophilologus* 37 (1953): 135–39.

Soyer, J. *A propos de Jean de Meung: Son Véritable Nom; la Date Exacte de sa Mort; Ce qu'il Pensait de son Style.* Orleans, 1945.

Spearing, Anthony C. *Medieval Dream-Poetry.* Cambridge, 1976. See pp. 24–31.

Stone, Donald, Jr. "C. S. Lewis and Lorris' Lady." *Romance Notes* 6 (1965): 196–99.

———. "Old and New Thoughts on Guillaume de Lorris." *Australian Journal of French Studies* 2 (1965): 157–70. Discusses Lewis's and Robertson's interpretations of the first part of the *Roman.*

Strohm, Paul. "Guillaume as Narrator and Lover in the *Roman de la Rose.*" *Romanic Review* 59 (1968): 3–9.

Thoss, Dagmar. *Studien zum 'Locus Amoenus' im Mittelalter.* Vienna, 1972. On the gardens in the *Roman*.

* Thuasne, Louis. *Le Roman de la Rose.* Paris, 1929. Especially useful for its discussions of the later influence of the *Roman*.

———. *Villon et Rabelais.* Paris, 1911. Chapter 1 treats the influence of the *Roman* on Villon.

Tillman, Mary K. "Scholastic and Averroistic Influences on the *Roman de la Rose.*" *Annuale Mediaevale* 11 (1970): 89–106.

* Tuve, Rosemond. *Allegorical Imagery: Some Mediaeval Books and their Posterity.* Princeton, 1966. See pp. 233–84 and passim. Contains valuable materials on the *Roman's* allegory and the ways it was interpreted.

Uitti, Karl D. "From *Clerc* to *Poète*: the Relevance of the *Romance of the Rose* to Machaut's World." In *Machaut's World: Science and Art in the Fourteenth Century*, edited by M. Cosman and B. Chandler, pp. 209–16. New York, 1978.

Vallone, A. "Personificazione, Simbolo e Allegoria del Medio Evo dinanzi a Dante." *Filologia e Letteratura* 10, no. 2 (1964): 189–224.

Verhuyck, P. "Guillaume de Lorris ou la Multiplication des Cadres." *Neophilologus* 58 (1974): 283–93.

Vitz, E. B. "The *I* of the *Roman de la Rose.*" *Genre* 6 (1973): 49–75.

Warren, F. M. "A Byzantine Source for Guillaume de Lorris' *Roman de la Rose.*" *PMLA* 31 (1916): 232–46.

———. "On the Date and Composition of Guillaume de Lorris' *Roman de la Rose.*" *PMLA* 23 (1908): 269–84.

Weinberg, B. "Guillaume Michel, dit de Tours." *Bibliothèque d'Humanisme et Renaissance* 11 (1949): 72–85.

* Wetherbee, W. "The Literal and the Allegorical: Jean de Meun and the *De Planctu Naturae.*" *Mediaeval Studies* 33 (1971): 264–91.

Wood, C. "*La Vielle*, Free Love, and Boethius in the *Roman de la Rose.*" *Revue de Littérature Comparée* 51 (1977): 336–42.

Zingarelli, N. "L'Allegoria del *Roman de la Rose.*" In *Studii Dedicati a Francesco Torraca nel 36 Anniversario della sua Laurea*, pp. 495–524. Naples, 1912.

Zumthor, Paul. "Autobiography in the Middle Ages." *Genre* 6

(1973): 29–48. Treats the *Roman* and other medieval allegorical and lyric texts.

———. "De Guillaume de Lorris à Jean de Meung." In *Etudes de Langue et de Littérature du Moyen Age Offertes à Félix Lecoy*, pp. 609–20. Paris, 1973.

———. *Essai de Poétique Médiévale*. Paris, 1972.

———. "Narrative and Anti-Narrative: *Le Roman de la Rose*." *Yale French Studies* 51 (1974): 185–204.

See also "Ancillary Materials for Study of the *Roman*: Miscellaneous Works": Wetherbee 1972.

29

Materials and Scholarship
Relating to the Quarrel

Baird, Joseph L., and Kane, John R. "*La Querelle de la Rose*: In Defense of the Opponents." *The French Review* 48 (1974): 298–307.

* ———. *La Querelle de la Rose: Letters and Documents*. Chapel Hill, 1978. The documents of the Quarrel in English translation: an admirable volume, and the only such collection. Bibliography.

Christine de Pisan. *Oeuvres Poétiques*. Edited by M. Roy. 3 vols. 1886–96. Reprint. New York, 1965. A collective edition, and a good one, of the poetry of the *Roman's* first notable detractor. For more recent critical editions of individual works, see Enid McLeod, *The Order of the Rose*, Totowa, N.J., 1976, pp. 178–82.

Combes, André. *Jean de Montreuil et le Chancelier Gerson*. Paris, 1942. 2d ed. Paris, 1973.

Coville, A. *Gontier et Pierre Col et l'Humanisme en France au Temps de Charles VI*. Paris, 1934.

* Fleming, John V. "Hoccleve's 'Letter of Cupid' and the 'Quarrel' over the *Roman de la Rose*." *Medium Aevum* 40 (1971): 21–40.

* Furr, Grover C. "The Quarrel of the *Roman de la Rose* and Fourteenth-Century Humanism." Ph.D. dissertation, Princeton University, 1979. A fresh attempt to understand the meaning of the Quarrel and motives of its participants. An important study. Bibliography.

Gerson, Jean. *Oeuvres Complètes*. Edited by P. Glorieux. 10 vols. Paris, 1961–73. The works of the *Roman's* most learned enemy. See especially vols. 2 and 7.

Hicks, Eric. "De l'Histoire Littéraire comme Cosmogonie: La Querelle du *Roman de la Rose*." *Critique* 32 (1976): 510–19. A review article on Potansky's study of the Quarrel, and on Poirion's edition.

————. "The 'Querelle de la Rose' in the *Roman de la Rose*." *Les Bonnes Feuilles* 3, no. 2 (1974): 152–69.

* ————, ed. *Le Débat sur le Roman de la Rose*. Paris, 1977. The only sound edition of the documents of the Quarrel. Unfortunately, the contents are arranged awkwardly, and the introduction is cluttered with modish obscurities. Even so, this edition is much to be preferred over that of C. F. Ward.

Hicks, Eric, and Ornato, Ezio. "Jean de Montreuil et le Débat sur le *Roman de la Rose*." *Romania* 98 (1977): 34–64, 186–219.

Hilder, Gisela. "Der Streit um den *Rosenroman*: Eine Britische Auseinandersetzung mit P. Potansky." *Zeitschrift für Romanische Philologie* 91 (1975): 79–94.

Langlois, Ernest. "Le Traité de Gerson contre le *Roman de la Rose*." *Romania* 45 (1918–19): 23–48. The French text of Gerson's treatise, with an account of the Quarrel.

* McLeod, Enid. *The Order of the Rose: The Life and Ideas of Christine de Pizan*. Totowa, N.J., 1976. Readable survey of Christine's life and writings. Chapter 6 is a concise account of the Quarrel, without much scholarly detail. (A good place to begin study of this subject.) Bibliography contains list of Christine's writings and recent publications about her.

Ott, Karl A. "Jean de Meun und Boethius: Über Aufbau und Quellen des *Rosenromans*." In *Philologische Studien: Gedenkschrift für Richard Kienast*, edited by U. Schwab and E. Stutz. Heidelberg, 1978.

Piaget, A. "Chronologie des Epîtres sur le *Roman de la Rose*." In *Etudes Romanes Dediées à Gaston Paris*. Paris, 1891.

* Potansky, Peter. *Der Streit um den Rosenroman*. Munich, 1972. An important study of the Quarrel. See review article by Eric Hicks, "De l'Histoire Littéraire comme Cosmogonie," *Critique* 32 (1976): 510–19.

Ward, C. F. *The Epistles on the Romance of the Rose and Other Documents in the Debate*. Chicago, 1911. A flawed edition, now supplanted by Eric Hicks's *Le Débat sur le Roman de la Rose*, Paris, 1977.

30

Ancillary Materials for Study
of the *Roman*

Miscellaneous Works

* Auerbach, Erich. "Figura." *Scenes from the Drama of European Literature*. New York, 1959. See pp. 11–76. A classic exploration of figurative language in Christian discourse.

* Barney, Stephen A. *Allegories of History, Allegories of Love*. Hamden, Conn., 1979. Contains valuable discussions of allegory (chapter 1), Prudentius's *Psychomachia* (chapter 2), and the *Roman de la Rose* (chapter 6). Useful bibliographical materials.

* Baron, Hans. *The Crisis of the Early Italian Renaissance*. 2 vols. Princeton, 1955. Rev. ed., 1 vol. Princeton, 1966.

* Bernardus Silvestris. *The Cosmographia*. Translated by W. Wetherbee. New York, 1973.

Bloomfield, M. W. "A Grammatical Approach to Personification Allegory." *MP* 40 (1963): 161–71.

Calin, William. "The Poet at the Fountain: Machaut as Narrative Poet." In *Machaut's World: Science and Art in the Fourteenth Century*, edited by M. Cosman and B. Chandler, pp. 177–87. New York, 1978.

Cornelius, R. *The Figurative Castle: A Study in the Medieval Allegory of the Edifice with Especial Reference to Religious Writings*. Bryn Mawr, 1930.

Crawley, Ernest. *The Mystic Rose: A Study of Primitive Marriage*. London, 1902.

* Curtius, Ernst R. *European Literature and the Latin Middle Ages*. Translated by Willard R. Trask. New York, 1953. An essential work of modern scholarship.

* ———. "Natura Mater Generationis." *Zeitschrift für Romanische Philologie* 58 (1938): 180–97.

* De Bruyne, E. *Etudes d'Esthétique Médiévale.* 3 vols. Bruges, 1946. A standard study of medieval aesthetics.

* Denomy, A. J. *The Heresy of Courtly Love.* New York, 1947.

De Wulf, Maurice. *Philosophy and Civilization in the Middle Ages.* Princeton, 1922.

Dronke, Peter. *Fabula: Explorations into the Uses of Myth in Medieval Platonism.* Leiden and Cologne, 1974. A suggestive study of the relations between myth, allegory, and philosophy.

* ———. *Medieval Latin and the Rise of European Love-Lyric.* 2 vols. Oxford, 1965–66. 2d ed. Oxford, 1968. See especially 1: 57–97.

———. *Poetic Individuality in the Middle Ages.* Oxford, 1970.

Dupire, Noël. *Jean Molinet.* Paris, 1932.

* Economou, George D. *The Goddess Natura in Medieval Literature.* Cambridge, Mass., 1972.

Fletcher, Angus. *Allegory: The Theory of a Symbolic Mode.* Ithaca, 1964.

Frank, R. W., Jr. "The Art of Reading Medieval Personification Allegory." *Journal of English Literary History* 20 (1953): 239–50.

Garin, E. *Studi sul Platonismo Medievale.* Florence, 1958.

Giamatti, A. B. *The Earthly Paradise and the Renaissance Epic.* Princeton, 1966.

Gilson, Etienne. "La Cosmogonie de Bernardus Silvestris." *Archives d'Histoire Doctrinale et Littéraire du Moyen Age* 3 (1928): 5–24.

Goldin, Frederick. *The Mirror of Narcissus in the Courtly Love Lyric.* Ithaca, 1967.

Gravereaux, Jules. *La Rose dans les Sciences, dans les Lettres, et dans les Arts: Documents pour Servir à l'Histoire de la Rose.* Paris, 1906.

Honig, Edwin. *Dark Conceit: The Making of Allegory.* New York, 1966.

Jauss, Hans R. "Form und Auffassung der Allegorie in der Tradition der Psychomachia (von Prudentius zum ersten *Romanz de la Rose*)." In *Medium Aevum Vivum: Festschrift Walter Bulst*, edited by H. R. Jauss and Dieter Schaller, pp. 179–206. Heidelberg, 1960.

———. *Genèse de la Poésie Allégorique Française au Moyen Age (de 1180 à 1240).* Heidelberg, 1962.

———. "La Transformation de la Forme Allégorique entre 1180 et 1240: d'Alain de Lille à Guillaume de Lorris." *L'Humanisme Médiéval dans les Littératures Romanes du XIIe au XIVe Siècle.* Paris, 1964.

Joret, C. *La Rose dans l'Antiquité et au Moyen Age.* Paris, 1892.

Knowlton, E. C. "The Allegorical Figure Genius." *Classical Philology* 15 (1920): 280–84.

———. "Genius as an Allegorical Figure." *MLN* 39 (1924): 89–95.

Levi, A. H. T., ed. *Humanism in France at the End of the Middle Ages and in the Early Renaissance.* New York, 1970.

Lot-Borodine, Myrrha. "Sur les Origines et les Fins du Service d'Amour." In *Mélanges de Linguistique et de Littérature Offerts à M. Alfred Jeanroy,* pp. 223–42. Paris, 1928.

* Macrobius, Ambrosius Theodosius. *Commentarii in Somnium Scipionis.* Edited by James Willis. Leipzig, c963.

* ———. *Commentary on the Dream of Scipio.* Translated by W. H. Stahl. 1952. Reprint. New York, 1966. Introduction has valuable discussion of Macrobius's influence.

* Ovid. *The Art of Love (Ars Amatoria) and Other Poems.* Edited and translated by J. H. Mozley. New York, 1929. Convenient Loeb Classical Library edition with original text and translation.

Pollmann, L. *Die Liebe in der Hochmittelalterlichen Literatur Frankreichs: Versuch einer Historischen Phänomenologie.* Frankfurt-am-Main, 1966.

* Prudentius. *Prudentius with an English Translation.* Edited by H. J. Thomson. 2 vols. Cambridge, Mass., 1949–53. The *Psychomachia* will be found in 1: 274–343 of this Loeb edition.

Quilligan, Maureen. *The Language of Allegory: Defining the Genre.* Ithaca, 1979.

* Rashdall, Hastings. *The Universities of Europe in the Middle Ages.* Edited by F. M. Powicke and A. B. Emden. New ed. 3 vols. Oxford, 1936.

Regalado, N. *Poetic Patterns in Rutebeuf.* New Haven, 1970.

Rougement, Denis de. *Love in the Western World.* Translated by Montgomery Belgion. New York, 1940. Rev. ed. New York, 1956. Translation of *L'Amour et l'Occident,* Paris, 1939.

Rutebeuf. *Oeuvres Complètes.* Edited by E. Faral and J. Bastin. 2 vols. Paris, 1959. Important introduction. Rutebeuf appears to have influenced the composition of the *Roman.*

Salter, Elizabeth. "Medieval Poetry and the Figural View of Reality." *Proceedings of the British Academy* 54 (1968): 73–92.

* Scaglione, Aldo D. *Nature and Love in the Late Middle Ages.* Berkeley, 1963.

Seigel, Jerrold E. *Rhetoric and Philosophy in Renaissance Humanism: The Union of Eloquence and Wisdom, Petrarch to Valla.* Princeton, 1968.

Seward, B. *The Symbolic Rose.* New York, 1968.

Stock, Brian. *Myth and Science in the Twelfth Century: A Study of Bernard Sylvester.* Princeton, 1975.

Vinge, Louis. *The Narcissus Theme in Western European Literature up to the Nineteenth Century.* Lund, 1967. See especially pp. 78–87.

Wenk, Linda T. "Irresolvable Dichotomies in the Twelfth-Century Debate Poem: A Study in Platonic Perspectives." Ph.D. dissertation, Cornell University, 1972.

* Wetherbee, Winthrop. *Platonism and Poetry in the Twelfth Century: The Literary Influence of the School of Chartres.* Princeton, 1972.

Special Topics

ALANUS DE INSULIS

* Bossuat, Robert, ed. *Anticlaudianus.* Paris, 1955. Best edition.

Brumble, Herbert D. "Genius and Other Related Allegorical Figures in the *De Planctu Naturae*, the *Roman de la Rose*, the *Confessio Amantis*, and the *Faerie Queene*." Ph.D. dissertation, University of Nebraska, 1970.

Cornog, W. H., trans. *The Anticlaudian of Alain de Lille.* Philadelphia, 1935. An unreadable translation, to be avoided. See Sheridan, below.

Delhaye, P. "La Vertu et les Vertus dans les Oeuvres d'Alain de Lille." *Cahiers de Civilisation Médiévale* 5 (1963): 13–25.

Economou, George D. "The Character Genius in Alan de Lille, Jean de Meun, and John Gower." *Chaucer Review* 4 (1970): 203–10.

* ———. *The Goddess Natura in Medieval Literature*. Cambridge, Mass., 1972.

* Green, R. H. "Alan of Lille's *De Planctu Naturae*." *Speculum* 31 (1956): 649–74.

* Häring, N. M., ed. *De Planctu Naturae. Studi Medievali*, 3d ser. 19, no. 2 (1978): 797–879. Best edition.

Migne, J. P., ed. *De Planctu Naturae, Anticlaudianus*. *Patrologia Latina*, 210. Paris, 1855. See cols. 429–82, 482–576.

Moffat, D. M., trans. *The Complaint of Nature by Alain de Lille*. 1908. Reprint. New York, 1972.

Raynaud de Lage, G. *Alain de Lille, Poète du XIIe Siècle*. Montreal, 1951.

* Sheridan, James J., trans. *Anticlaudianus or the Good and Perfect Man*. Toronto, 1973. Fine translation (the only good one), with useful commentary.

* ———, trans. *The Plaint of Nature (De Planctu Naturae)*. Toronto, 1980. Excellent translation, with commentary and notes.

* Wetherbee, Winthrop. "The Function of Poetry in the *De Planctu Naturae* of Alain de Lille." *Traditio* 25 (1969): 87–125.

* ———. "The Literal and the Allegorical: Jean de Meun and the *De Planctu Naturae*." *Mediaeval Studies* 33 (1971): 264–91.

See also "Ancillary Materials for Study of the *Roman*: Miscellaneous Works": Wetherbee 1972.

Andreas Capellanus

* Denomy, A. J. "The *De Amore* of Andreas Capellanus and the Condemnation of 1277." *Mediaeval Studies* 8 (1946): 107–49.

* Parry, John J., trans. *The Art of Courtly Love*. New York, 1941.

* Robertson, D. W., Jr. *A Preface to Chaucer: Studies in Medieval Perspectives*. Princeton, 1962. See pp. 84–85, 393–448, and passim.

* ———. "The Subject of the *De Amore* of Andreas Capellanus." *MP* 50 (1953): 145–61.

* Trojel, E., ed. *De Amore Libri Tres*. Copenhagen, 1892. 2d ed. Munich, 1964. The standard edition of the original text.

Zaddy, Z. P. "*Le Chevalier de la Charrete* and the *De Amore* of Andreas Capellanus." In *Studies in Medieval Literature and*

Languages in Memory of Frederick Whitehead, edited by W.
Rothwell, pp. 363–99. Manchester, 1974.

Zumthor, Paul. "Notes en Marge du Traité de l'Amour d'André le
Chapelain." *Zeitschrift für Romanische Philologie* 63 (1943):
179–91.

Boethius

* Courcelle, P. *La Consolation de Philosophie dans la Tradition
Littéraire*. Paris, 1967.

Crespo, R. "Jean de Meun, Traduttore della *Consolatio Philosophiae*
di Boezio." *Atti dell'Accad. delle Scienze di Torino* 103 (1969):
65–170.

Dedeck-Héry, V. L. "Un Fragment Inédit de la Traduction de la
Consolation de Boèce par Jean de Meun." *Romanic Review* 27
(1936): 110–24.

———. "Jean de Meun et Chaucer, Traducteurs de la *Consolation*
de Boèce." *PMLA* 52 (1937): 967–91.

Lowes, J. L. "Chaucer's Boethius and Jean de Meun." *Romanic
Review* 8 (1917): 383–400.

* Stewart, H. F., ed. *The Consolation of Philosophy*. 1918. Reprint.
Cambridge, Mass., 1962. A Loeb Classical Library text, with
English translation on facing pages.

See also "Scholarship and Criticism of the Twentieth Century":
Fenzi.

Jean de Meun

Charrier, Charlotte, ed. *Traduction de la Première Epître de Pierre
Abelard*. Paris, 1934. Latin text with Jean's French version.

Dedeck-Héry, V. L., ed. "*Li Livres de Confort de Philosophie*."
Mediaeval Studies 14 (1952): 165–275. Jean's translation of
Boethius.

* Langlois, Ernest, ed. *Le Roman de la Rose*. Vol. 1. Paris, 1914. See
pp. 18–25 for account of various works ascribed to Jean.

Méon, M., ed. Jean's *Testament* and *Codicile*. In *Le Roman de la
Rose*, 4: 1–121. Paris, 1814.

Robert, Ulysse, ed. *L'Art de Chevalerie*. Paris, 1897. Jean's translation of Vegetius.

See also "Scholarship and Criticism of the Twentieth Century": Bourneuf, Francon 1944, A. B. Friedman, Lionel J. Friedman 1959–60 and 1962, Hatzfeld.

"Echecs Amoureux"

* Fleming, John V. *The Roman de la Rose: A Study in Allegory and Iconography*. Princeton, 1969. See pp. 62–66.

* Galpin, Stanley L. "*Les Eschez Amoureux*: A Complete Synopsis, with Unpublished Extracts." *Romanic Review* 11 (1920): 283–307.

* Jones, Joan M. "*The Chess of Love*: Translation of Prose Commentary on *Echecs Amoureux* from a MS 1390–1430." Ph.D. dissertation, University of Nebraska, 1968.

Lydgate, John. *Reason and Sensuality*. Edited by Ernst Sieper. EETS-ES, vols. 84, 89. London, 1901–03. Lydgate's fifteenth-century translation and adaptation of the *Echecs Amoureux*.

Sieper, Ernst. *Les Echecs Amoureux: Eine Altfranzösische Nachahmung des Rosenromans und ihre Englische Übertragung*. Weimar, 1898. A study of the poem and of its English version by Lydgate.

"Il Fiore" and Italian Literature

* Benedetto, Luigi F. *Il Roman de la Rose e la Letteratura Italiana*. Halle, 1910.

* Bertoni, Giulio. *Il Duecento*. Milan, 1930. 4th ed. Milan, 1954. See pp. 350–52 in the 1954 edition for discussion of Italian versions of the *Roman*.

* Boccaccio, Giovanni. *Boccaccio on Poetry*. Translated by Charles G. Osgood. 1930. Reprint. New York, 1956. Boccaccio's ideas about poetry, especially poetic allegory, in books 14 and 15 of the *Genealogia Deorum Gentilium*, with a long and important introduction by Osgood.

Castets, F., ed. *Il Fiore, Poème Italien du XIIIᵉ Siècle en CCXXXII*

Sonnets, Imité du Roman de la Rose. Paris, 1881.

Contini, Gianfranco. "Un Nodo della Cultura Medievale: La Serie *Roman de la Rose, Fiore, Divina Commedia.*" *Lettere Italiane* 25 (1973): 162–89.

Fenzi, Enrico. "Boezio e Jean de Meun: Filosofia e Razione nelle Rime Allegorische di Dante." In *Studi di Filologia e Letterature Dedicati a Vincenzo Pernicone.* Genoa, 1975.

Govra, E. "Lange Abhandlung über den *Fiore* und den *Rosenroman* (ohne Titel)." In *Inventario dei Manoscritti Italiani delle Biblioteche di Francia,* edited by G. Mazzatinti, 3: 419–610. Rome, 1888.

Morpurgo, S., ed. "*Detto d'Amore:* Antiche Rime Imitate dal *Roman de la Rose.*" *Il Propugnatore,* new ser. 1, no. 1 (1888): 18–31.

* Parodi, E. G., ed. *Il Fiore, e il Detto d'Amore.* Florence, 1922. Texts of these early Italian adaptations of the *Roman,* with glossary and notes.

Spitzer, Leo. "Osservazioni al Testo del 'Detto d'Amore.'" *Giornale Storico della Letteratura Italiana* 134 (1957): 77–85.

Took, John. "Towards an Interpretation of the *Fiore.*" *Speculum* 54 (1979): 500–527.

Controversy Concerning the Friars

Allen, Judson B. *The Friar as Critic: Literary Attitudes in the Later Middle Ages.* Nashville, 1971.

* Congar, Yves M.-J. "Aspects Ecclésiologiques de la Querelle entre Mendiants et Séculiers dans la seconde Moitié du XIIIᵉ Siècle et le Debut du XIVᵉ." *Archives d'Histoire Doctrinale et Littéraire du Moyen Age* 36 (1961): 35–151. Summarizes the matter, and provides extensive bibliography.

* Dahlberg, Charles. "The Secular Tradition in Chaucer and Jean de Meun." Ph.D. dissertation, Princeton University, 1953.

Dufeil, M.-M. *Guillaume de Saint-Amour et la Polémique Universitaire Parisienne, 1250–1259.* Paris, 1972.

* Glorieux, P. "Le Conflit de 1252–1257 à la Lumière du Mémoire de Guillaume de Saint-Amour." *Recherches de Théologie Ancienne et Médiévale* 24 (1957): 364–72.

Perrod, M. *Etude sur la Vie et sur les Oeuvres de Guillaume de Saint-Amour.* Lons-le-Saulnier, 1902.

31

Romaunt of the Rose

Editions

Furnivall, F. J., ed. *The Romaunt of the Rose: A Reprint of the First Printed Edition by William Thynne A.D. 1532.* London, 1911.

Kaluza, Max, ed. *The Romaunt of the Rose: The English Fragments, from the Unique MS. V.3.7. in the Hunterian Museum, Glasgow, with their French Original.* Chaucer Society pubs., 83. London, 1891.

Nichols, Stephen G., ed. *Le Roman de la Rose par Guillaume de Lorris.* New York, 1967. Langlois text, and *Romaunt* to line 1705 (fragment 'A'). No notes or glossary.

* Robinson, F. N., ed. *The Works of Geoffrey Chaucer.* Boston, 1933. 2d ed. Boston, 1957. See pp. 564–640.

* Skeat, Walter W., ed. *The Complete Works of Geoffrey Chaucer.* Vol. 1. 2d ed. Oxford, 1899. See pp. 93–259. Skeat prints the French text for fragment 'A' only, and the entire *Romaunt*.

* Sutherland, Ronald, ed. *The Romaunt of the Rose and Le Roman de la Rose: A Parallel-Text Edition.* Oxford, 1967. Extensive introduction and attempt to show textual affiliations. Uses Thynne's text of 1532, emended from the Glasgow MS and the French original.

Scholarship and Criticism

Brusendorff, Aage. *The Chaucer Tradition.* London, 1925. See chapter 5.

Caie, Graham D. "An Iconographic Detail in the *Roman de la Rose* and the Middle English *Romaunt*." *Chaucer Review* 8 (1974): 320–23.

Fleming, John V. "Chaucer's Squire: The *Roman de la Rose* and the *Romaunt*." *Notes and Queries* 14 (1967): 48–49.

French, R. D. *A Chaucer Handbook.* 2d ed. New York, 1947. See pp. 75–82.

Huppé, Bernard F. "The Translation of the Technical Terms in the Middle English *Romaunt of the Rose*." *JEGP* 47 (1948): 334–42.

Kaluza, Max. *Chaucer-Handbuch für Studierende*. Leipzig, 1915. See pp. 27–36.

Kittredge, George L. "The Authorship of the English *Romaunt of the Rose*." (Harvard) *Studies and Notes in Philology and Literature* 1 (1892): 1–65.

Morley, Henry. *English Writers; an Attempt Towards a History of English Literature*. 11 vols. London, 1887–95. See 4: 1–17.

Nordahl, Helge. "Ars Fidi Interpretis: Un Aspect Rhétorique de l'Art de Chaucer dans sa Traduction du *Roman de la Rose*." *Archivum Linguisticum*, new ser. 9 (1978): 24–31.

Root, Robert K. *The Poetry of Chaucer*. 2d ed. Boston, 1922. See pp. 45–56.

Schoch, A. D. "The Differences in the Middle English *Romaunt of the Rose* and Their Bearing upon Chaucer's Authorship." *MP* 3 (1905–06): 339–58.

Skeat, Walter W. *The Chaucer Canon*. Oxford, 1900. See chapters 6–8.

Sutherland, Ronald. "The *Romaunt of the Rose* and Source Manuscripts." *PMLA* 74 (1959): 178–82.

32

Chaucer's Relation to the
Roman de la Rose

* Cipriani, Lisi. "Studies in the Influence of the *Romance of the Rose* upon Chaucer." *PMLA* 22 (1907): 552–95.

* Dahlberg, Charles. "The Secular Tradition in Chaucer and Jean de Meun." Ph.D. dissertation, Princeton University, 1953.

Economou, George D. "Januarie's Sin Against Nature: The *Merchant's Tale* and the *Roman de la Rose*." *CL* 17 (1965): 251–57.

* Fansler, Dean Spruill. *Chaucer and the Roman de la Rose*. 1914. Reprint. Gloucester, Mass., 1965. More concerned with verbal influences and allusions than with larger matters of style or substance.

Ferster, Judith I. "Chaucer and *l'Art Véritable*: The Epistemology of Art in Two Early Dream Visions and Two of their French Sources." Ph.D. dissertation, Brown University, 1974. Discusses relationships between *Roman* and the *De Planctu Naturae* and Chaucer's *Book of the Duchess* and *Parlement of Foules*.

* Kaluza, Max. *Chaucer und der Rosenroman: Eine Literargeschichtliche Studie*. Berlin, 1893.

Kittredge, George L. *Chaucer and his Poetry*. Cambridge, Mass., 1915.

Knopp, Sherron. "Chaucer and Jean de Meun as Self-Conscious Narrators: The Prologue to the *Legend of Good Women* and the *Roman de la Rose* 10,307–10,680." *Comitatus* 4 (1973): 25–39.

Koeppel, E. "Jehan de Meung." *Anglia* 14 (1891–92): 238–67. Discusses Jean's influence on Chaucer.

Lounsbury, Thomas R. *Studies in Chaucer: His Life and Writings*. Vol. 2. New York, 1892.

Magoun, F. P. "Chaucer and the *Roman de la Rose,* vv. 16,096–16,105." *Romanic Review* 17 (1926): 69–70.

Morgan, Gerald. "The Self-Revealing Tendencies of Chaucer's Pardoner." *MLR* 71 (1976): 241–55.

* Muscatine, Charles. *Chaucer and the French Tradition.* Berkeley, 1957.

Thompson, Nasta M. "A Further Study of Chaucer and the *Romance of the Rose.*" Ph.D. dissertation, Stanford University, 1926.

See also "Scholarship and Criticism of the Twentieth Century": Robertson 1962.

Appendix

Tables of Lineation

TABLE I
Roman de la Rose

Lecoy	Langlois (Dahlberg, Robbins)
1–370	1–370
370 a–b	371–372
371–890	373–892
891–892	[omitted]
893–1,044	893–1,044
[omitted]	1,045–1,046
1,045–2,074	1,047–2,076
2,074 a–j	2,077–2,086
2,075–2,452	2,087–2,464
2,452 a–b	2,465–2,466
2,453–2,680	2,467–2,694
[omitted]	2,695–2,696
2,681–3,328	2,697–3,344
[omitted]	3,345–3,346
3,329–3,908	3,347–3,926
3,908 a–j	3,927–3,936
3,909–4,020	3,937–4,048
[omitted]	4,049–4,050
4,021–4,028	4,051–4,058
[End of Guillaume's part.]	
4,029–21,750	4,059–21,780

There are differences in the lineation of the several editions of the *Roman* and the *Romaunt* which often make it difficult to compare texts. The following tables should facilitate such comparisons. (Table I is adapted from Charles Dahlberg's translation, p. 427.)

The English versions of Harry Robbins and of Charles Dahlberg are both based upon the Langlois text, whose lineation will therefore serve approximately for these translations as well. F. S. Ellis based his translation on the Marteau text; both text and translation are now obsolete, and of only historical interest. (See the survey of texts and translations in chapter two.)

TABLE II
Romaunt of the Rose

	ROBINSON (REV. ED.)	SUTHERLAND	LECOY	LANGLOIS (DAHLBERG, ROBBINS)
Frag. A	1–1,705	1–1,705	1–1,668	1–1,670
Frag. B (Guillaume)	1,706–4,432	1,706–4,430	1,669–4,028	1,671–4,058
Frag. B (Jean)	4,433–5,810	4,431–5,810	4,029–5,124	4,059–5,154
Frag. C	5,811–7,696	5,811–7,696	10,649–12,330	10,679–12,360

Notes

Part One

1 Throughout this book, line numbers for the *Roman* refer to the three-volume edition of Félix Lecoy (Paris, 1965–70). For equivalences in the Langlois text, see the Appendix.

2 Cf. *Le Conte du Graal* (45,379 lines), or, in the fourteenth century, Gower's *Mirour de l'Omme* (29,945 lines), among others.

3 Thus, for example, the elaborate gloss in Philadelphia Museum of Art MS Collins 45-65-3, discussed above, makes no distinction between the two parts of the *Roman*, though acknowledging the two authors. Cf. also Christine de Pisan (in the letter excerpted on pp. 191–202): "But you will tell me that de Lorris caused this. My answer: I consider the work a single entity . . . for the whole work comes to a single purpose in the conclusion, interpret as you will."

4 C. S. Lewis, *The Allegory of Love* (London, 1936), chapter 3.

5 Cf. the 1735 preface of Lenglet du Fresnoy (p. 218–21), which, though sympathetic, also expresses this condescending opinion.

6 Cited by Alan Gunn, *The Mirror of Love* (Lubbock, 1952), p. 6.

7 Lewis, *Allegory*, p. 157.

8 Ibid.

9 Gunn, *Mirror*, pp. 7–8.

10 J. L. Baird and J. R. Kane, eds., *La Querelle de la Rose: Letters and Documents* (Chapel Hill, 1978), pp. 114, 63. See also the letters reprinted in chapter seventeen of the present volume.

11 Gunn, *Mirror*, p. 6.

12 Ibid., pp. 8–9.

13 For biographical summaries, see Ernest Langlois, ed., *Le Roman de la Rose* (Paris, 1914), 1:1–3; Félix Lecoy, ed., *Le Roman de la Rose* (Paris, 1965), 1:v–vi.

14 All English translations of the *Roman* in this book are from Charles Dahlberg, trans., *The Romance of the Rose* (Princeton, 1971).

15 Langlois, ed., *Roman*, 1:2.

16 Lecoy, ed., *Roman*, 1:viii.

17 Langlois, ed., *Roman*, 1:3–4.

18 Lecoy, ed., *Roman*, 1:vi, n.

19 Ibid., pp. xiii–xvi.

20 For biographical material on Jean, see Langlois, ed., *Roman*, 1:8–25; Lecoy, ed., *Roman*, 1:vi–x, includes a bibliography of Jean's writings.

21 Ibid., p. x.

22 Because of their common *Orléanais* origins, Guillaume's and Jean's dialects differ only slightly, however. For discussions of language and versification, see Daniel Poirion, *Le Roman de la Rose* (Paris, 1973), pp. 215–18, and Langlois, ed., *Roman*, vol. 1, which provides the fullest account of the poem's language.

23 Northrop Frye, *Anatomy of Criticism* (1957; reprint ed., New York, 1966), p. 56.

24 See chapters six and seventeen.

25 Langlois, ed., *Roman*, 1:32.

26 Quoted by Gunn, *Mirror*, p. 12, from Lewis, *Allegory*, pp. 137–42.

27 Charles Muscatine, *Chaucer and the French Tradition* (Berkeley, 1957), p. 79.

28 Lecoy, ed., *Roman*, 1:xix.

29 Ernest Langlois, *Les Manuscrits du Roman de la Rose: Description et Classement* (Lille, 1910). In his edition of the *Roman*, 1:32, Langlois says that "il en existe aujourd'hui encore au moins 300 manuscrits," and this figure has been cited by some later scholars; but Langlois does not explain what he means, and we may assume that he was including MSS which are likely to exist but have not yet been identified.

30 Lecoy, ed., *Roman*, 1:xxxv–xxxvi. In a note on p. xxxvi, Lecoy lists the MSS discovered since Langlois's researches.

31 Carleton Brown and R. H. Robbins, *The Index of Middle English Verse* (New York, 1943), p. 737; Thomas G. Bergin, *Dante* (Boston, 1965), p. 303.

32 Langlois, *Manuscrits*, knew of seventy-two MSS in the Bibliothèque Nationale; MS n.a.fr. 11387 was acquired in 1917. I am grateful to Mme. Florence Callu of the B.N. for providing me with this information. The Bodleian, in addition to its own nine MSS, has on deposit a late fourteenth-century MS from the collection of the late Viscount Astor (Dep. Astor A.12); and the British Library has three MSS in addition to the thirteen which Langlois noted there: Add. 42133, Yates Thompson 21, and Loan 55/1. This information was kindly sent me by Dr. Bruce Barker-Benfield of the Bodley, and Mr. T. A. J. Burnett of the B.L.

33 MSS 48, 120, 132, 181, 185, 245, 324, 372, 503.

34 See Lecoy, ed., *Roman*, 1:xxxvi, n. Also: S. De Ricci, *Census of Medieval and Renaissance Manuscripts in the United States and Canada*, 3 vols. (New York, 1935); and W. H. Bond and C. U. Faye, *Supplement to the Census of Medieval and Renaissance Manuscripts in the United States and Canada* (New York, 1962).

35 Langlois, *Manuscrits*, p. 121.

36 Maxwell Luria, "A Sixteenth-Century Gloss on the *Roman de la Rose*," *Mediaeval Studies*, 44 (1982).

37 F. W. Bourdillon, *The Early Editions of the Roman de la Rose* (London, 1906), p. 23.

38 For bibliography, see chapters twenty-three and twenty-eight, "Scholarship on Manuscripts of the *Roman de la Rose*" and "Scholarship and Criticism of the Twentieth Century." The earliest monograph on the illustrations in the *Roman* MSS is Alfred Kuhn, "Die Illustration des Rosenromans," *Jahrbuch der Kunsthistorischen Sammlungen der Allerhöchsten Kaiserhauses* 31 (1913–14): 1–66.

39 Complete color microfiches of the Bodleian MSS may be obtained from Oxford Microform Publications Ltd., 19a Paradise St., Oxford OX1 1LD.

40 Cf., for example, F. S. Ellis, trans., *The Romance of the Rose* (London, 1900), 1: xi.

41 Bourdillon, *Early Editions*, pp. 35–68.
42 Ibid., pp. 77–78. Part Two of this monograph is devoted to the illustrations in the early printed editions.
43 Ibid., pp. 97–130.
44 "How, after this fine talk, the Lover—motivated by deceiving Youth—humbly pays homage to the God of Love, who receives him." "How Reason, beloved of God, has come down from her tower, and chastises and berates the Lover about how he undertakes foolish love." "Here is the very beautiful Reason, who is always ready to give good advice to all who are lazy about saving themselves." "How Reason shows the Lover Fortune with her turning wheel, and tells him that if he wishes it, all Fortune's power cannot bring him unhappiness."
45 For a bibliographical listing of the principal modern editions, see chapter twenty-four, "French Printed Editions."
46 M. Méon, ed., *Le Roman de la Rose* (Paris, 1814), 1:xxi–xxii.
47 Sections of this preface are reprinted below in chapter twenty-one.
48 Méon, ed., *Roman*, 1: xxii; Langlois, ed., *Roman*, 1: 45.
49 Quoted in Langlois, ed., *Roman*, 1: 46. The MS used by Méon is B.N. fr. 25523.
50 Ibid., pp. 46–47.
51 Ibid., pp. 47–48.
52 For a list of some translations into other languages as well as English, see chapter twenty-six.
53 Ellis, trans., *Romance*, 3: 212.
54 Dahlberg used Langlois's text, but his translation can easily be read in conjunction with the Lecoy text by using Dahlberg's Table of Concordances (p. 27) or the Appendix in the present volume.
55 Dahlberg, trans., *Romance*, p. 358, n. 38.
56 Lecoy, ed., *Roman*, 1: xv.
57 Ibid., n. 1.
58 Ernest Langlois, *Origines et Sources du Roman de la Rose* (Paris, 1891). The materials in this book should be supplemented with the notes to Langlois's edition of the *Roman*.
59 John J. Parry, trans., *The Art of Courtly Love* (New York, 1941), p. 17.
60 See John F. Benton, "The Court of Champagne as a Literary Center," *Speculum* 36 (1961): 551–91.
61 Parry, trans., *Art of Courtly Love*, pp. 21, 17–18.
62 Lewis, *Allegory*, pp. 32–43.
63 Parry, trans., *Art of Courtly Love*, p. 187.
64 Ibid., pp. 18–19.
65 Lewis, *Allegory*, p. 42.
66 D. W. Robertson, Jr., *A Preface to Chaucer: Studies in Medieval Perspectives* (Princeton, 1962), pp. 447–48.
67 Charles Muscatine, *Chaucer and the French Tradition* (Berkeley, 1957), pp. 13–14.
68 Lewis, *Allegory*, p. 2.
69 D. W. Robertson, Jr., "The Concept of Courtly Love as an Impediment to the Understanding of Medieval Texts," in his *Essays in Medieval Culture* (Princeton, 1980), pp. 258–60.
70 Robertson, *Preface*, p. 98.
71 See Lecoy, ed., *Roman*, 1: xiv.

72 For the origins of classical allegorism, see Jean Pépin, *Mythe et Allégorie: les Origines Grecques et les Contestations Judéo-Chrétiennes* (Paris, 1958); and F. Buffière, *Les Mythes d'Homère et la Pensée Grecque* (Paris, 1956). There are in English a number of modern theoretical and historical studies of allegory. Some of the most important of these are listed in chapter thirty, "Ancillary Materials for Study of the *Roman*: Miscellaneous Works."

73 *Jewish Encyclopedia*, s.v. "allegory," "allegory in the Old Testament," "Midrash"; *Oxford Dictionary of the Christian Church*, s.v. "Midrash."

74 See, e.g., Charles G. Osgood, trans., *Boccaccio on Poetry* (1930; reprint ed., New York, 1956). This volume contains Boccaccio's ideas about poetic allegory from books 14 and 15 of the *Genealogia Deorum Gentilium*.

75 H. J. Thomson, ed., *Prudentius with an English Translation* (Cambridge, Mass., 1949), 1: 310–20 (lines 454–598). I have modified Thomson's translation in a few small matters.

76 Charles Dahlberg, "First Person and Personification in the *Roman de la Rose*: Amant and Dangier," *Mediaevalia* 3 (1977): 37.

77 For Macrobius's typology of dreams, to which Guillaume refers at the very beginning of the *Roman*, see the excerpt from his commentary on the *Somnium Scipionis* in chapter thirteen of this book.

78 Lewis, *Allegory*, p. 126.

79 John V. Fleming, *The Roman de la Rose: A Study in Allegory and Iconography* (Princeton, 1969), p. 32. See also the now classic paper by D. W. Robertson, Jr., "The Doctrine of Charity in Medieval Literary Gardens," *Speculum* 26 (1951): 24–49; reprinted in his *Essays in Medieval Culture* (Princeton, 1980), pp. 21–50.

80 See p. 207, and the discussion of the Collins gloss beginning on p. 72.

81 See Luria, "Gloss," gloss note 43.

82 Dahlberg, "First Person," p. 42.

83 See p. 209.

84 See p. 209–10.

85 See p. 207.

86 Ibid.

87 But cf. Collins gloss note 31, p. 209.

88 See Collins gloss note 88, p. 211; and Luria, "Gloss," gloss note 36.

89 For a discussion of Nature and Genius, see p. 54–58.

90 See H. Paolucci, ed., *The Enchiridion on Faith, Hope and Love* (Chicago, 1961), p. 139 (chapter 121). The scriptural passage is I Tim. 1.5: "Now the end of the commandment is charity, out of a pure heart, and of a good conscience, and of faith unfeigned."

91 See Luria, "Gloss," gloss notes 9 and 24.

92 See Fleming, *Roman de la Rose*, passim; Dahlberg, trans., *Romance*, pp. 12–22; Robertson, *Preface*, pp. 91–104, 196–207.

93 Lewis, *Allegory*, p. 122.

94 Gunn, *Mirror*, p. 498.

95 Lecoy, ed., *Roman*, 1: xvi–xvii.

96 See p. 208.

97 Robertson, *Preface*, pp. 74–75, shows that medieval Ovidians often associated Narcissus's condition with St. Augustine's notion of the fall of man's lower reason by self-indulgence in pleasure of thought, or *delectatio cogitationis*. The Collins glossator deftly employs this conventional interpretation to imply that Narcissus is emblematic of the *Roman*'s Lover.

98 Cf. Collins gloss note 140 in Luria, "Gloss"; Robertson, *Preface*, p. 102.
99 For bibliography, see chapter thirty, "Ancillary Materials for Study of the *Roman*: Special Topics: Controversy Concerning the Friars."
100 Dahlberg, trans., *Romance*, p. 18.
101 Genius, also, delivers himself of brutally antifeminist doctrine: see lines 16,293–16,698.
102 Langlois, ed., *Roman*, 1: 29.
103 René Louis, *Le Roman de la Rose: Essai d'Interprétation de l'Allégorisme Erotique* (Paris, 1974), pp. 128 ff.
104 Lecoy, ed., *Roman*, 1: xxi.
105 Lewis, *Allegory*, p. 151.
106 Gunn, *Mirror*, p. 403.
107 The Collins glossator agrees: cf. gloss note 158, p. 215, and gloss note 143 in Luria, "Gloss".
108 Robertson, *Preface*, pp. 200, 202.
109 Rosemond Tuve, *Allegorical Imagery* (Princeton, 1966), pp. 269–278.
110 Fleming, *Roman de la Rose*, pp. 197–99.
111 For bibliography on Alanus, see chapter thirty, "Ancillary Materials for Study of the *Roman*: Special Topics: Alanus de Insulis." See also the excerpts from Alanus's writings in chapter fourteen and fifteen.
112 James J. Sheridan, trans., *The Plaint of Nature* (Toronto, 1980), pp. 32–33.
113 Langlois, ed., *Roman*, 1: 32.
114 For bibliography, see chapters twenty-six and thirty, "Translations" and "Ancillary Materials for Study of the *Roman*: Special Topics: *Il Fiore* and Italian Literature."
115 Langlois, ed., *Roman*, 1: 40–41.
116 Ibid., pp. 38–41; Lecoy, ed., *Roman*, 1: xxxiv.
117 Langlois, ed., *Roman*, 1: 5–7, 32, 35; Lecoy, ed., *Roman*, 1: xiv, xxix.
118 Robertson, *Preface*, p. 233.
119 Ibid., p. 236.
120 For bibliography, see chapter thirty, "Ancillary Materials for Study of the *Roman*: Special Topics: *Echecs Amoureux*."
121 Fleming, *Roman de la Rose*, p. 63.
122 Ibid.
123 Ibid., p. 62.
124 Ibid., pp. 64–65. Fleming quotes from MS B.N. fr. 9197, fols. 237v–238v. For Fleming's major discussion of the *Echecs*, see pp. 12, 55, 62–65, 78 n. Cf. Collins gloss note 166, p. 216 above.
125 For bibliography, see chapter twenty-nine, "Materials and Scholarship Relating to the Quarrel."
126 Langlois, ed., *Roman*, 1: 35.
127 A good introduction to Christine, with bibliography, is Enid McLeod, *The Order of the Rose: The Life and Ideas of Christine de Pizan* (Totowa, N.J., 1976).
128 C. F. Ward, *The Epistles on the Romance of the Rose and Other Documents in the Debate* (Chicago, 1911), pp. 6–10; Ernest Langlois, "Le Traité de Gerson contre le *Roman de la Rose*," *Romania* 45 (1918–19): 23; Eric Hicks, ed., *Le Débat sur le Roman de la Rose* (Paris, 1977); Joseph L. Baird and John R. Kane, *La Querelle de la Rose: Letters and Documents* (Chapel Hill, 1978); Peter Potansky, *Der Streit um den Rosenroman* (Munich, 1972).
129 Baird and Kane, *Querelle*, pp. 71–73.

130 Ibid., p. 90. In Pierre Col's letter to Christine de Pisan which is printed in chapter seventeen of the present volume, along with Christine's reply, there are many references to Gerson's *Treatise*, and numerous allusions to its author.

131 Grover C. Furr, "The Quarrel of the *Roman de la Rose* and Fourteenth-Century Humanism" (Ph.D. Diss., Princeton University, 1979), p. 205. See also Baird and Kane, *Querelle*, pp. 18–28.

132 Tuve, *Allegorical Imagery*, p. 274, n. But cf. Baird and Kane, *Querelle*, pp. 11–12: "The evidence seems to indicate that the debate was quite a live issue of real and earnest moral interest to a large number of people. The fact that the notable Jean Gerson addressed himself to the subject in a series of sermons is, in this regard, most significant."

133 Ibid., p. 12.

134 Ibid., p. 153 (document 16).

135 Ibid., p. 57 (document 7).

136 Ibid., pp. 103–04 (document 13).

137 Langlois, ed., *Roman*, 1: 36: "There is none like him in French."

138 Ibid., 1: 36.

139 Silvio Baridon, ed., *Le Roman de la Rose par Guillaume de Lorris et Jean de Meung. Dans la Version Attribuée à Clément Marot* (Milan, 1954), 1: 14–15.

140 Langlois, ed., *Roman*, 1: 32.

141 Fleming, *Roman de la Rose*, p. 6.

142 Bourdillon, *Early Editions*, pp. 64–68, 147, 160, 162; Baridon, ed., *Roman*, p. 15.

143 Fol. a i recto. The book was printed by Vérard at Paris in 1500.

144 Ibid., fols. ii and ii recto. Excerpts from this prologue are reprinted in chapter eighteen of the present volume.

145 Bourdillon, *Early Editions*, p. 162.

146 Ibid., pp. 157–59.

147 Fols. A ii verso, iii recto (Paris, 1531).

148 Tuve, *Allegorical Imagery*, p. 227.

149 Fleming, *Roman de la Rose*, p. 6.

150 Excerpts from the Collins gloss are reprinted in chapter twenty.

151 The *Bible des Poetes* was first issued by Mansion at Bruges in 1484. For an edited text of the Collins gloss, and detailed discussion of its provenance, see Luria, "Gloss."

152 Baridon, ed., *Roman*, vol. 1, chapter 2.

153 Ibid., p. 43.

154 Ibid., p. 27, quoting Louis Thuasne, *Villon et Rabelais* (Paris, 1911), p. 168.

155 Quoted in Ibid., p. 28.

156 Ibid., p. 29.

157 Albert C. Baugh, *The Middle English Period (1100–1500)*, in *A Literary History of England*, ed. Baugh, 2d ed. (New York, 1967), p. 252.

158 Surprisingly, there is no modern study devoted exclusively to this important literary connection. Dean Spruill Fansler, *Chaucer and the Roman de la Rose* (1914; reprint ed. Gloucester, Mass., 1965) is full of small matters but evades the large ones. It is both unsatisfactory and out of date. Charles Muscatine, *Chaucer and the French Tradition* (Berkeley, 1957), gives a good deal of attention to the *Roman*, as does D. W. Robertson, Jr., *A Preface to Chaucer* (Princeton, 1962): both are essential works.

159 Richard L. Hoffman, *Ovid and the Canterbury Tales* (Philadelphia, 1966), p. vii.

160 Walter W. Skeat, ed., *The Complete Works of Geoffrey Chaucer*, 2d ed. (Oxford,

1899), 1: 10.

161 F. N. Robinson, ed., *The Works of Geoffrey Chaucer*, 2d ed. (Boston, 1957), p. 872.

162 Ronald Sutherland, ed., *The Romaunt of the Rose and Le Roman de la Rose: A Parallel-Text Edition* (Oxford, 1967), introduction.

163 All Chaucer citations are from the Robinson text (2d ed.).

164 For the date, see Robinson, ed., *Chaucer*, p. xxix.

165 Cf. Robertson, *Preface*, pp. 233–38.

166 Ibid., Part Three, "Late Medieval Style."

167 Fansler, *Chaucer and the Roman de la Rose*, pp. 162–64.

Part Four

1 The selection printed here is from Macrobius, *Commentary on the Dream of Scipio*, trans. W. H. Stahl (New York, 1952), pp. 87–92, and is included by permission of Columbia University Press. As we see in this passage, Macrobius believed that certain kinds of dreams could give us information about ourselves and our future. It is not surprising that an epoch such as the Middle Ages, whose biblical culture provided many examples of prophetic dreams, read him with great interest, or that poets like Guillaume de Lorris and Chaucer used him to authenticate their own poetical dreams. For further discussion, see pp. 40–47 above, and for analysis of Macrobius's sources, see the notes in Stahl's edition.

2 *Aeneid* 6.896.

3 *Aeneid* 4.3–5, 9.

4 Stahl's note: "One his father by nature, the other his grandfather by adoption. The dreaming Scipio (commonly called Scipio the Younger or Scipio Aemilianus, destroyer of Carthage in 146 B.C. and founder of the Scipionic Circle) was the natural son of Aemilius Paulus, famous Roman general and Hellenophile, and the adopted son of Scipio Africanus, the oldest son of Scipio the Elder (conqueror of Hannibal)."

5 *Iliad* 2.56–83.

6 *Aeneid* 2.604–606.

7 The description of the island of Fortune was adapted by Jean de Meun for Reason's discourse to the Lover (lines 5,891–6,084). In this work, as in the *De Planctu Naturae*, Alanus was deeply influenced by Boethius (cf. *Consolatio* 2.1–2), as were Jean, Chaucer, and many other medieval authors. We have here a characteristic instance of how ideas and iconography were transmitted in the Middle Ages. In the *Anticlaudianus*, Nature proposes to create a perfect man, and receives the collaboration and contributions of such personifications as Prudence, Reason, et al. At this point, Fortune's daughter Nobility comes on the scene.

8 The selection printed here is from Alanus de Insulis, *The Complaint of Nature*, trans. D. M. Moffat (New York, 1908), pp. 1, 24–26, 29, 34–35, 45, 47–50, 83–86, 93–95, and is included by permission of Yale University Press. We have somewhat modified the translation in places for the sake of accuracy and clarity, and in the light of more recent scholarship. The *De Planctu Naturae* is an early, stylistically self-conscious work of Alanus, and no one who tackles its Latin comes away undaunted or unscathed. Nor does it make easy reading

even in translation. The work was, however, much admired in the Middle Ages, and very influential. It is the model and chief source for the important Nature-Genius section of the *Roman*, and Nature's "confession" is based directly upon it. As James J. Sheridan—whose translation (Toronto, 1980) is accompanied by an invaluable preface—notes, the *De Planctu* was itself closely modelled on Boethius's *De Consolatione Philosophiae* (p. 62). We thus see once again the enormous and seminal importance of Boethius to later medieval humanistic culture. For further discussion, see pp. 54–58 above; for bibliography on Alanus, see chapter thirty, "Ancillary Materials for Study of the *Roman*: Special Topics: Alanus de Insulis."

9 The selection printed here is from Andreas Capellanus, *The Art of Courtly Love*, trans. John J. Parry (New York, 1941), pp. 28–33, 81–82, 184–86, and is included by permission of Columbia University Press. For a discussion of the *De Amore* and its relation to the *Roman de la Rose*, see chapter three, "'Li Romanz . . . ou l'Art d'Amors est Tote Enclose'"; for bibliography on Andreas Capellanus, see chapter thirty, "Ancillary Materials for Study of the *Roman*: Special Topics: Andreas Capellanus."

10 The selection printed here is from J. L. Baird and J. R. Kane, *La Querelle de la Rose: Letters and Documents* (Chapel Hill, 1978), pp. 92–144, and is included by kind permission of University of North Carolina Studies in the Romance Languages and Literatures. For a discussion of the Quarrel, see chapter six, "The Poem's Reception"; for bibliography, chapter twenty-nine, "Materials and Scholarship Relating to the Quarrel." The two letters excerpted here are the longest of the Quarrel documents, and embody characteristic arguments pro and contra. They are numbered 13 and 14 in Baird and Kane, and III.3 and III.4 in Eric Hicks's edition of the original texts (Paris, 1977).

11 *Col* refers to Christine's letter of mid-1401 to Jean de Montreuil (Baird and Kane 6), which he later quotes or paraphrases.

12 The allusion is to Ballade 856 of Eustache Deschamps: "Vous vous tuez, com fait li pellicant."

13 *Ars Poetica* 9–10.

14 *De Officiis* 1.25.127–128.

15 See Deut. 23.1.

16 *Andria* 68.

17 The reference is to Jean Gerson's allegorical *Traictié d'une Vision contre le Roman de la Rose* (Baird and Kane 12).

18 Ecclus. 42.14.

19 These excerpts from Jean Molinet's prologue to his *Roman de la Rose Moralisie* have been translated from the folio edition of 1500, printed at Paris by Vérard: fols. b i verso, b ii recto, b iii verso, b iiii recto. For discussion of Molinet's allegorism, see chapter seven, "After the Quarrel"; for a listing and description of Molinet's several editions of the *Roman*, see chapter two, "Manuscripts, Editions, and Translations."

20 These excerpts from Clément Marot's *Preambule* to his modernized version of the *Roman de la Rose* have been translated from the folio edition of 1531, printed at Paris by Galliot du Pré: fols. A ii verso, A iii recto. For a discussion of Marot's allegorism, see chapter seven, "After the Quarrel"; for a listing and description of the editions of his version, see chapter two, "Manuscripts, Editions, and Translations."

21 Apuleius, *Metamorphoses* 11.1.

22 Ecclus. 24.18.

23 These excerpts from the Collins gloss have been translated from MS Collins 45-65-3 in the Philadelphia Museum of Art, and are printed here by permission of the Museum. For an edited text of the complete gloss, with commentary, see Maxwell Luria, "A Sixteenth-Century Gloss on the *Roman de la Rose*," *Mediaeval Studies* 44 (1982). For a discussion of the gloss, see chapter seven, "After the Quarrel." The gloss notes are numbered as they appear in the article just cited; in parentheses are line numbers of the Lecoy text to indicate where the notes appear in the MS.

24 As Hoffman, *Ovid*, p. 74, pointed out, the glossator has both misquoted Ovid (though in an inspired way, substituting "Cupid's arts" for "Cupid's bow") and incorrectly cited the *Ars Amatoria*. This verse, much quoted in the Middle Ages, is *Remedia Amoris* 139: "Otia si tollas, periere Cupidinis arcus." ("Take away leisure and Cupid's bow is broken.") According to Robertson, *Preface*, p. 92, n. 69, this verse is the locus classicus of Idleness.

25 Ezek. 16.49: "Behold, this was the iniquity of Sodom thy sister, pride, fulness of bread and abundance, and the idleness of her and of her daughters."

26 Boethius, *Consolatio Philosophiae* 3.met.12.47–48: "Who can give law to lovers? Love is a greater law unto itself." Chaucer's use of these lines in the *Knight's Tale*, I(A)1163–66, is one of many medieval allusions to Orpheus as lawless lover in whom wisdom has been overthrown.

27 The allusion may be to *Ars Amatoria* 1.269–274.

28 These excerpts from Lenglet du Fresnoy's preface to the *Roman de la Rose* have been translated from the complete text of the preface as it appears in M. Méon, ed., *Le Roman de la Rose* (Paris, 1814), 1:1–38. For discussion of Lenglet's preface and edition, see chapter seven, "After the Quarrel."

Index

Index